PRVDENTIA

IVSTITIA

ASAPH

AEMAN

DAVIDREXETPROP

CERETHI

ETPHE

LETHI

AETHAN

IDITHUN

FORTITVDO

JERUSALEM: A HISTORY

JERUSALEM
A HISTORY

FOREWORD BY E. O. JAMES

EDITED BY J. BOUDET

G. P. PUTNAM'S SONS · NEW YORK

PHOTO CREDITS

Bibberkraut—D. Brihat—A. Duncan—Leonard Freed—M. Hayaux du Tilly—Izis—R. Leconte—Chris Marker—Merry Ottin—W. Van de Poll—David Rubinger—A. Vigneau—Sabine Weiss.

Alliance Israélite Universelle—Ashmolean Museum—Dazy Collection—Giraudon—Magnum (Brake, Glinn, Morath, Rodger, Seymour)—Marburg Institut—Matson Photo Service—Dresden Museum—National Gallery, London— Photo-Haus, Turin—Rapho—Rijksmuseum, Amsterdam—André Sauret—Scala—Skira—Staedelsches Kunstinstitut, Frankfurt—Jerusalem University—Roger Viollet.

The publishers wish to thank the Israeli authorities, and in particular the department of the Prime Minister, the Ministry of Foreign Affairs and the municipality of Jerusalem, for the assistance brought to the realisation of this book.

Nihil obstat, John M. T. Barton, S.T.D., L.S.S.
Imprimatur + Patrick Casey Vic. gen.
Westminster, die 1st March, 1967.
The Nihil obstat *and* Imprimatur *are a declaration that a book or pamphlet is considered to be free from doctrinal or moral error. It is not implied that those who have granted the* Nihil obstat *and* Imprimatur *agree with the contents, opinions or statements expressed.*

First American Edition 1967
Jerusalem: a History translated from *Histoire de Jérusalem*
first published in France in 1965 by Editions Robert Laffont, Paris.

Library of Congress Catalog Card Number: 67-17933.
Printed in France by Editions Robert Laffont.

The Scripture quotations in this publication are from the *Revised Standard Version of the Bible,* copyrighted 1946 and 1952 by the Division of Christian Education, National Council of Churches, and used by permission.

CONTENTS

JERUSALEM: A HISTORY

FOREWORD

by E. O. James, D. Litt., D.D., F.S.A.
Professor Emeritus of the History of Religion
in the University of London

This lavishly illustrated history of Jerusalem will be widely welcomed as a most handsome production devoted to a fascinating subject. In this volume the chequered history of the city which became the meeting place of East and West is comprehensively outlined from the earliest settlement of the Semitic invaders round about 3000 B.C. to the arrival of the British forces under Allenby on December 9th 1917 and the visit of Pope Paul VI on January 4th 1964.

As will be seen in this book, much has been done in the field of archaeology to recover the remains of Jerusalem's chequered history, though it has proved to be a disappointing site for exploration, it is true, because it presents so many difficulties for excavation. Thus the Canaanite town on the hill of Ophel, inhabited by a tribe of so-called Jebusites in the second millenium B.C., and part of the fortress captured by David about 1000 B.C. lie under the modern city and the site of the Temple. This fact has hampered excavation, especially since the Moslem mosque, known as Haram Ash-Sharif, and the Dome of the Rock, now occupy what may have been the rock on which the altar of burnt-offering stood, to the west of the present walled city.

On this part of the hill remains of the Early Bronze Age walls have been found, and during the Middle Bronze Age the city seems to have expanded to the north, as traces of its walls, dated about 1800 B.C., have been discovered along the eastern side of Ophel.

About 1000 B.C. David captured the Jebusite fortress and made it the capital of the united Israelite monarchy in neutral territory between Benjamin and Judah. Here with Phoenician help he built his palace at the north end of Ophel, and at the height of his glory his son Solomon erected the Temple—primarily as a royal chapel—on the northern section of the eastern ridge, employing skilled workmen and materials supplied by Hiram, King of Tyre. The Temple eventually became the central sanctuary of the worship of Yahweh until it was destroyed by Nebuchadnezzar when he beleagured the city in 597 B.C. Its reconstruction after the return of the exiles in 539 B.C. was on a much smaller scale, while the walls of Jerusalem herself were not built by Nehemiah (and even then in the face of strenuous opposition from the Samaritans) until 433 B.C.

This course of events in the Israelite occupation of Jerusalem is very clearly described and graphically illustrated in the opening chapters of this book, and placed in the context of the Old Testament narratives. It is followed by an account of the 'abomination of desolation' in the reign of Antiochus Epiphanes in 167 B.C., the Maccabaean revolt, subjection to the Roman Empire in 63 B.C. and the ambitious reconstruction of the Temple by Herod as it stood in all its splendour in the time of Christ and before its final destruction when the city was captured by Titus in A.D. 70.

The Christian period is introduced by the tradition of the birth of the Virgin Mary in its various portrayals in art, depicted and narrated in some detail, together with the Anunciation, Visitation and Incarnation, the offerings of the Magi, the Massacre of the Innocents and the Presentation in the Temple. The rest of the salient features and events in the life of Christ are then recorded and illustrated, reaching their climax in the Passion narratives and those of the Resurrection and Ascension.

The discovery of the alleged site of the burial and Resurrection of Christ and the finding of the cross on the Mount of Olives by St. Helena, mother of Constantine, when she visited Palestine in 326, is discussed as a legend expressing and embellishing the historical reality of the triumph of Christianity in the Roman world. Jerusalem (the Aelia Capitolina of Hadrian) acquired a unique status after Constantine's edict of 312 as the Holy City in which the erection of the great basilica known as the Holy Sepulchre (Anastasis) about 325 on the traditional site of the tomb of Christ, and the Invention or Discovery of the cross by St. Helena became the centre of interest and controversy, which culminated in the Crusades and their aftermath.

In the chapter entitled 'Jerusalem of the Crescent and the Cross' this turbulent period in her history is elucidated from the seventh century onwards when, in the early days of the expansion of Islam, she became a centre of pilgrimage for Moslems as well as for Christians, after being sacked by the Persian Chosroes II in 614 and surrendered to caliph Omar in 638. As a rival to Mecca, Jerusalem became the centre of pilgrimage: 'for him who dies therein it is as if he had died in heaven, and for him who dies close by it, it is as if he had died in the city.'

The liberation of the Holy City became the concern of Christendom, and in 1099 it was seized by the Crusaders and the Church of the Holy Sepulchre was restored and enlarged to cover the alleged site of Calvary. The fortifications and citadel were rebuilt and the churches restored. The conflict continued, however, and attempts to regain the holy places in the fourteenth and fifteenth centuries failed. Quarrels for the custody of the holy places never ceased among the warring rival elements and, as is pointed out in the text, to this day 'Arabs, Jews and Christians have lived side by side without merging with one another'. The Dome of the Rock marks the hallowed spot in the Temple region sacred alike to them all and (with the Mosque of el-Aksa) has become for Moslems the place of pilgrimage like the Holy Sepulchre for Christians.

After the capture of Jerusalem by British forces under General Allenby in 1917 a national home for the Jewish people was established in Palestine without prejudice to the civil and religious rights of non-Jewish communities, which was ratified by the League of Nations in 1922. A new era began and the city was transformed into a flourishing capital brought up to date through rapid cultural, educational and economic developments.

Religious and national rivalries have produced perpetual conflicts, riots and feuds culminating in armed agression and the partition of Palestine into a Jewish and an Arab state at enmity with each other.

The production of a book dealing with the history of Jerusalem in a single volume is an ambitious undertaking requiring much thought and care in the apportionment, interpretation and evaluation of the available evidence from so many different sources. This has been done with conspicuous success. In the best sense it is introductory, selective and comprehensive, based on a wide and accurate knowledge of this specialised field presented in a manner readily understandable to the general reader and superbly illustrated. In short, it admirably fulfils its purpose as an outline of the history of Jerusalem throughout the ages.

Capital cities have always burned with an inner fire whose flames illuminate the ages: in Jerusalem it is the Rock of Abraham, both funeral pyre and hearth of a city seventeen times destroyed and eighteen times reborn.

For centuries Jerusalem was, for the Western mind, the foremost city in the world, the earthly archetype of an ideal city, the supreme goal of the 'pilgrimage of human life'. Sovereigns among cities, capitals always have some fixed point around which they collect their energies, group their offspring and accumulate their treasures—the mother cell, the inner fire and life-giving nucleus from which everything springs. Rome grew up around the Palatine, Moscow around the Kremlin and Paris around a principal island. Jerusalem sprang from a simple rock and ruled by it. It was there that Abraham took the great step forward, the step decisive for civilisation. Hé substituted animal sacrifice for human sacrifice, an extraordinary spiritual and intellectual progress—in spite of appearances—which was still unknown to the Aztecs (although so learned in so many matters) when the Conquistadores landed in the Americas. And if, in the earliest periods of history, gods crowded the earth on every side stealing into all things living or inanimate, if thé famous triad of Mars, Jupiter and Quirinus held sway on the Capitol, it was a single god who ordered Abraham not to sacrifice Isaac. There, too, the new step forward of advancing humanity was an essential one.

But the Rock of Mount Moriah has had many successive proprietors since David bought it from a Jebusite, a member of the tribe which, prior to the Hebrews, occupied the junction of three meagre valleys: Hinnom, Tyropoean and Kidron. From the Euphrates to the Tiber, from the Nile to the Seine, from the midst of Europe and Asia, conquering armies have marched towards it and delivered their assaults, but the numbers of these warlike cohorts were far less than those of the men of goodwill who have come here, and the din of their cries far less than the murmur of their simple prayers.

Indeed the history of Jerusalem has always taken place on two planes, one invisible or mystical, the other visible or political. It is a history that is neither easy to write nor, above all, to illustrate.

View of Jerusalem with, in the foreground, the cupola of the Dome of the Rock.

Jews, Christians and Moslems all claim kinship with the patriarch who, in obeying his God, took an important step forward for civilisation.

In Jerusalem the three great religions—Jewish, Christian and Moslem—which regard Abraham as their father have had the freedom of the city for thousands of years. In the lifetime of their teacher the disciples of Mohammed themselves prayed prostrated towards the city; she was the first and, for a long time, only city to bring together travellers from the most distant nations of the earth. In the Scriptures the unseen Jerusalem is present in the voices of the prophets and the four evangelists, and later through the accounts of the Apocrypha and the chronicles of the Crusades. She is again present in traditions and legends. All

these are authentic and impassioned voices, though sometimes naïve, that mingle, join in unison, diverge and occasionally contradict each other.

There is little in Jerusalem that provides visual excitement or spectacular photography. There is no river bearing life and the unexpected through the city. The soil, the rock and the barren earth were the unique and eternal dowry of the daughters of Zion. The landscape itself is calculated to exalt the mind, and the mind alone. *Cuius regio eius religio* (In a [prince's] country, the [prince's] religion): Jerusalem bears witness, if there is need for witness, to

the secret harmony between geography and the fate of men. This barren, even lunar, landscape devoid of terrestrial life or rich, material wealth was predestined from the beginning of eternity to serve as the stage for the most tremendous spiritual adventure of all time. Yet if it is true that Jerusalem is in the spirit, in the letter which is the symbol of the Spirit and in the Scriptures which are its translation, and if it is true that nothing there consents to speak to the senses or the imagination, what is the function of this book?

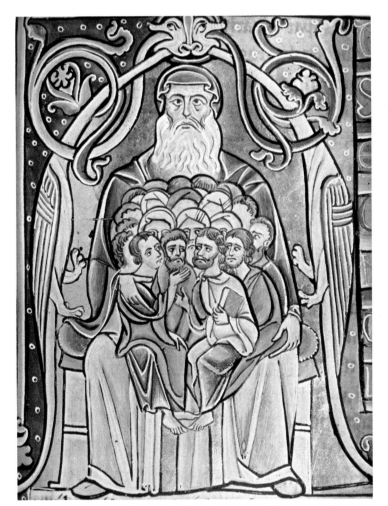

Christians, Jews and Moslems in Abraham's bosom (twelfth-century miniature).

English pilgrim leaving for the Holy Land (early sixteenth-century wood-cut).

Christ's genealogical tree starting from Jesse, the father of David (fourteenth-century Windmill Psalter).

Scenery of Palestine from Mount Nebo, from which Moses gazed upon the Promised Land. On the horizon the silhouettes of Jerusalem and Bethlehem, and the Mount of Olives

On the summits of the hills, in an almost lunar setting, actors refuse to become incarnate and perform the unseen drama which, in spite of themselves, will inspire two thousand years of art.

The sea, when there is one, slumbers miles away. It is the Dead Sea. At Jerusalem man did not want to create anything that could give flesh to dreams or the facile powers of the imagination. There were no sumptuous art treasures, only useful shapes intended for man's daily use. A strict law forbad even the representation of the face or the body and exalted the symbol instead. Abstraction abounded, geometry blossomed and the non-figurative held sway, whether Jewish, Christian or Moslem. Israel dictated a style to the Mediterranean East. 'Only the god of the Jews was never linked with a place. He is he who was, who is, who will always be.

An art that was pleasing to Yahweh could not be one of varied or ordered spaces but of time measured and controlled, of music, of speech and ultimately of memory. Judaism remained irreconcilably opposed to any attempt to imprison the divine in space and thus subject it to the destructive empire of time. (Manes Sperber). Moreover the tendency towards non-figurative art was not a characteristic of Islam, and in fact although Moslem doctrine finally came to proscribe images the Koran is silent on this subject. The doctors take their stand on a declaration of Mohammed's: 'Image-makers will be punished', because they attempt to

can be seen. In the foreground are the Dead Sea and the River Jordan with its muddy waters. (Infra-red telephoto).

Clay pitcher (about 2100–1500 B.C.).

Coin of King Amaury I (twelfth century).

Pulpit of the Mosque of el-Aksa (detail).

imitate and equal the creative act of God. The only historical fact is the decree promulgated in 792 by the Omayyad Caliph Yazid II, four years before the iconoclastic edict of Leo III, the Isaurian—a synchronism which corresponded to a political intention. It was not ascribable to an essential philosophy and applied to specific areas. 'In Assyria, in Palestine, in the Islamic world, already under strong Semitic influence, the ground was prepared.' (Georges Contenau).

That Mohammed should thus have been in agreement with David and that painters, image-makers and manufacturers of idols alike should have been condemned to a cruel Gehenna, does not make the task of preparing the history of Jerusalem any easier. More especially as the temptation to write a history of Palestine has been studiously avoided. The narrative has been confined to the immediate vicinity of the city with only the occasional, sometimes fleeting, reference to localities that are both near at hand and famous; Jericho and Bethlehem; Qumran, too, because the Essenes played an unquestionable role in Jerusalem; Masada and the Negeb because the people of Jerusalem confronted their enemies there; and the banks of the Jordan because it was there that John baptised Jesus.

13

Life has become fruitful again, but no witness remains to a past whose very reality appears fabulous. The Jerusalem of the imagination defies history.

The train opposite, bringing to the city young people filled with thoughtful enthusiasm, reminds us that Jerusalem lives again and grows anew. So little remains that can still be seen at Jerusalem dating from the earliest periods, described and recounted the most by oral tradition or written in the Scriptures. There is even less than of Paris, Rome or Moscow: the walls of an esplanade, at the foot of which thousands of Jews have come to wail, and a few almost indecipherable signs carved in stone.

The young nation of Israel can pride itself today on a museum of art worthy of itself *(see below right)* and which is to undergo numerous developments, but again it is not there that one finds reflections of the great days of Jerusalem.

To find these traces and reflections it has been necessary to seek them in the imaginary world of the artist. Some time during the third century people began to illustrate the Bible—and in the Middle East itself. A fresco painter was able to decorate the synagogue at Dura-Europas, on the confines of Syria and Mesopotamia, because Jewish rigorism had begun to be relaxed as a result of subtle rabbinical distinctions between the idol and narrative illustration. And Christ was never to come so fully to life as in medieval art. But can the historian silence his scruples before this too fanciful art? The miniaturists frequently turned the soldiers of Titus or the companions of the Maccabees into the combatants of Crécy or Agincourt while the great bibles of the seventeenth century deliberately confused the Israelite soldiers marching in the desert with the armies of the Thirty Years War, or the tribes of Judah with the Swiss cantons. For Holbein the aged David was a notable of Germany.

Archaeologists may reproach the many naïve stories, pious fallacies and clothes and monuments taken from their own periods, but dress has evolved more during the last 200 years than in 2,000. Between the robes and cloaks of Van Eyck and the tunics and veils of Palestine the relationship, or at least the similarity, can be glimpsed well enough. And it is all to the good if we can learn a little on the way of what family or social life was like in twelfth- or sixteenth-century Europe.

Sabras in the Tel-Aviv-Jerusalem train.

View of the city, with the Temple esplanade and the Mosque of el-Aksa in the foreground.

The facade of the Bezalel Museum with a large seven-branched candlestick in wrought iron.

Israeli girl carrying the ritual cakes of Purim, the feast days which, in the spring, commemorate Esther and the liberation of the Jews of Persia.

A long impassioned and enthralling destiny full of blood and fires, alleluias and songs, and promises of peace. Even the present has the appearance of eternity.

Nevertheless an attempt has been made, as far as possible, to avoid any anachronisms or peculiarities of decor and dress which are too conspicuous or are too obviously Gothic or baroque. Preference has been given to Giotto, or at least to his Paduan cycle, as his faces and attitudes have a timeless humanity, over and above the 'accident' of dress and actuality.

In a landscape, and for minds which are so little concerned with external detail, anachronism is, furthermore, of

little importance. The old and the new exist side by side with such perfect naturalness and lack of concern that it is not always possible to separate them. What is important here is what one believes and not what one wears. The most punctilious upholders of the ancient Jewish laws are those who, paradoxically, wear European dress, while Arab dress has remained untouched through the centuries, and it is not difficult to encounter on the slopes of the Mount of Olives some member of a procession who

Arab arguing at the Mandelbaum Gate on the Israel-Jordan frontier.

The traditional Palm Sunday procession returning to the city.

could have come straight out of the Middle Ages.

In our search for authenticity biblical archaeology, which has proved so fertile in the Near East and is so developed in Palestine, but whose discoveries on the site of Jerusalem itself are, alas, too scanty as yet—will they be more plentiful one day?—has provided us with some pieces of evidence. Fiction has furthermore sometimes succeeded in overtaking reality with astonishing perspicacity. If, today, Masada is a place filled with the memory of Herod which fires researchers with enthusiasm, we can ask ourselves how an engraver of the eighteenth century was able to reproduce its perspectives so accurately (see p. 195).

Finally, it is very true that certain aspects of what the Jewish way of life may have been like at Jerusalem for centuries, its liturgy or its actual setting, persist almost unchanged in some Middle Eastern communities and even in North Africa. It is such scenes that have been chosen to illustrate this book. The reader may make the necessary transpositions both in space and time.

The abiding concern throughout has been to be thorough and accurate in a stirring and enthralling subject full of mysteries, blood and clamour but also of promising assurances of peace for men of goodwill.

Jacques Boudet.

1

THE PREDESTINED
STRONGHOLD

from Abraham to David

Those who trust in the Lord are like Mount Zion, which cannot be moved, but abides for ever.

   As the mountains are round about Jerusalem, so the Lord is round about his people, from this time forth and for evermore.

Ps. CXXV. 1-2

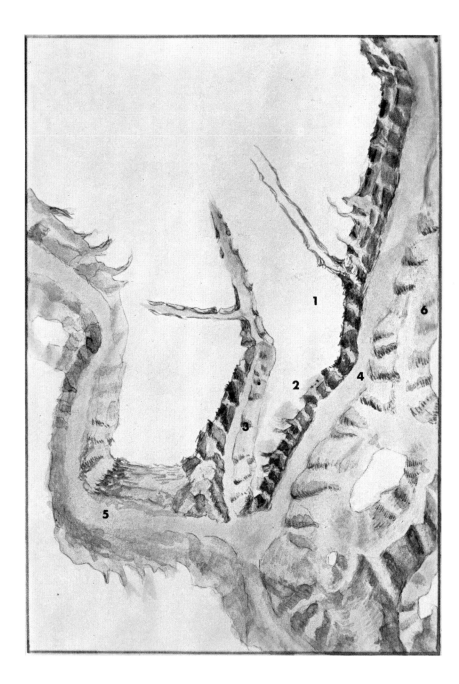

Geographical situation of the city:
1. Mount Moriah (with the Rock of Abraham),
the site of the Temple esplanade.
2. Ophel, a hill whose declivity prolongs Mount Moriah,
and upon which the City of David
(called Zion, from the name of the original citadel) was built.
3. Valley of the Tyropoean, half filled in before the Christian era,
separating Mount Zion (on the left) from the Ophel.
4. Valley of Kidron.
5. Valley of Gehenna.
6. Mount of Olives.
The maps on pages 40, 88 and 200
show the successive stages in the growth of the city.

Nomads of the Near East. In their journeys from well to well the patriarchs already employed the camel as a beast of burden.

The epic of Israel begins. Abraham leaves Mesopotamia and goes towards the

Jerusalem was only a minor stronghold and probably in no way distinguishable from other Canaanite towns when, about the year 2000 B.C., a nomadic tribe left Ur at the eastern end of the Fertile Crescent. This migration was the starting point of the historical development of Israel which was to make of Jerusalem its capital.

The Semites, who at that time held sway over most of the kingdoms of northern Mesopotamia, had assimilated the 1500 years of Sumerian culture. Bronze working technique had reached a high level of refinement, laws were engraved on tablets, trade was international, and temples and towns bore witness to a powerful architecture. The people of Mesopotamia worshipped the lunar deities Sin and Nannar and their religion was now marked by the need for a personal relationship with the deity.

The documents that have come down to us, in particular the tablets discovered at Mari dating from about 1700 B.C., describe an unstable political situation. The security of the Amorite towns was constantly troubled by bands of invaders who nomadised in the region and sometimes waged war. Two peoples existed side by side, one settled, the other still seeking to establish itself.

The migration of the clan of Terah, the father of Abraham, formed part of this general movement and must have been very similar to that of any nomadic tribe of today. Terah left Ur, following the Euphrates towards the north, and settled at Haran, a city of upper Mesopotamia between the Tigris and the Euphrates. At his death Abraham took to the road again, but in a new direction. With Sarah, his wife, Lot his nephew, his slaves and his flocks, he left his clan and set out towards the south and the unknown land of Canaan.

We can picture his itinerary, determined by pasture for the flocks. The Euphrates would have to be crossed at Carchemish or Tell Barsip, then the route would pass through Aleppo and Damascus, about 125 miles from Shechem in the heart of Samaria. The Canaanite towns skirted by the caravan looked like stone-built fortresses, reflecting an aristocratic and warlike civilisation.

Their ramparts protected temple and palace, while the population lived outside the walls in cob houses with conical roofs, still found in some Middle Eastern villages. Objects unearthed in Palestine supply us with evidence about the crafts and mode of life encountered by the new arrivals.

The tribe would move forward from grazing-ground to grazing-ground in time with the flocks, anxious to find wells. Breeders of small live-stock, the nomads lived on milk and its products, wove the hair of the goats and, from the skins, made the black tents of the desert.

The tribe lived in accordance with precise customs and an oral law originating in Mesopotamia. The clan was the initial unit of the tribe, whose leader was appointed for his prestige and personality and the exploits of the ancestor who had given his name to the group were handed down from generation to generation.

The clans had their gods. These were the Teraphim, family idols whose possession implied all the privileges of the birthright, and the Elohim, protectors of

Abraham goes into Canaan. It was from Ur in Chaldea that the 'Father of all them that believe' set out towards the south (seventeenth-century engraving).

land of Canaan, but he is still a 'stranger in a strange land'.

the individual and the clan who were linked to the deity by an intimate relationship which rested on a covenant: by virtue of a covenant Abraham set off on the call of his God who had promised him a country. The religion of the clan,

like the judicial traditions, reflected the degree of civilisation attained in the Middle East in the Middle Bronze Age. (Elohim was the name commonly given to the God of the patriarchs, but He was worshipped under numerous other

names.) The cult was still permeated with magic, but because of the personal covenant which it implied between God and man, it already differed from the great Mesopotamian state religions, and bore the seed of the faith of Israel.

Syrian village with conical cob roofs whose style recalls those of Biblical times.

Basalt mortar (Nablus, 5000 B.C.).

Shechem, in Samaria, where Elohim appeared to Abraham for the first time and designated Canaan to him as the land promised to his descendants.

Cult stones in the Sinai region. Symbols of power, these stones are similar to those of the Canaanite sanctuaries evoked by the Bible.

The patriarchs settle in Canaan.

Along the route of wells and mountain pastures Shechem, in Samaria, was the first important town encountered by Abraham on his arrival in Palestine from the north. At this time (2000 B.C.) Egypt had already established her authority over the country, but this suzerainty made itself little felt. The then Pharaoh, who had to contend with domestic difficulties, only replied to the defection of the Canaanite princes with magical formulas. The small towns fought with one another, incapable of providing themselves with a central administration. This unstable and confused situation would facilitate the evolution of the nomads, and eventually the descendants of the inhabitants blended with the different strains of successive invaders, both Semitic and Indo-European.

The Canaanites were sedentary farmers and had a religion profoundly linked with nature. They camped in the vicinity of the oak tree of Moreh, a holy place. Trees, like springs, mountains and stones, were religious objects by virtue of the force of life which they demonstrated. Around the terebinth or spring walls were built to delimit the abode of the god; stones were raised and altars for sacrifice. The gods had their history. El was power, the father, the supreme god of the Semitic pantheon; he had a wife, Ashera of the Sea, and children: Baal, Mot and Astarte. Baal, the god of fertility, was worshipped at Shechem in one of its most ancient sanctuaries. He caused the earth to bring forth, and died and was born again to the rhythm of the seasons; his name signified master, possessor. Mot, the god of death, was his enemy. Astarte, the goddess of fertility, who is found in clumsy representations, was his ally. In the East people still often ward off the baleful power of Mot by means of amulets and medals.

Shechem represents a decisive moment in the biblical traditions, for Elohim appeared to Abraham and designated Canaan to him as the country promised to his descendants. After this vision Abraham erected, on the very floor of the Canaanite sanctuary, an altar destined to receive the sacrifice. There was no organised priesthood in the religion of the clan; the head of the household or the leader of the clan performed the sacrifice. The victim was generally an animal from the flock.

Stage by stage Abraham reached the Negeb on the Egyptian frontier, having crossed the whole of Palestine. The Negeb was not yet a desert and Abraham was able to lead the same life there, pitching camp near towns to barter the produce of their flocks for oil and flour. Periods of drought would oblige them to take off again, and they would cross over into Egypt.

On one of these occasions Sarah's beauty was noticed by the Pharaoh. Abraham, afraid that the Pharaoh would kill him, declared that she was his sister. Sarah went into the harem while Abraham had riches heaped upon him by the Pharaoh for having such a beautiful sister. Having left Egypt considerably more wealthy than when they arrived, Abraham and Lot decided to separate because the shepherds were quarrelling over the wells and pastures. They had become too numerous to live off the same land. Lot settled in the Jordan valley, close to Sodom, in a very fertile region. Abraham dwelt at Hebron in the oak-grove of Mamre.

Both abandoned the completely nomadic life; when they sowed a field it was only to abandon it the following year. But they no longer left the south of Palestine and the confines of Egypt; the great migration was at an end.

Fertility goddesses (3000 B.C.).

Hebron, among the mountains of Judah, with the olive trees that have replaced the oaks of Mamre.

The town of Salem enters biblical history for the first time. Her priest-king, Melchizedek, offers bread and wine there to Abraham, whose flocks are grazing in the forest of Mamre.

The mountains of Judah became the setting of Abraham's life. Hebron is only about fifteen miles from Jerusalem. The town is only named once in the biblical narrative of the patriarchal period, under the name of Salem. Salim, or Salem, was a known deity of the Semitic pantheon: a Phoenician poem discovered at Ras Shamra mentions him when describing the birth of the 'graceful and beautiful' gods. He was probably the Canaanite god of Jerusalem, whose name *Urusalim*, meant 'City of Salim'. The god was undoubtedly benevolent, and the Semitic root of his name *slm*, is that of prosperity.

The region had been inhabited since the Stone Age: the archaic type of homo sapiens has left numerous traces there. Around 3000 B.C. a Semitic invasion ushered in the historical period.

The newcomers, whose social organisation led them to prefer elevated sites, installed themselves on the hill of Ophel, at the junction of the Kidron and the Tyropoean, at the south-east corner of the modern city. Protected on the south and east by a hill, accessible on the north, the spot was easy to defend and was close to springs. The rock, hollowed out by cavities, south of the Haram must have been the site of a primitive religious installation. The highest point was occupied by a rustic sanctuary which served as an abode for the god and for the prince who repre-

The mountains of Judah where Abraham's tribe settled, one of the most rocky and deserted regions in the whole of Palestine.

sented him. Below this the town spread out over the lower terraces as far as the junction of the valleys which seemed to enclose it like two pincers.

It was on Abraham's return from a warlike expedition that Jerusalem entered biblical history. Abraham was leading his peaceful shepherd's existence at Hebron when he heard that a coalition of kings from the north had laid waste the country. To the south of the Dead Sea five towns which had tried to resist had been defeated and sacked; among them were Sodom and Gomorrah. Lot formed part of the booty. Abraham immediately organised the pursuit. With the help of neighbouring tribes he assembled 318 men, caught up with the allied kings in the north at Dan on the other side of Damascus and compelled them to restore the booty.

The long return route passed through the hills dominated by Jerusalem. At the gates of the town Melchizedek offered Abraham bread and wine and in return the patriarch gave him a tenth of the booty. Christian tradition was to regard the priest-king's gesture of hospitality as a prefiguration of the sacrament of the Eucharist. Melchizedek's meeting with Abraham also heralded the Three Kings, a subject dear to medieval artists, but the sober austerity of the original meeting which inspired them has subsequently been restored by numerous objects discovered by archaeologists *(see below right)*. A dignified warrior, Abraham refused all booty for himself. 'I have sworn to the Lord God Most High . . .,' he said, 'that I would not take a thread or a sandal-thong or anything that is yours, lest you should say, I have made Abram rich. I will take nothing but what the young men have eaten, and the share of the men who went with me: let Aner, Eshcol, and Mamre take their share.' He became the peaceful shepherd of Mamre again.

On this occasion he received an ethnic epithet for the first time: Abraham the Hebrew. Abraham was descended from Eber, the great-grandson of Shem, himself the son of Noah. Eber figured as the eponymous ancestor of the tribe. This name had a topographical sense also: Eber meant 'beyond the river'. Abraham would accordingly be a Semite hailing from beyond the Euphrates. People have sometimes connected Hebrews with *habiru*, the name given to the nomads who sacked the towns, but this word does not seen to have designated a single people. Tradition has it that Abraham was an Aramaean and no argument really disproves this hypothesis.

The meeting of Abraham and Melchizedek, King and high priest of Salem (D. Bouts, fifteenth century).

Pottery of the twentieth century B.C. Lamp with four wick holders; dish on three ring-shaped feet.

A nomad in the tradition of the patriarchs.

'Abraham's oak' near Hebron, photographed by Bonfils in 1877, but since dead.

'I will make my covenant between me and you, and will multiply you exceedingly.' (Gen. XVII. 2)

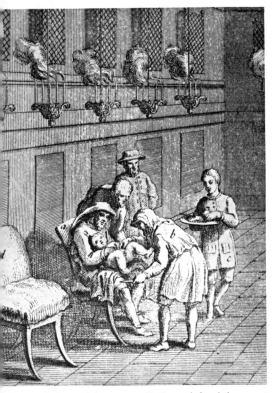

A circumcision scene with the *mohel* and the vacant seat of Elijah (seventeenth-century engraving).

After some ten years of life at Mamre the aging and childless Sarah chose one of her maidservants, Hagar the Egyptian, from among the women who accompanied the tribes and gave her to Abraham to have a child by her. The custom was recognised and the law specified that the concubine and her children could not be ill-treated by the wife. The pregnant Hagar despised the barren wife and Sarah ill-treated her to such a degree that the servant fled into the wilderness. She returned, however, and gave birth to Ishmael, the ancester of the Arabs. Later set aside, Ishmael was not to become Abraham's heir. Elohim had promised a legitimate offspring and He returned to reiterate his promise.

The patriarch was at the foot of his oak tree at Mamre 'at the door of his tent in the heat of the day. He lifted up his eyes and looked, and behold, three men stood in front of him. When he saw them, he . . . bowed himself to the earth . . .' Hospitality was the rule of life in the tents: to take a meal with one's guests turned passing strangers into blood brothers. Elohim was one of the three visitors and He foretold the birth

of a son to Sarah. Hidden within her tent, Sarah laughed as she thought of her age and of that of Abraham. So it was that her son was called Isaac: 'He laughs'.

After this promise various rites established the covenant between Elohim and Abraham more closely. The first of these revived a strange and ancient manner of concluding a contract. Three victims would be split into two halves and aligned on either side of the altar; the contracting parties would pass between the pieces and in this way assimilate themselves to the victims in the event of the covenant being broken. Circumcision, a second sign, was an African rite transmitted via Egypt and anterior to the Bronze Age. The Hebrews made use of stone knives to perform it. Originally a clan initiation ceremony, it was performed at the age of puberty; Ishmael was circumcised at the age of thirteen. Having become a sign of the covenant with God, circumcision was practised on children and on adults. Isaac was circumcised at eight days, Abraham at ninety-nine years.

Abraham's vision near the oak of Mamre (fifth-century mosaic, Rome).

'... now I know that you fear God, seeing you have not withheld your son, your only son, from me.' (Gen. XXIL. 12)

Only thirty-seven miles from the Mediterranean, Jerusalem was completely cut off from the littoral by the mountains of Judah and turned towards the east and the strange landscapes of the wilderness of Judaea and the depression of the Dead Sea, which the Bible calls the Salt Sea. Leaving Mamre, Abraham's two visiting angels made their way to Sodom in order to test the sinful inhabitants and, if there were not ten righteous men there, accomplish their mission of destruction. At the gates of the city they chanced upon Lot and accepted his hospitality offered in the nomadic tradition. This gesture was to save him. Very quickly the Sodomites surrounded the house and demanded the strangers in order to misuse them. It was their death sentence. The messengers of God warned Lot of the fate in store for the town and he fled at dawn with all his family before the rain of fire came down. Having reached the mountains, Lot and his daughters were to beget the ancestors of the Moabites and the Ammonites, the future enemies of Israel. Abraham, for his part, had temporarily left the Mamre-Hebron region.

Archaeology has confirmed, even in Hebron itself, that human masks were employed in agrarian rites to call down rain and make grain germinate, or were employed in the rites of war to ward off the power of the enemy. But the Babylonians, the Canaanites—and probably the Hebrews—went as far as human sacrifice, the sacrifice of children (most frequently the first-born), as well as of the first beasts and the first-fruits of the harvests.

Isaac was born at Gerar, in the south, near the littoral, in the kingdom of Abimelech. From there he set off with his father and some servants to sacrifice to Elohim. He did not know of the order that Abraham had received: that he should take his only son, lead him up to a mountain top and offer him up to God. The patriarch obeyed and climbed the slopes of Jerusalem, but just as he was preparing to slay Isaac an angel intervened to prevent him from doing so. The God of Abraham, while retaining the idea of sacrifice, refused to take human life and sanctioned the substitution of an animal.

Abraham's sacrifice on Mount Moriah where Solomon was to build the Temple. (Psalter of St Louis)

The sacred Rock, the foundation of the Holy of Holies, carved by the Templars into an altar.

Ritual mask found near Hebron (1600 B.C.).

Jerusalem prepares from afar; the covenant sealed between Jahweh and His

Jacob-Israel, the son of Isaac, begot the twelve tribes who crossed over into Egypt. At first they lived there freely, then, under a more cruel Pharaoh, were reduced to bondage. About the year 1300 B.C. the Hebrew slaves, set free by Moses, fled from Egypt. Canaan seemed the only possible refuge, but the coastal route was blocked by some new invaders from the sea who were both armed and organised, the Philistines (in Hebrew *peliochtim*, i.e. invaders, whence the name of Palestine). There only re-mained the desert route, upon which Israel embarked for what was to be a long march; a generation was to spend its life there. During this exodus Moses succeeded in giving to the tribes scattered by the life of the desert a conscious-ness of their community of interests and race, which enabled them later to accom-plish the conquest of Canaan, to federate and eventually unite in the kingdom of which Jerusalem was to be the capital. It was under Moses' influence that Israel passed beyond the bounds of the tribe and attained the concept of nationhood. The religion of the clan was replaced by the cult of Yahweh who appeared to Moses on Mount Horeb and revealed to him His name *Yw/Yhwh* 'I am that I am'. The God who refused to be represented or defined bound Himself to the destiny of a people whom he chose and set free. In exchange for His election He gave the Law. Abraham had only received a sign, that of circumcision; Moses re-ceived a system of laws.

In its shortest and most ancient form

Semite prisoner, walking-stick of Tutankhamen.

Moses receives the Tables of the Law; below, Joshua and the people (ninth-century Tours Bible).

people on Mount Sinai puts its mark on the destiny of a nation in search of itself.

the Decalogue sanctified a faith in one god, who was beyond appearances. It was accompanied by religious and civil laws, all of which were attributed to Moses, although in fact written after the installation at Jerusalem. The laws were engraved on stone tablets which Moses broke in great anger on his descent from the mountain. For forty days he had talked with Yahweh on the mountain, but when he returned the people were merry-making around a statue representing a calf. They had demanded an image of their god and had brought the jewels stolen from the Egyptians to Aaron, the brother of Moses, in order to cover the wooden statue with gold. Tradition has made of this episode a symbol of idolatry, but we can consider it with more subtlety. In the desert the Golden Calf was not just an idol. The Israelites did not worship in it the animal, in the manner of the Egyptians, but rather the symbol of divine power. It was doubtless at Jerusalem that the Golden Calf was to become completely incompatible with the worship of Elohim.

But at the time of the Exodus the relics of old cults were not incompatible with a belief in Yahweh. The episode of the brazen serpent is another demonstration of this. Moses set up an image at the top of a pole in order to cure of reptile bites whoever looked at it. Under the name of Nehushtan this serpent, a sort of ex-voto which 'wards off the evil eye', was to have incense burned before it in the Temple of Jerusalem.

The rites of the greatest Jewish festival, the Passover, go back in the same way to ancient traditions of nomadic times. It was celebrated at night, standing, with a pilgrim's staff in the hand, ready to depart. A lamb whose bones had not been broken was eaten, as in the days when the firstlings of the flocks were offered up. A sign was drawn on the lintels of the doors with a bunch of hyssop dipped in the blood of the lamb, and this had protective power. To this feast was added the offering of unleavened bread.

On becoming a national feast of liberation in commemoration of the departure from Egypt, the Passover would be celebrated exclusively at Jerusalem, on a fixed date, and in order to participate it was necessary to be circumcised. But the sign of blood was done away with, as though people suspected its pagan origin.

The brazen serpent (seventeenth-century engraving).

The original Passover; the lamb, whose blood has marked the door lintels, is eaten by the participants, one staff in hand (seventeenth-century engraving).

'When the cloud was taken up from over the tabernacle,' the people of Israel, without realising, went towards their city.

The scarcely realistic picture of life in the wilderness left by the most ancient tradition, and one which was for long preserved in the iconography, was that of twelve tribes grouped in order around the Tent of the Congregation, each one beneath its standard bearing the name of the son of Jacob-Israel who was its eponymous ancestor. The biblical text is very precise on this subject and enables us to picture fairly accurately what the Tabernacle—sanctuary of Yahweh and place of sacrifice—was like.

It comprised two parts: the Tabernacle and the court. The Tabernacle was a simple construction of boards, divided into the Holy Place and the Most Holy Place. The Most Holy Place was a cube of ten cubits to the side, the symbol of perfection, and contained a chest, the Ark of the Covenant. (The traditional equivalent of the cubit is eighteen inches, but standards varied in different places and at different times, so that no attempt will be made to give accurate modern measurements.) Made of acacia wood, this was two-and-a-half cubits in length and a cubit-and-a-half in width and height, and supported the Mercy Seat, a slab of pure gold, which bore two cherubim. This precious covering was the place where Yahweh communicated with Moses, dictated His wishes and manifested His presence. It was the residence of the invisible god. On the Day of Atonement the high priest would enter the Holy of Holies and, taking with his finger the blood of the bullock offered up as a sacrifice, he would sprinkle the Mercy Seat with it. The wooden Ark contained the two Tables of the Law. It was not only the throne of God but

With his rod Moses makes a fountain well up and twelve streams gush forth for the twelve tribes (third-century fresco at Dura-Europas).

the instrument of His power, merged with Him; when people set eyes upon the Ark, they said: Yahweh. It put in concrete form the power of a divine king who had guided Israel in the wilderness.

The Holy Place measured twenty cubits in length, ten in width and ten in height. It contained the seven-branched candlestick, the table for the shewbread and the altar of incense. As in all oriental cults, the liturgy made great use of incense for which a special altar was reserved. The shewbread, twelve in number like the twelve tribes, remained for a whole week before the Ark and could only be eaten by priests. Near this, on the table, bowls received the incense and libations.

The court which surrounded the Tabernacle was encircled by linen hangings which prevented the sanctuary from being seen. In the middle of the court stood the altar of burnt-offerings. Made of acacia wood, it had four horns at the corners which constituted its most sacred part; these were sprinkled with the blood of the victims and rendered inviolable any criminal who took hold of them. Near the altar was a brass vessel of which the exact significance is not known. There were also basins for the purification of the priests.

Sacrifices came into the following categories: the sacrifice of adoration (the burnt offering) in the course of which the entire victim was offered up to God and was totally consumed by the fire on the altar; offerings of vegetable produce grown by man and used as his food; and the sacrifices of atonement (sacrifices of animals) only the oblation of the blood of which was required in order to wipe out sin. Distinct from the burnt-offering, the *zebah,* or peace offering in which the flesh of the victim was in part consumed in a sacred meal, seemed intended to establish communion with God by commensality.

All this liturgy implied an organised priesthood. One particular tribe, that of Levi, had been chosen by Yahweh to dedicate itself to His worship, and priests and Levites, entrusted with His service, would come from that tribe. Aaron, the brother of Moses, was the first high priest of the Old Testament, anointed by Moses by order of Yahweh. He wore a special costume: the ephod of gold, blue, purple and scarlet, the pectoral (borrowed from Egyptian personages of high rank) the robe fringed with pomegranates alternating with gold bells which enabled the congregation to follow the high priest's movements and the diadem engraved with the inscription: 'Holiness to the Lord.'

Objects for the cult. From left to right: the altar of burnt-offering, the altar of incense, the candlestick the Ark of the Covenant and the table for the shewbread (seventeenth-century engraving).

The Tabernacle in the midst of the tents of the twelve tribes (seventeenth-century engraving).

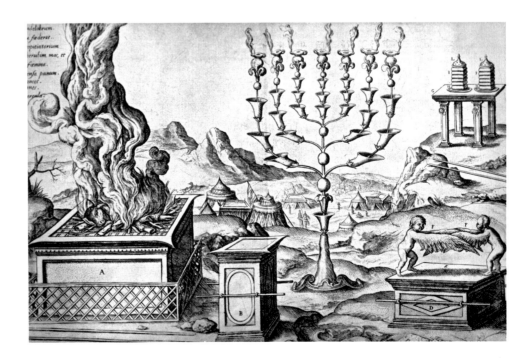

The triumphal advance of the armies of Israel in the wilderness, setting out to conquer the Promised Land. At their head is the Ark of the Covenant (seventeenth-century engraving)

After the euphoria of victory the tribes have to learn to construct peace.

The covenant concluded between Yahweh and Moses on Mount Sinai comprised two terms: the people were to observe the Law and Yahweh was to give them a country. Grouped around the Tent of the Congregation, the tribes set off to conquer Canaan in the thirteenth century B.C. The south resisted their attempts at invasion and the nomads who had already settled on the shores of the Salt or Dead Sea refused them a passage through their territory. The Hebrews made their way round every obstacle, however, and headed for the north, giving battle several times to the kings of Transjordania beyond the Arnon. Some of the clans settled in the conquered lands, the majority prepared to cross the Jordan. Before he died, Moses gazed down from the top of Mount Nebo upon the panorama of the Promised Land.

Yahweh appointed Joshua war leader. With the Ark carried in front by the Levites, the people crossed the river whose waters divided. The trumpets sounded, Jericho, the mighty walled city of palms, was taken and its inhabitants were anathematised according to the rite of holy war and massacred as a sacrifice to Yahweh.

Other towns fell; the Hebrews were making headway. But the resistance of the Canaanites became organised and they attempted to withstand the invasion by forming a coalition. The war would be a long one. Surrounded by enemies, the tribes of Israel fought as individuals, but a common sanctuary was created at Shiloh and the presence of the Ark perpetuated the bonds that had been created in the wilderness. Shiloh consequently became the official religious centre of the confederation.

Joshua divided out the conquered lands *(see map opposite)*; Asher, Naphtali, Zebulum and Issachar established themselves in the north; the Plain of Esdraëlon, which remained in the hands of the Canaanites, separated from the tribes in the centre: Ephraim, Manasseh, Dan and Gad, Benjamin, Judah, Simeon and Reuben settled in the southern part. After the death of Joshua, 'judges' were entrusted with ensuring the functioning of the confederation, and they travelled round the country to enforce the law. Israel was to live for about 200 years

under this regime without accepting the idea of a monarchy. The King of the Jews was Yahweh, the tribes were independent. They ran the risk of being absorbed by the Canaanite civilisation, but songs appeared to revive national sentiment and bring them together again in the face of enemy attacks. These songs are among the most ancient Hebrew poems:

'In the days of Shamgar, son of Anath, in the days of Jaël, caravans ceased and the travellers kept to the byways.

'The peasantry ceased in Israel, they ceased until you arose, Deborah, as a mother in Israel.'

Individual efforts were no longer sufficient to defend the Israelite possessions when the menace of the Philistines, who had invaded the country by sea at the same time as the Hebrews arrived by land, grew worse. The period of the judges was to last for about two centuries. In fact Palestinian archaeology dates the destruction of various Canaanite settlements at the end of the thirteenth century B.C. The Philistine attack, which

The capture of the city of Jericho by Joshua, on the seventh day, to the sound of trumpets.

made the Israelites feel the necessity for a stronger political link between the tribes, occurred about 1050. The people then called for a king. Samuel was judge at the time of the military disasters which ended in the capture of Shiloh and upset the confederation, and although he was attached to the old order he was compelled to appoint a king. Saul, a brave warrior and the conqueror of the Ammonites, was anointed by Samuel and acclaimed by the people as *melech*.

Saul did not alter the structure of Israel in any way, the tribal organisation remained intact and the last representatives of the priesthood accompanied him as in the days when they were the principal link of the confederation. Saul had neither court nor officers and his residence at Gibeah, three miles to the north of Jerusalem, was of a rustic simplicity.

Aided by his son Jonathan, Saul undertook the struggle against the Philistines. He achieved a striking success at Michmash and freed the mountain without, however, removing the danger. The conqueror of the Philistines was to be David.

Canaan (shown horizontally north to south) as divided out among the twelve tribes: (1) Asher. (2) Naphtali. (3) Benjamin. (4) Zebulun. (5) Issachar. (6) Manasseh. (7) Ephraim. (8) Gad. (9) Dan. (10) Judah. (11) Reuben. (12) Simeon.

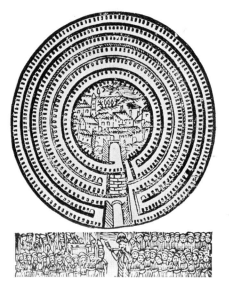

The seven symbolic walls of Jericho (seventeenth-century Hebraic engraving).

Excavations on the presumed site of the city of Jericho.

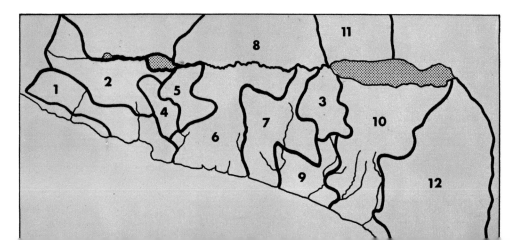

The prompt gesture of a young shepherd acquires unexpected renown.

Shepherd boy with a sling.

Two parallel accounts introduce the figure of David at the court of Saul. One presents him as the conqueror of Goliath, the other as the king's poet page. The war against the Philistines, which occupied the whole reign, appears under different guises: pitched battle, surprise attack or the challenging of a champion. At one point, when the Philistines and the Israelites were face to face in Judah, the giant Goliath stepped forward and asked to fight a Hebrew champion. For forty days and forty nights he repeated his challenge. A young shepherd, the son of Jesse of Bethlehem, had come to bring food to his brothers who were soldiers of Saul. He saw Goliath, took his sling and five smooth stones and advanced towards the Philistine. Although young and without a proper weapon of combat, David triumphed over the giant. After this astonishing defeat the Philistine army fled, pursued by the soldiers of Israel.

This brilliant feat of arms is attributed in another passage to a certain Elhanan whose exploit may have been ascribed to David. Be that as it may, David arrived at court covered in glory, made friends with Saul's son, Jonathan, and continued his warlike exploits. The people revered him as a hero and the women of Israel praised him in songs: 'Saul has slain his thousands, and David his ten thousands'. Confronted with such a reputation, the king became jealous and attempted to kill David, who decided to escape with the help of Jonathan. The priestly family of Shiloh, which had settled near Jerusalem, came to David's assistance and was consequently massacred by Saul in his fury. David then took to the hills, surrounded himself with guerrilla fighters and became their leader. He contracted two marriages into powerful families in the hope of strengthening his position, but ended by going over to the side of the Philistines and offering his services to their king, Achish, at Gath. The latter believed David and said to himself, 'He has made himself utterly abhorred by his people Israel; therefore he shall be my servant always.'

David, armed with a sling, advances against the giant Goliath in reply to the challenge made to the armies of God (seventeenth-century engraving).

Sorrowful, but triumphant, David holds up the bloody head of the Philistine giant (Caravaggio).

Fleeing Saul's jealousy David is proclaimed king. The whole of Israel recognises his authority, but the Philistine menace persists.

David's other aspect was that of the poet and musician and as a youth he soothed the king's period of melancholy with his music. Although highly religious, Saul had been unable to gain the goodwill of the priesthood in the difficult passage from collegiate leadership to the monarchy and Samuel, who had anointed him with a great many restrictions, ended by abandoning and cursing him. The king was then seized with attacks of madness which David calmed by playing his harp. Artists of all periods continue to illustrate the glory of David as a musician, who might well be compared with Apollo the lyre-player of paganism. However primitive his harp may have been, it nevertheless accompanied poems which are still numbered among the masterpieces of world literature. When Saul fell upon his sword on the day of the battle of Gilboa and three of his four sons were killed on the same day, David composed the famous elegy upon the death of his friend, Prince Jonathan, and upon that of the king. Many psalms are attributed to David with likelihood, and he doubtless inspired those not directly composed by him.

The disaster at Gilboa, in the Plain of Esdraëlon, in 1010 B.C., delivered Israel into the hands of the Philistines but they did not, however, venture as far as the provinces of Transjordania. It was there that Saul's last surviving son (Ishbosheth) was to proclaim himself king. He claimed sovereignty over the whole of Israel but lacked the authority to impose it, while the clans did not recognise the principle of heredity in any case. Judah proclaimed David king at Hebron, probably with the co-operation of the Philistines who saw an opportunity of dividing the country. However, David immediately organised the territory of Judah and the neighbouring provinces. Two years later, on the death of Saul's son in the year 1000 B.C., the people went to Hebron and offered David the kingship over the whole of Israel. Once unity had been accomplished war with the Philistines was inevitable and the last phase was enacted near Jerusalem, which was still in the hands of the Canaanites. The Philistines concentrated their army in the valley of Rephaim, but were compelled to retreat before David.

David with psaltery (ninth-century miniature).

'. . . whenever the evil spirit . . . was upon Saul . . . David took the lyre and played . . .' (Rembrandt).

Archaic harp found in Egypt. The shape recalls the instrument of the time of David.

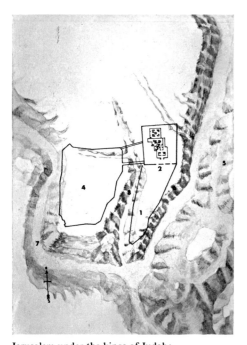

Jerusalem under the kings of Judah:
(1) City of David. (2) The Ophel. (3) Temple of
Solomon. (4) Upper City. (5) Mount of Olives.
(6) Valley of Kidron. (7) Valley of Gehenna.
(8) Valley of Tyropoean.

It was only after he had definitely averted
all danger from outside that David
decided to seize the Jebusite city of
Jerusalem and make it his capital.
There would be no battle. The city was
impregnable by ordinary methods. Confined at that period to the hill of Ophel,
defended by the fortress of Zion, protected naturally by its situation up above
the moat formed by the Kidron and the
Tyropoean and enclosed on the north by
a rampart, it defied the king. 'You will
not come in here, but the blind and the
lame will ward you off.'

David sought a weak point without
attacking. It was by slipping into one of
the town's water conduits that Joab, a
nephew of David and a future general,
opened the gates of the fortress to the
army. He does not seem to have
massacred the indigenous population,
which remained on the spot and the
Israelites gradually blended with it.

The fortress of Zion had become the
'City of David', the king's personal
possession and the capital of the kingdom. It had, indeed, the advantage over
Hebron of occupying the position of a
bridge between the tribes of the south
and north. Jerusalem, like the person of
the king, became the symbol of the
difficult unity between the north and
south. David built a palace there with
the aid of Hiram, King of Tyre, who
sent his cedar trees, his carpenters and
his masons. He did not alter the appearance of the town however.

To the left, at the foot of the wall, the site of the
original City of David.

steep fortress of Zion by a ruse and makes it his capital.

'David and all the house of Israel were making merry before the Lord . . .' while bringing the Ark back to Jerusalem (seventeenth-century engraving).

Once a year pilgrims singing psalms climb to 'the tomb of David' on Mount Zion, with the scrolls of the Law.

With great rejoicing Jerusalem welcomes the Ark of the Covenant. 'David danced before the Lord with all his might.'

Shortly after the capture of Jerusalem David decided to transfer the Ark of the Covenant to the new capital from Kirjath-jearim, where it had remained for more than a generation after being captured by the Philistines. In this way he showed his intention of resuming the ancient Israelite traditions. A sanctuary was erected in the shape of a tent and, after a three months' wait in the house of Obed-edom of Gath because of the terror which it inspired, the Ark made its entry with great pomp into Jerusalem. David appears here as much in the role of a priest as of a king: he himself offered up the sacrifice and broke out in ecstasy in a ritual dance.

Dances and acclamation are two very ancient elements of Jewish worship and remain important elements of it. When the Hebrews visited the sanctuaries of Yahweh on feast days or the Ark was brought into their camp, they uttered such violent acclamations that they were sometimes mistaken for war cries. The moment when the crowd was to give these sacred acclamations was indicated in the liturgy by the signal *Hallelujah* (Praise ye Yahweh). These acclamations were accompanied by dances or processional rounds about the holy object, the altar of the victim (in Hebrew the same word *hag* denotes both feast and dance).

When the procession had reached its objective and the Ark had been set down beneath the Tabernacle prepared for it, David offered the sacrifice which consisted of both burnt offerings and peace offerings. This religious festival was the occasion of the breach between David and his wife Michal, the daughter of Saul, who had mocked at her husband's dance. 'It was before the Lord,' David replied, 'who chose me above your father, and above all his house, to appoint me as prince over Israel, over the people of the Lord—and I will make merry before the Lord. I will make myself yet more contemptible than this, and will be abased in your eyes; but by the maids of whom you have spoken, by them shall I be held in honour.' 'And Michal the daughter of Saul had no child to the day of her death.' We must see in this incident the narrator's desire to emphasise everything that separated David from Saul. David's success was not only military and political, but also religious. He depended upon the priesthood. To minister to the new sanctuary he called upon Abiathar, a

Two young Israeli girls in traditional costume perform the ritual staff dance.

priest of the sacerdotal line of Shiloh. Jerusalem became the religious centre of the kingdom, the Ark legitimised the new order and the new state appeared as the continuation of the sacred institutions of the past. In all these designs, David showed himself to be far more wise and clever than Saul, who had not hesitated to massacre the priests and had neglected the Ark which had been captured by the Philistines. It was doubtless David who prepared detailed plans for the Temple. The difficult union of the priesthood and monarchy was realised in his person.

From the terrace of his palace David surprises Bath-sheba taking a bath in the open air, and is filled with desire (Feanciabigio, sixteenth century).

'The Lord is my rock, and my fortress, and my deliverer.'

The concentration of power in the hands of the king entailed a new administration of the state and gave to the court a prestige unknown in the days of Saul. As a sign of his wealth David had numerous wives, a great many children, a guard of honour and a table at which a multitude of guests took their places.

Of David's wives Bath-sheba was his favourite. He caught sight of her one day from the roof of his palace when she was taking her bath, a famous scene that has enchanted poets and painters. He was filled with such desire that he sent for her immediately. Within a short space of time Bath-sheba was pregnant, but her husband, Uriah, was at the wars and could not pass for the child's father. David sent for him and tried to persuade him to fulfil his conjugal duties, but Uriah refused. A man did not have relations with a woman in times of war; war was sacred. David therefore dismissed Uriah and asked his general to expose him deliberately to the greatest

danger in battle. The prophet Nathan heard of this and rebuked David, who repented. 'And the Lord struck the child that Uriah's wife bore to David, and it became sick. David therefore besought God for the child; and David fasted, and went in and lay all night upon the ground . . . On the seventh day the child died.' But Bath-sheba later gave birth to another son, Solomon.

During this period the wars conducted by Joab continued. Before launching out into foreign wars, David unified the territory of Israel by subduing the numerous Canaanite cities still holding out in the Plain of Esdraëlon, in Galilee and along the coast. Israel, which formerly only designated the confederation of the tribes, thus became a geographical entity embracing increasingly extensive areas of Palestine. The Canaanites became part of this and their kings became vassals of the King of Israel.

At this point the problem of opposi-

tion or assimilation to the Canaanite culture arose. Abroad, Joab was fighting on several fronts. An insult offered to the ambassadors sent by David to the Ammonites in Transjordania provided the opportunity for a punitive expedition. The Ammonites, who were being assisted by the Aramaeans, were annihilated and David received the Ammonite crown. To the east of Palestine, Moab and Edom were conquered and treated with great harshness. The King of Moab became David's vassal and Edom became an Israelite province. In the north David defeated the Aramaeans and the King of Zobah. Then at the end of his reign, David signed an agreement with Hiram, King of Tyre, probably with the object of trade, so that his authority ultimately extended over the whole of Palestine from the desert to the Mediterranean.

A census was taken. Joab travelled throughout the country and returned a total of 800,000 men-at-arms in Israel and 500,000 in Judah. This census was

King David questions Uriah, the husband of Bath-sheba, about the fighting and gives him wine and food from his table (seventeenth-century engraving).

regarded as a sin and an act of impiety which interfered with the prerogatives of Yahweh, who alone was responsible for increasing families and nations. David was punished and a pestilence was sent down upon Israel. As an expiation David was ordered by the prophet to offer up a sacrifice at the gates of the city on the threshing-floor of Araunah the Jebusite. This site, on the hill which dominated the original city of Jerusalem on the north, was bought by the king. It was there that the temple of Solomon would be built.

The Bible furnishes few particulars about the domestic structure of the kingdom. It seems, however, that David modelled his administration on that of Egypt, from which country he even brought in certain officials. Yet this brilliant king never really succeeded in uniting the two parts of the kingdom; he remained the King of 'Israel' and Judah'. The affair of Absalom was soon to reveal this division tragically.

David's repentance (Pesellino, fifteenth century).

Absalom's short lived conspiracy and the sudden revolt of Sheba expose the

ABSALON·VIDI·PENDER·PECHAPELLI·POI·CHE·FEDO·LACHAMERA·PATERNA·ET·VCTO·ERA·FILCATO·DIQVADRELLI

Joab pierces Absalom's heart as he hangs in the branches of a terebinth, caught by his hair while attempting to escape (P. del Minella, Sienna detail).

flaws of the kingdom.

King David grown old and sick (Aert de Gelder, seventeenth century, Rijksmuseum, Amsterdam).

The shadow cast over David's glittering life was that of his third son, Absalom, whose intrigues epitomised all the rebellions and oppositions of the end of his reign. 'In all Israel there was no one so much to be praised for his beauty as Absalom'. His first noteworthy action was a gesture of retribution when he killed his half-brother, Amnon, who had violated his sister, Tamar, but had been left unpunished by his father. Whether it was the crime of a lover of justice or simply a murder which removed a candidate to the throne, this incident obliged Absalom to go into exile for three years. He was recalled through the influence of Joab, who induced David to pardon him.

On his return Absalom set about exploiting all the tribes' causes for discontent, thus preparing his accession to the throne. The centralised administration of the state, despite David's political ability, offended the independent spirit of the tribes. Absalom stirred up all the dissatisfied elements, was ready to listen to grievances and made contact with the whole of the country. After four years he had himself proclaimed king by a powerful conspiracy at Hebron, the former capital which the Judaeans had seen with resentment abandoned by David. This rebellion seemed to be the outburst of a general hostility. The king, however, retained the loyalty of certain groups: the priesthood, his personal troops and the court officials. As he did not have sufficient time to organise the resistance, David left Jerusalem and took refuge with trustworthy tribes on the other side of the Jordan. When the two armies eventually came face to face, Absalom was defeated, and as he attempted to escape was the victim of a curious accident. His mule passed beneath the branches of a terebinth in which his hair became entangled. The news was brought to Joab, who dispatched the traitor with a lance.

This turbulent life, which ended so ingloriously, has lent a mysterious glamour to the curious tomb which still stands beneath the walls of Jerusalem and which, although supposed to be that of Absalom, was not built until hundreds of years after his death (see p. 248).

Before David could return to Jerusalem a new revolt broke out. It occurred this time among the northern tribes and constituted a separatist manoeuvre: the personal union realised by David, now advanced in years, was fragile. The leader

When David had grown old they gave him Abishag (wood-cut by Holbein, fifteenth century).

this time was Sheba, a Benjamite who possibly belonged to the family of Saul. But this last rebellion was quickly put down by Joab. David remained victorious and the story of Abishag, the Shunammite, brings some light into the sombre end of his reign.

'Now King David was old and advanced in years; and although they covered him with clothes, he could not get warm. Therefore his servants said to him, Let a young maiden be sought for my lord the king, and let her wait upon the king, and be his nurse; let her lie in your bosom, that my lord the king may be warm. So they sought for a beautiful maiden throughout all the territory of Israel, and found Abishag the Shunammite, and brought her to the king.'

'Zadok the priest took the horn of oil . . . and anointed Solomon . . . and all the people said, Long live King Solomon' (seventeenth-century engraving)

Tombs brought to light by excavations in the rock of Ophel and believed to be a royal necropolis of Israel (tenth to seventh centuries B.C.).

'So Solomon sat on the throne of David his father; and his kingdom was firmly established.' (1 Kings II. 12)

The problem of the succession was now acute. Eastern dynasties did not have a fixed law of succession recognised unanimously. In Israel there was a presumption in favour of the eldest son, but the rank or whim of the mother, the discretion of the king or the manifest favour of Yahweh could give the preference to a younger son. The women of the harem wove sinister plots to ensure the triumph of their offspring and violent hatreds grew up between the young princes. At David's court two factions vied with one another. Joab, leader of the army, and Abiathar, the priest, supported the eldest son and legitimacy: they were for Adonijah. The prophet Nathan, Benaiah, captain of the mercenaries and Joab's rival, and Zadok, the rival priest to Abiathar, took the side of Solomon, the son of the beautiful Bath-sheba, the king's favourite wife, to whom he had promised that he would appoint their son as successor. Adonijah tried his luck and had himself proclaimed king. Solomon's party informed David of what was happening and urged him to announce that Solomon was to succeed him. David ordered that Solomon should be invested, and he was anointed king by Zadok.

Before he died, David left Solomon a kind of testament: he was to keep the statutes of Yahweh in the Law of Moses and carry out those acts of revenge which he had been unable to perform himself: these concerned Joab in particular, who had served him faithfully but had shed the blood of his son who had been guilty of murder. The house of David was not to be called to account by Yahweh for the crimes committed on its behalf. He advised his son to show kindness to those who had remained loyal and had received and succoured him at the time of Absalom's rebellion.

'David slept with his fathers' and was buried in the City of David with the other kings of Judah, on the hill of Ophel where archaeologists have discovered the presence of a very ancient royal necropolis. Since the tenth century, however, it is to a vast arched burial vault on Mount Zion that pilgrims have come to venerate the tomb of David. It is covered with a cloth embroidered with twenty-two crowns and pomegranates symbolising the twenty-two kings issued from the line of David.

The legendary tomb of David: three crowns surmount the three consonants of his name.

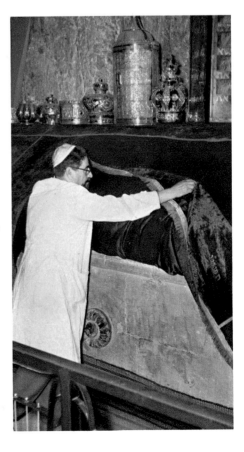

Moslems and Jews have a common veneration for the 'tomb of David'.

The covering of the tomb is decorated with twenty-two crowns and pomegranates.

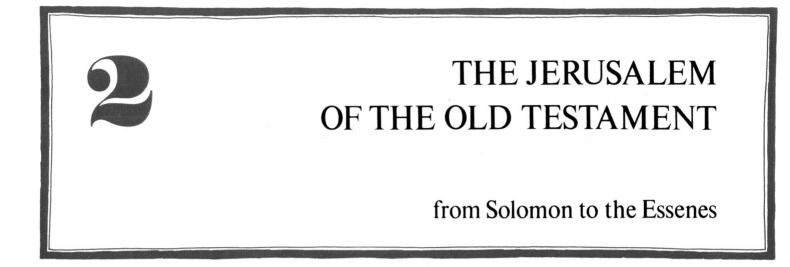

2

THE JERUSALEM OF THE OLD TESTAMENT

from Solomon to the Essenes

Many times he delivered them, but they were rebellious in their purposes, and were brought low through their iniquity. Nevertheless he regarded their distress, when he heard their cry.

Ps. CVI. 43-44

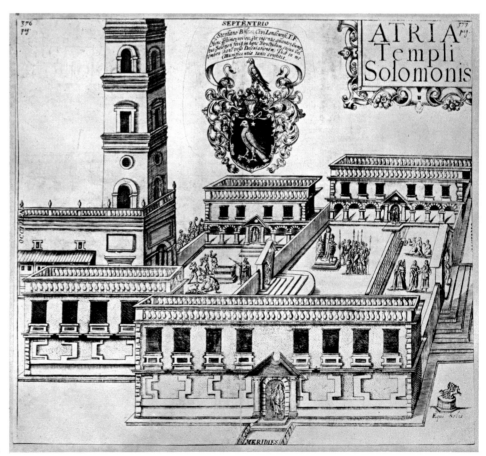

The Temple esplanade (seventeenth-century engraving).

In 960 B.C. Solomon begins building the Temple on Mount Moriah (seventeenth-century engraving).

'... neither hammer nor axe nor any tool of iron was heard

Solomon had been given understanding to 'discern between good and evil'.

An able administrator, Solomon swept Jerusalem and Israel into a veritable race towards prosperity. Destroying the old structures and utilising all resources to the full, he created a new state. The country could not keep up the pace; it was not yet fully ready for the changes that the young king wanted to impose. His first action was to do away with the past in the shape of the court. Adonijah was condemned to death for trying to lay claim to David's harem, which was considered a sign of royal power. His supporters were exiled, like the priest Abiathar, or done away with, like Joab, the general who had killed Absalom with his own hands and sided with Adonijah, the pretender to the throne. He had taken refuge in the sanctuary and it was there that his rival, Benaiah, struck him down without regard for the law which spared the life of whoever grasped the horns of the altar. Shimei, the former leader of a revolt against David, was executed.

At the beginning of his reign frontier incidents obliged Solomon to surrender part of his Syrian possessions, but he did not attempt to contest this, preferring to devote himself to administration and a

great building programme. He had a magnificent conception of the monarchy and desired peace and wealth. One of his first preoccupations was to furnish it with the external signs by which a great power is recognised. He ushered in his policy of grandeur by undertaking extensive building operations in the capital.

Jerusalem now left the confines of the City of David and began to extend towards the north, over the hill which rose some sixty feet above the old city. David had bought the field of a Jebusite there and probably planned to build the Temple on this site. Solomon expanded this project and embarked on a great architectural ensemble which grouped together the Temple and the palace in several buildings, the throne room, hall of pillars, House of the Forest of Lebanon and private residence.

Defensive works were set on hand throughout the country. At Jerusalem the Millo, the citadel which protected the City of David at its weak point on the north, was completed. The frontier towns were given fortifications in the Canaanite style: Hazor in Galilee defied the Aramaeans, Megiddo commanded the defile leading to Mount Carmel and

assured the protection of the north of the country, while Gezer and Beth-horon did the same on the west as did Tamar on the Edomite frontier. These undertakings constituted a definite policy: the centralisation and unification of the state around Jerusalem and its equipment with a national army. This centralisation was carried out to the detriment of the autonomy of the tribes and the institutions of provincial life. The country was divided into twelve districts, each administered by an officer who was entrusted with levying the taxes in kind destined to provide for the upkeep of the king and his court and harem, together with that of the civil servants. The provinces satisfied these requirements in rotation, for a month each.

Only the tribe of Judah—the royal tribe —was exempt, in flagrant violation of the principle of equality which had operated in the federation until then. This system transformed the life of the peasants: the harvests were supervised and the peasants themselves were subjected to statute labour and poll-tax. The king raised a personal army, made military service obligatory, renewed the armaments, equipped his soldiers with Canaanite war

in the temple, while it was being built', at which one hundred and seventy thousand workmen laboured for over seven years (engraving by Luycken).

chariots and formed a cavalry corps; great troops of horses were to make his four thousand stables famous.

This proud monarchy was of divine right. Solomon did not forget that he was the anointed of Yahweh. He inaugurated his reign by offering up a gigantic holocaust of a thousand beasts at Gibeon, a high place in the vicinity of Jerusalem. That same night Yahweh appeared to Solomon in a dream and the king asked Him for 'an understanding mind'. He soon gave proof that his wish had been granted when two prostitutes presented themselves before him to obtain justice. They had each given birth to a son in the same house, but one of them had died. Both claimed to be the mother of the survivor. Solomon allotted them half the child each, and the real mother revealed herself by refusing to let it die.

The Judgment of Solomon (painting attributed to Giovanni Balduccio, sixteenth century).

The finest cedars of Lebanon and the best craftsmen of Sidon build a Temple which will be filled with the 'glory' of Yahweh.

Cedars of Lebanon like those which the King of Tyre exchanged with Solomon for wheat and oil.

The language spoken on the building yards of Jerusalem was Phoenician. The Hebrews had never built anything; as nomads they had occupied towns already completed. So to help him in his vast project Solomon called upon his father's old ally Hiram, King of Tyre, who in exchange for the oil and wheat Solomon required supplied him with timber and his best craftsmen from Sidon, employed by Egypt herself since 3000 B.C.

Nothing remains at Jerusalem today of the splendour of Solomon. Only a few pieces of evidence unearthed by archaeologists, and above all the texts relating to the Temple, form the basis of hypotheses and reconstructions. The biggest part of the vast architectural ensemble undertaken on the northern hill was given over to the palace. The Temple proper was of limited proportions, which is somewhat surprising when one considers Solomon's characteristic love of display. But for the Semites the Holy Place was first and foremost an open area, the court, of which the building occupied only a small part. The extent of the court conspicuously increased the importance of the house itself. The first Temple of a jealously national god, who until then had resided beneath a tent, posed a problem of invention. The Phoenicians had a tradition of their own, but this was bound up with their own religion and their dealings with Egypt. There was, however, a constant in the Semitic religions: the Temple was above all a house standing on a court, the House of Yahweh, the dwelling-place of the Ark which represented Him and upon or in which resided His 'glory', and it is to the plan of a secular house that one must turn to understand its appearance.

The House of Yahweh was a rectangular edifice sixty cubits by twenty cubits, with a flat roof. It was set east to west with the entrance facing the rising sun. The main walls were built of ashlar, the only material which could be found in abundance at Jerusalem, as too were the foundations, but with wooden clamps like those discovered on several excavation sites in Phoenicia. Annexes consisting of storehouses and quarters for the priests were built up against the Temple on the west, north and south.

The building of Solomon's Temple.

Solomon enthroned (Poussin, Louvre. Paris, detail).

Only the high priest has access to the mysterious gloom of the Holy of Holies where the Ark of the Covenant rests upon the sacred rock.

The Temple of Yahweh was not generally accessible. The congregation only had -access to the court which was, strictly speaking, the place of worship. The house was preceded by a porch, the *ulam*, which had a double door. In front of the porch were two pillars of brass, each of which had a name: that on the right was called Jachin and that on the left, Boaz. Their significance is not explained; they served no useful purpose architecturally and their function appears to have been symbolic.

Only the priests had the right to pass through the porch and enter the first chamber which was the most spacious: this was the *hekal*, a rectangular room forty cubits by twenty cubits and thirty cubits in height. It was lit by bays set in the upper part. The *hekal* housed certain accessories of the cult: the alter of incense, which was made of gold, the table for the shewbread, ten candlesticks, and lamps, knives, cups, basins and braziers. Only the high priest entered the *debir*: the Holy of Holies, a dark mysterious room twenty cubits square in which the Ark of the Covenant was lodged.

The plan of the Temple has given rise to numerous theories concerning the symbolism which may have inspired it. The three parts of the building have

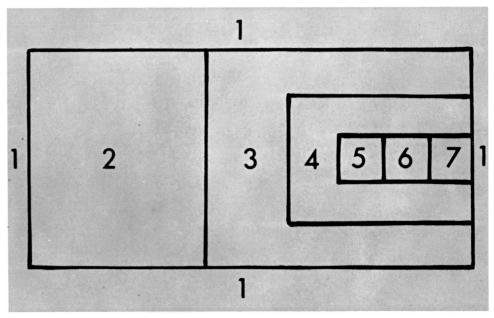

Solomon's Temple. (1) Court of the Gentiles. (2) Women's Court. (3) Court of Israel. (4) Court of the priests. (5) Porch. (6) The Holy Place. (7) The Holy of Holies.

been held to represent the three parts of the cosmos: water, earth and sky, which would correspond to the cosmogony of the Bible. The two pillars of brass placed before the cosmos would then recall those upon which the earth rests. The Temple of Jerusalem was both the national sanctuary of the Israelite people because the Ark reposed there and, at the same time, a dynastic sanctuary and royal chapel, the priest in charge of which (appointed by the king) was a member of the council. The king, who was himself a sacred personage, was worshipped.

The esplanade of the Mosque of Omar, the Haram Ash-Sharif where formerly stood the first Temple of Jerusalem, that of Solomon (960-587 B.C.).

The Temple interior with the wreathed columns, the ritual pool and the Holy of Holies, as pictured in the Middle Ages.

The court and the southern gateway; a reconstruction of the Temple, inspired by the sanctuaries of Egypt and Syria, by Chipiez in the nineteenth century.

Mythological figurine from Nimrud (eighth century B.C., British Museum, London).

A sarcophagus which possibly reproduces the pillars of the Temple.

Incense, precious woods and symbols are the only witnesses to the presence of God.

The external decoration of the Temple was deliberately restrained and, in order to comply with the precepts of Moses, the sanctuary was devoid of any anthropomorphic representation of Yahweh. Only the Ark revealed the divine presence. But the sumptuousness of the project necessitated some decoration, which was carried out by the Phoenician craftsmen using the repertory they possessed and which Solomon left them free to employ.

It was in this way that Syro-Phoenician and Egyptian symbolism was introduced into Jerusalem. The walls, ceiling, floor and doors were completely covered with cedar-wood, cypress-wood or wild olive, and this carved wood was itself overlaid with gold. The decorative motifs took up again the subjects of winged personages, flowers, palmettes and rosettes like those on ivories discovered on several excavation sites in Syria-Phoenicia.

The whole ensemble of buildings, which were doubtless smaller in size than reconstructions have supposed, was no more than the repository of the Ark. The Ark itself was dominated by two cherubim in olive wood overlaid with gold ten cubits high and ten wide. Influenced by the Egyptian style of sphinxes and protecting goddesses, they seem to have acted as guardians. The

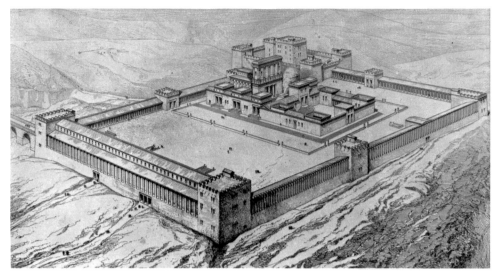

Reconstruction of the Temple of Herod, on the site of the first Temple, by M. de Vogüé.

Temple liturgy made great use of incense and among the order of Levites was found, not surprisingly, a special order with responsibility for the incense. The candlesticks of the *hekal* were ten in number, five to the north and five to the south, and it seems that this number was symbolic. It is not known whether they burned day and night like the seven-branched candlestick in the second Temple. The *debir*, in its cubical proportions and obscurity, also appears to express symbols which are again difficult to interpret. Yahweh dwelt, and had wished to dwell, in darkness, as is stated in the prayer of dedication (I Kings VIII. 12). This characteristic recalls the temples of Egypt in which one passes from the bright light of the colonnaded courts into the darkness of the sanctuary through a series of increasingly gloomy halls.

The Ark of the Covenant in the Holy of Holies with the cherubim (seventeenth-century engraving).

Altar of incense (seventeenth-century engraving).

Twenty-two thousand oxen and a hundred and twenty thousand sheep are sacrificed so that the Spirit might reign.

Ten lavers of brass, each with a capacity of forty baths (a bath is about nine gallons), were used for the ablutions of the priests and for purification. They were placed on quadrangular bases with wheels, four cubits square and three in height, and decorated with a whole symbolic fauna of bulls, lions and cherubim, and plant subjects consisting of palmettes and scrolls.

The significance of the 'molten sea' has not been explained. This basin, which was ornamented with colocynths, was ten cubits across and five cubits high and had a capacity of two thousand baths. It rested on a base representing twelve oxen which were arranged in groups of three set at each of the cardinal points. It was doubtless symbolic and recalled the sacred lakes of Egyptian temples or the 'body of waters beneath the earth' of the Babylonians, or the 'Heavenly Ocean'. The bulls call to mind the Canaanite cults where they were the symbol of fertility; the same symbol is found on the capitals of the two pillars, Jachin and Boaz, which were decorated with pomegranates. A whole set of objects was required for the preparation of animal sacrifices: vases, shovels and basins for aspersion. The objects were made of bronze, like the mobile lavers of

Hiram, the bronze-founder of Tyre, who worked on the banks of the Jordan where there was excellent clay.

The court reserved for the throng and for sacrifices was an important part of the Holy Place. It corresponded to the present esplanade of the Haram, but its dimensions were doubtless considerably smaller. On this flat area were placed the various large utensils required for the sacrifice, the most important being the brazen altar, upon which the priests climbed to deposit the victims sacrificed as burnt offerings and which was twenty cubits square and five cubits high.

When the temple was finished (in 960 B.C.), the great feast of dedication was held. Solomon offered up a holocaust of twenty-two thousand oxen and a hundred and twenty thousand sheep. The brazen altar was too small and the king had to consecrate the middle of the precinct to turn it into a place of sacrifice. This was, in fact, the Rock of Ornan, the Jebusite (the former owner of the threshing-floor), which emerged at this spot. In great pomp the sacred Ark left the City of David to enter the *debir*, the Holy of Holies. Solomon ascended the dais and addressed a solemn prayer to Yahweh, who descended in the form of a cloud upon the Temple He was to inhabit.

On the building yards of the Temple, Hiram, the bronze-founder

Dedication of the Temple by Solomon. As soon as the priests

One of the ten brass lavers of the Temple.

The molten sea, whose significance is uncertain.

of Tyre, directs Solomon's workmen. 'He was full of wisdom, understanding and skill, for making any work in bronze', the Bible says of him.

had left the sanctuary a cloud suddenly appeared inside it: 'the glory of the Lord filled the house of the Lord' (seventeenth-century engraving).

At the foot of these tall cliffs the deposits of copper known as 'Solomon's mines' were worked from the times of the earliest kings.

Enamelled copper pot and bronze nails from Solomon's mines (tenth century).

Small jug with a strainer to filter beer (twelfth century B.C.).

The Jerusalem of ivory and spices. Solomon gives his fleet and caravans trading papers for Africa and Asia.

With the reign of Solomon Jerusalem became a cosmopolitan city. The king took advantage of the geographical situation of Palestine on the caravan routes, which led from Egypt and Arabia to Syria, to secure huge revenues for himself from trade, which was turned into a royal monopoly. He sold Cilician horses to Egyptian enterprises and Egyptian chariots to Syria, while he exchanged the corn and oil of his own country for the timber of Lebanon.

One of his great economic successes is not mentioned in the Bible: the excavations at Ezion-Geber on the Gulf of Elath have brought blast-furnaces to light in which Solomon's workers smelted the copper and iron ore extracted from the mountains on both sides of the valley. A solidly equipped merchant fleet was built in the same port with the aid of Hiram of Tyre, and this ventured as far as Ophir, from which the Israelite vessels brought back gold and silver, precious woods, ivory, jewels, and monkeys for the king's amusement.

Coinage was not yet in use, wealth being put in reserve in the shape of objects, vessels, golden shields for the Temple and jewels, which were stored in the arsenal, the treasury constituted by the House of the Forest of Lebanon, which formed part of the palace. Although remaining a state monopoly, Solomon's enterprises brought an economic prosperity to Israel never before attained. Thousands of people were in employment, craftsmen brought their products to perfection, private enterprises were stimulated and the standard of living was raised. Society suffered a profound transformation, however, and passed from an agrarian to an industrial and commercial state. A class division became more and more pronounced between an exploited proletariat and an aristocracy of civil servants and nouveau riche merchants.

Israel moved away from its former proud, independent tribal way of life, state control having stifled the spirit of collegiate direction. An opposition to this development manifested itself in the north of the country and took as its pretext the desire of the house of David to create a dynasty. Many Israelites refused to accept Solomon's rule as a divine institution and protested against the tyranny of a Judaean. A revolt broke out at the instigation of Jeroboam, the Ephrathite who was in charge of statute labour for the tribes of Joseph, but it was vigorously put down and Jeroboam was obliged to flee to Egypt. A rift had opened up, however, between the two parts of the kingdom and, even before his death, Solomon had managed to alienate the northern tribes. The provinces were already opposed to Jerusalem, the capital.

King Solomon draws up the inventory of his treasures stored in the House of the Forest of Lebanon (Koninck, seventeenth century, Berlin Museum).

Caravans come to Jerusalem from the heart of Arabia. Solomon gives a magnificent reception to Balkis, from the distant kingdom of Sheba.

Jewish dancer from the Yemen, the land of Balkis.

Jerusalem welcomed the Queen of Sheba with great ceremony. She came from a kingdom of the eastern Yemen where a Jewish colony exists to the present day. Its people, who were originally nomadic, had settled down and controlled the commercial activity of almost the whole of Arabia from Ethiopia to Somaliland, the land of gold. The caravans which carried the incense and spices from these distant lands converged upon Israel and, contrary to the legend, it was doubtless an economic mission which was at the origin of this visit.

The queen arrived from these colourful, legendary regions with all her suite. Her camels bore gold and spices and precious stones. The king awaited her at the palace, in the sumptuous throne room where his magnificence was seen at its most brilliant. The throne was of ivory covered with pure gold and two lions stood beside the arms, one on each side. The contents of the House of the

Forest of Lebanon impressed the queen. Unlike poorer constructions or the tents of the desert, its walls were of stone, the floors of cedar wood, the interior walls were embellished with carved ornament and the upper part was painted in bright colours. The palace buildings were connected by colonnades and open air terraces and clumps of trees. The roofs and walls were decorated with stones inlaid with gold as had been done for the Temple of God. Queen Balkis asked Solomon riddles; the king replied with his legendary wisdom, and Balkis presented him with all the riches that she had brought with her: 'The report was true which I heard in my own land of your affairs and of your wisdom', she said to Solomon, 'but I did not believe the reports until I came and my own eyes had seen it; and behold, the half was not told me; your wisdom and prosperity surpass the report which I heard'.

Balkis, Queen of Sheba, attracted by Solomon's fame, pays him a visit (P. della Francesca, fifteenth century, Church of S. Francesco, Arezzo).

The meeting between the Queen of Sheba and Solomon in which medieval exegesis saw the meeting between Christ and the Church (Veronese, Turin).

The love of foreign women and the love of Molech lead to a scandal.

A Lebanese girl playing the ritual tambourine.

'Flee strange women.'

Israeli girl dancing to the rhythm of the tambourine as did Miriam the prophetess.

The policy of foreign alliances had started as early as Solomon's marriage: his first wife, an Egyptian princess, the daughter of a Pharaoh of the XXIst dynasty, had brought him Gezer as her marriage portion. Since then Solomon's harem had considerably increased. Tradition credits him with 700 wives, all foreign, a symbol of his wealth and alliances. It is moving to discover again today, on the beautiful faces of the women of the countries of the Near East, something of what must have been the fascinating spectacle of the court of Solomon at Jerusalem, resounding with dances and songs, and humming with the processions of ambassadors and great caravaneers.

This love of foreign marvels led Solomon into going as far as to sacrifice on the high places to idols, the various gods of his wives. Thus, paradoxically, the sovereign who had built the Temple of the jealous God, himself introduced foreign gods into his country. A hill which prolongs the Mount of Olives recalls by its name, the Mount of Corruption, the memory of these idolatrous cults, while into the valley of Gehenna was even introduced the worship of the Ammonite god, Molech, who demanded the sacrifice of children.

The king's name is also linked with literature and the admirable *Song of Songs*. Critics, however, reject this attribution on philological grounds: both by its language and style, this celebrated work would appear to belong to post Exilic literature, since it contains Persian words, Aramaic neologisms and late Hebrew expressions. In addition its optimistic character is in keeping with the period of peace and prosperity which the reforms of Ezra and Nehemiah were to bring to the community *(see* p.88), and with the political calm enjoyed by Palestine in the fourth century. The term 'song of songs', like 'holy of holies' or 'king of kings', is a typical Hebraic form of the superlative: the most beautiful song, the poem *par excellence*.

It is a collection of nuptial songs, a literary genre for long held in honour in the Mediterranean East. This book which does not mention God and employs a language of lyrical love, both tender and passionate, has always been held to be canonical and inspired. Jewish tradition interpreted it as an allegory of the love between God and Israel; Christian theologians as that of the mysti-

Solomon worshipping idols: 'when Solomon was old his wives turned away his heart after other gods' (Koninck, seventeenth century, Rijksmuseum, Amsterdam).

cal marriage of Christ and the Church.

Others have preferred to leave it its literal meaning as the most beautiful poem ever to celebrate human love and the marriage of husband and wife.

'I am very dark, but comely, O daughters of Jerusalem, like the tents of Kedar, like the curtains of Solomon.

'Do not gaze upon me because I am swarthy, because the sun has scorched me . . . they made me the keeper of the vineyards; but, my own vineyard I have not kept'.

Thus starts the first song of the bride.

Even if it is certain that Solomon was not the author of the *Song of Songs* and even if it is impossible to attribute the *Proverbs* and the maxims of *The Wisdom of Solomon* to him with certainty, it can be asserted that his court saw the flowering of an historical literature without equal in the ancient world. It is generally admitted that he had the first collections of national songs made; the sculptures of the temples and the palace bear witness to his interest in the arts while he spoke, according to the Bible, 'of trees, from the cedar tree that is in Lebanon to the hyssop that grows out of the wall; he spoke also of beasts, and of birds, and of reptiles, and of fish'.

Miniature from the *Song of Songs*, traditionally ascribed to Solomon (twelfth century, Rheims).

Already the new kingdom is torn apart.
Pharaoh launches an onslaught on the riches of the late great king.

Around 922 the death of Solomon precipitated Jerusalem into a new phase of her history, one both unsettled and confused. The future of the town was closely linked with the dynasty of David which had made the fortune of this royal city. She shone thanks to the toil of an entire nation and the commercial and diplomatic genius of Solomon. She held the rank of a cosmopolitan capital in a land still largely agricultural and traditionalist. Without hesitating she chose Solomon's son Rehoboam as king. But the tribes gathered together at Shechem demanded the abolition of statute labour. Rehoboam's uncompromising refusal created a schism which split the country in two irrevocably. Judah and Benjamin remained faithful to the principal of heredity and kept Rehoboam as king and Jerusalem as capital; the other ten tribes formed the kingdom of Israel. Shechem became the capital of the North and challenged Jerusalem's role not only as the political, but also as the religious capital. One of the first preoccupations of Jeroboam, the King of Israel, was to establish not one but two official sanctuaries which could vie with Jerusalem: Bethel, linked with the patriarchal tradition, and Dan, which prided itself on a priesthood going back to Moses. At

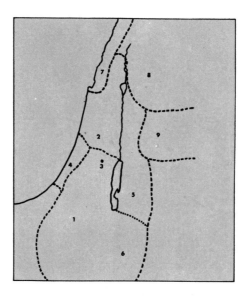

Palestine at the period of the schism:
(1) Judah. (2) Israel. (3) Jerusalem. (4) Philistines.
(5) Moab. (6) Edom. (7) Phoenicia. (8) Aram.
(9) Ammon.

Bethel the worship of the 'pedestal' bull of Yahweh harked back to the tradition of the golden calf of the Exodus, and to the animal symbolism of earliest times. The cult of Yahweh and that of Baal, whose force was symbolised by a bull,

Rehoboam, Solomon's eldest son (931–913 B.C.) responsible by his harsh and unrelenting behaviour for the schism between Judah and Israel.

were very soon confused, however, and the religious policy of the king, originally intended to be a return to the fountain-head, was rapidly condemned by the prophetic circles, who were the guardians of the purity of the Law.

The altar is rent during Jeroboam's sacrifice (seventeenth-century engraving).

Jeroboam restores the cult of the golden calf (seventeenth-century engraving).

The hills of Samaria where Omri, King of Israel, established a capital to rival Jerusalem.

The first consequence of the schism for both states was their parallel weakening, which the neighbouring countries took advantage of. Egypt immediately attacked. The Pharaoh launched a lightning campaign, destroyed a large number of towns, laid waste the copper mines, entered Jerusalem and pillaged the Temple treasures and the riches of Solomon. External difficulties did not prevent the two rival states from making war on each other, however. Hostilities continued without a break for some fifty years and Jerusalem was often threatened.

A period of calm and internal peace began in 876 with the accession of Omri in Israel and Jehoshaphat in Judah. The real rival of Jerusalem now appeared. In the sixth year of his reign Omri abandoned Shechem and made Samaria into a luxurious capital into which poured the wealth from trade recovered with the help of his Phoenician allies. The house of Omri initiated a policy of alliances and dynastic marriages with their neighbours and with Judah. Phoenician princesses married the Israelite princes and arrived at Samaria with their cults and their gods. One of them, Jezebel, the daughter of King Ethbaal of Tyre and the wife of King Ahab, wished to make Baal the only official god of the kingdom. The prophets of Yahweh, and Elijah the first, then assumed direction of the opposition in conditions almost identical with those that had produced the schism: economic prosperity reserved for a limited class of officials and nobles who ensured that gross social injustice prevailed. The destitution of the peasants drove them into revolt. In the name of the malcontents and the respect of Yahvism Elisha, assisted by some officers, gave the signal for Israel's most bloody revolution of which Jehu assumed the leadership. Not only was the King of Israel butchered but also Ahaziah, King of Judah, who had come to his aid from Jerusalem, and all his brothers. Queen Jezebel, who awaited Jehu decked out in all her finery, was hurled out of an upper window and thrown to the dogs. In Samaria the worshippers of Baal, who had taken refuge in the temple, were massacred. This was the *herem*, the total sacrifice demanded by holy war.

Jezebel hurled to her death from a window on the orders of Jehu (illustration for the Bible by G. Doré).

'And this was so, because the people of Israel . . . had feared other gods . . .
Asherim on every high hill, and under every green tree; and there they burned

Catastrophes followed one another. At Jerusalem the queen mother, Athaliah, the daughter of Jezebel, remained in sole command. Her first action was to have all the remaining members of the royal family of Judah put to death, except for Joash, her grandson, who was still only a child, and who was concealed in the Temple, where he remained until the age of seven. Following her mother's fatal policy, Athaliah set up the worship of Baal at Jerusalem, the very cult which had just been eradicated from Israel. Joash, however, was presented to the people by the clergy and was then acclaimed and given the royal unction. Athaliah declared this to be treason but was swiftly silenced and executed. Under the influence of the high priest, Joash undertook a religious reform, but after the death of his protector he became slack and tolerant of paganism. Little esteemed as a king, he was finally assassinated.

The end of the ninth century ushered in a period of decline for both Judah and Israel. Jehu's revolution had saved Israel from pagan encroachment, but had at the same time destroyed the system of alliances upon which the economy of the kingdom was based. The execution of Jezebel embroiled Israel and Phoenicia, while the King of Judah's murder ended the alliances between the two kingdoms.

It was at this period that Assyria appeared on the scene. Archaeological discoveries, together with the Assyrian documents which have been deciphered since 1852, have thrown further light on the period of the kings which is only related in a fragmentary manner in the Bible. Thus the Black Obelisk discovered in 1846 was found to bear the annals of the Assyrian king Shalmaneser III whose name is not mentioned in the Bible

The young Joash, the only survivor of the royal family, is anointed while Athaliah rends her clothes (seventeenth-century engraving).

They built for themselves high places . . . they set up for themselves pillars and incense . . . as the nations did whom the Lord carried away before them'.

2 Kings XVII. 7–11).

Fertility goddess (930–620 B.C.).

Royal seal found at Ramat Rachel.

any more than it recounts the humiliating submission of Jehu, paying tribute to his conqueror. The Assyrians laid waste Syria, reached the coast and exacted tribute from Tyre and Sidon, and from Jehu in Israel and Joash in Judah.

At the beginning of the eighth century, the Assyrians being momentarily weakened and the kingdom of Damascus rent by internal discord, Israel and Judah revived. The authors of the Books of the Kings, who doubtless based themselves on ancient documents, mention various measures on behalf of agriculture and stock-breeding, together with the exten-

sion and strengthening of the line of fortifications around Jerusalem and the reorganisation of the army. The kings enjoyed a power and prosperity unequalled since the days of David and Solomon. Amaziah reigned in Judah and Jehoash in Israel. Amaziah, however, proud of a few victories over the Edomites, decided to challenge the King of Israel, whom he believed to be exhausted by his struggles with the Aramaeans. He was defeated and taken prisoner. Jehoash of Israel entered Jerusalem, ransacked it, destroyed its ramparts and took away hostages.

Jehu at the feet of his conqueror (Obelisk of Shalmaneser, British Museum, London).

Cultivation of desert lands with implements as rudimentary as in the days of the Bible. A spade in the shape of a ploughshare.

Jerusalem, the capital of Judah, slowly rises from her ashes but does not recover her spiritual purity of royalty.

The kings of Judah succeeded each other without dynastic crises at Jerusalem, which remained faithful to the house of David. Around 780 B.C. Uzziah, the son of Amaziah, ascended the throne at the age of sixteen and took advantage of the improved international situation to carry out a programme of expansion which gave a renewal of activity to Jerusalem. He had the ramparts restored, reorganised the army, which he equipped with new siege engines, and plunged into several offensive wars. Edom was held in check, the works at Ezion-Geber were reopened and the caravan routes were supervised. He decided to dig reservoirs to irrigate the lands which he had had put under cultivation. The Negeb and southern desert, and the north and east of the Philistine plain came under his authority again, as did some ancient Philistine towns. The copper, weaving and dyeing industries flourished.

The economic prosperity manifested itself in important enterprises and works. The fortress of Ramat Rachel, a few miles from Jerusalem, was possibly the residence of Uzziah when, stricken with leprosy, he was obliged to leave the city and transfer his powers to his son, Jotham, though continuing to rule from a distance.

It was said that the king was smitten with this terrible disease because he had set himself up against the priests by wishing to usurp their functions. One day when he wished to do the censing of the incense on the altar himself, a function which was reserved for the Levites, 'eighty priests of the Lord who were men of valour . . . withstood King Uzziah, and said to him, It is not for you, Uzziah, to burn incense to the Lord . . . Go out of the sanctuary; for you have done wrong . . .
. . . and when he became angry with the priests leprosy broke out on his forehead . . .' He was then brutally thrust out of the Temple. The authors of the Books of the Kings and of the Chronicles account for the anger of Yahweh against Uzziah and most of the kings of Judah on the grounds of their impiety. Perhaps a remainder of the Hebrews' primitive conception of the

Uzziah (783–742), the leper king, celebrates the Passover (seventeenth-century Bohemia Bible).

retributive justice of God should be seen in this accusation, all illnesses being seen as the punishment for a transgression.

The king remained in 'a separate house' until the day of his death, says the Book of Kings. It seems indeed that this term, which was synonymous with *sheol* (Hades), was merely a circumlocution to describe the house of the leper king. The excavations carried out on the site of Ramat Rachel in 1962 have confirmed the theory that the fortress brought to light was the house of the contagious king. No remains prior to the eighth century have been discovered. The perfection of the surrounding wall, the vast central courtyard and the capitals and potsherds which have been unearthed prove it to be a royal fortress built with the most advanced and costly techniques of the period. This leper king, despite his long-standing former piety and the prosperity which he brought to his country, consequently did not escape the accusations of the authors of the Books of the Kings any more than did the others. Only two kings, Hezekiah and Josiah, the kings of the religious reform, found favour in

their sight. Indeed, the history of Israel and Judah is judged by these chroniclers only from the religious point of view. It is not so much a question of relating the happenings of this period as of explaining the failure of the two kingdoms by the impiety of their leaders; only complete faithfulness to the Law in the only Temple of Jerusalem could have saved the Jewish nation.

It is true that the whole of this period of economic well-being was linked with a malaise of a social and religious nature. The system which was already hard on the poorer classes was still further aggravated by the greed of the ruling class, who, with the complaisance of the government, turned this poverty to their own account by the most illegal methods. This state of affairs was very far removed from the tribal confederation, based on the Covenant of Yahweh, without class distinctions and governed by the Law. Moreover the religious decline was alarming. Yahvism appears to have assimilated the pagan rites which contaminated it, the prophetic circles had degenerated and the priests were the tools of the state.

Walls of the royal fortress of Ramat Rachel to which Uzziah, the leper king, retired.

Capital of the eighth century B.C. from Ramat Rachel.

Royal profile on eighth-century pottery fragment.

Assyrian warriors before a besieged city. From 750 B.C. onwards the Assyrians embarked on the conquest of the two states of Palestine which they had long coveted (bas-relief.

'They . . . made for themselves molten images . . . and worshipped all the host

From 737 B.C. onwards the fate of Palestine was in the hands of the Assyrians. Israel and Damascus conspired against Assyria and attacked Ahaz, King of Judah, who refused to join them. Judah was invaded from the north and Jerusalem besieged. In spite of the advice of the prophet Isaiah, Ahaz, seeing his kingdom laid waste, called for help to Tiglath-pileser III, the King of Assyria. Syria was pillaged, Israel reduced to the territories of Manasseh and Ephraim, and King Hoshea made a vassal of Assyria. At the death of Tiglath-pileser he revolted, refused to pay tribute and tried to enter into a political alliance with Egypt. In 724, Shalmaneser attacked: Israel was occupied and Samaria was besieged for two

years. In the course of the siege the Assyrian king died and was succeeded by Sargon II, who seized Samaria in 721. A large number of its inhabitants were deported, but Judah was preserved thanks to Ahaz's refusal to enter the conspiracy. It lost its autonomy, however, and became an Assyrian satellite.

The first consequence of this submission was the adopting of the religion of the suzerains. The King of Judah was compelled to go to Damascus, where he saw an altar dedicated to the gods of Assur. A copy of this altar was erected in the Temple of Jerusalem. Ahaz sacrificed his own son to Molech and his reign remains one of the most troubled in the religious history of Judah. To pay the formidable tribute demanded by

the Assyrians, Ahaz plundered the Temple treasury and also emptied that of the state. The hostility between the peasants in the villages and the aristocracy in Jerusalem created a social malaise which was aggravated by the revival of paganism and the slackening of the links of the Covenant. In the midst of this religious and moral crisis two great prophets, Isaiah and Micah, comforted Judah and reminded the people of the Covenant and the Law:

'O my people, who dwell in Zion, be not afraid of the Assyrians when they smite with the rod, and lift up their staff against you'.

Prophecy was the animating spirit of the political and religious life of this period of the kings. The prophets were

British Museum, London).

Isaiah weeps over Jerusalem and foretells its downfall (wood-cut by Holbein, sixteenth century).

# of heaven, and served Baal.'
(2 Kings XVII. 16)

the opponents of the regime, morals and institutions and, without fear of offending, predicted the worst. Elisha had brought about the revolution of Israel and Isaiah, the greatest prophet of Judah and an aristocrat from Jerusalem, foretold the destruction of the two kingdoms and bewailed his city. One hope sustained him, however, that of faith in Yahweh whom he had had the privilege of 'seeing' one day in the Temple, surrounded with six-winged seraphim. 'Woe is me! For I am lost', he cried, 'for I am a man of unclean lips . . . for my eyes have seen the King, the Lord of hosts'.

The call of Isaiah (seventeenth-century engraving).

Yahweh said 'By the way that he came, by the same he shall return, and he shall not come into this city . . . For I will defend this city to save it'. (2 Kings XIX. 33–34)

After the downfall of Samaria and the dismemberment of the kingdom of the North, Jerusalem tried to decide on its policy. Open rebellion against Assyria could not be absolutely sure of success and was therefore tantamount to suicide. Submission to a suzerain involved the worship of Assur, the god of the victors, and would provoke the anger of Yahweh. The prophets declared this unceasingly. When Hezekiah ascended the throne in 715 B.C. Sargon II was King of Assyria. The latter had just lost Babylon and was fighting in the north. Some Philistine cities, hoping for help from Egypt, judged the moment favourable for trying to throw off their yoke and drawing Judah, Moab and Edom into their coalition. Isaiah advised abstention.

Throughout his life the prophet was to remain faithful to the same idea; the main thing was not to regain political liberty because Judah's mission was not a temporal one. The Assyrians were only the instruments of God to punish His unfaithful people and would themselves pass away like all earthly dominion. Much more essential was the inner, moral reform, the return to Yahweh and repentance to obtain forgiveness. A new

mission was given to Judah. In the midst of downfalls, idolatry and scandal, a small group of the faithful would keep the Covenant and save the world.

This voice was not alone at Jerusalem in the seventh century B.C.; it was echoed in the strata in which Yahvism was still deeply rooted. Events often bore it out and gave it its force. It corresponded to a reality: Judah did not have the breadth of an empire.

Hezekiah was king and approached events from a point of view different from that of Isaiah. At the beginning of his reign he followed the prudent course prescribed by the prophet and kept aloof from the coalition which, as it turned out, proved abortive. He set on hand a religious and social reform. Formal repudiation of the Assyrian gods was not yet possible, but in the limits within which he was allowed to act the king did away with the pagan customs introduced by Ahaz and with the cult objects which had become the occasion for idolatry, such as the brazen serpent which had been preserved in the Temple from time immemorial. He tried to make the survivors of the Northern kingdom adhere to the form of worship practised

at Jerusalem, but he seems to have failed. The Assyrians had very cleverly opened a centre for instruction in Yahvism at Bethel.

Under the influence of the prophet Micah, who was less aristocratic and more realistic than Isaiah and who increasingly denounced abuses, Hezekiah attempted a social and economic reform.

On the death of Sargon, Hezekiah felt that he could discharge himself from the heavy tribute which had to be paid to the Assyrians. All over the Fertile Crescent the countries which had been subject now united against Sargon's son, Sennacherib, who appeared to be less able. The King of Tyre made himself leader of the insurrectionary movement of the West. Some Philistine and Syrian cities joined him, as did Hezekiah, in spite of Isaiah.

In order to withstand all reprisals the King of Judah organised the defence of Jerusalem, overhauled the ramparts, and dug the tunnel of Siloam which brought the water from the fountain of Gihon, to the east of Jerusalem, into the capital through 500 yards of rock.

In 701 Sennacherib finished pacifying Babylon and turned towards Palestine. He kept to the coast and took Tyre. Some members of the coalition surrendered, but Judah and her Philistine allies held out. In spite of Egyptian intervention in support of the Philistine cities, Sennacharib invaded Judaea, occupied forty-six fortified cities, including Lachish which defended the road into Jerusalem, then besieged Jerusalem herself. Hezekiah was abandoned by part of his army and Isaiah advised him to sue for peace. The conditions dictated by Sennacherib were very harsh: the territory of Judah was broken up and shared out between several Philistine kings, while the tribute demanded was so heavy that Hezekiah was compelled to have recourse to the Temple treasure. Sennacherib contented himself with this immense booty of silver, however, and abandoned the siege, the details of which have been preserved in writing.

Hezekiah, King of Judah, abolishes the worship of idols (seventeenth-century engraving).

The underground conduit: (1) The fountain of Gihon on the slopes of the Ophel. (2) Walls of Jerusalem. (3) Pool of Siloam.

The outlet of the conduit into the pool.

Account of Sennacherib's siege engraved on a hexahedral prism.

In order to supply Jerusalem with water Hezekiah constructs a conduit from the fountain of Gihon to the pool of Siloam (seventeenth-century engraving).

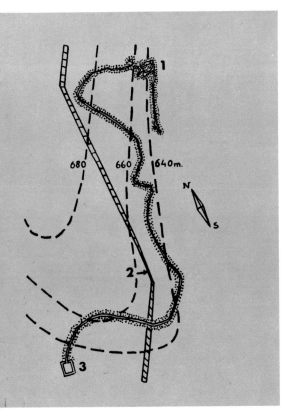

'I will wipe Jerusalem as one wipes a dish, wiping it and turning it upside down

Jerusalem had escaped destruction and its inhabitants deportation, but it was now nothing more than a very small speck on the map of the Assyrian empire. For the moment there was no longer any power capable of resisting Assur. Manasseh, the son of Hezekiah who had ascended the throne in 687, had no other hope of survival than to act as an abject vassal.

The tragic death of Isaiah, who was sawn in two by Manasseh's executioners, intimated clearly that all national awareness had disappeared for a time, even on the spiritual plane. Manasseh's religious policy differed completely from that of his father and followed the example of Ahaz. Once again the conqueror's gods were worshipped at Jerusalem: Assur, the

father of the gods, the Sun God and 'the Host of heaven'. Sacred prostitution invaded the temple and divination and magic enjoyed an extraordinary vogue. Human sacrifice made its appearance again, Manasseh himself offering up one of his sons, and a place was consecrated—the Valley of Slaughter—'to burn their sons and daughters'. Baal,

The foreign gods (A) Teraphim. (B) Baal. (C) Tammuz, a Syrian god whose eyes wept tears of melted lead. (D) Aphis, bull god of Egypt. (E) Molech, an Ammonite god

'. . because they have done what is evil in my sight and have provoked me to anger.'

(2 Kings XXI. 13, 15)

who had never ceased to appear and disappear during the course of the city's eventful history, was victorious.

Generally considered a docile vassal by the Assyrians, Manasseh made one attempt to free himself in the course of his reign, around 650 B.C. He had cause to rue it. He was carried off into captivity at Nineveh, but seems to have been well treated there, and at some time reascended the throne. Warning signs of a coming crisis in the Assyrian empire appeared in a number of quarters at this period, however. In Babylonia discontent was threatening to break out; at Susa the Elamites were continually on the verge of revolt; Egypt was gradually freeing herself from Assyrian control and, in 665, refused to pay tribute; in Iran the Medes were becoming a danger and the Cimmerians, a tribe of Caucasian warriors, were threatening in the north. A first general rebellion was crushed by Assur-bani-pal who deported some of the Elamite and Babylonian peoples to Samaria. But in 642 when Manasseh died, the situation was in full evolution.

to whom children were sacrificed. (F) Philistine dragon. (G) Temple of Venus (seventeenth-century engraving).

Baal, a Canaanite god, the male principle, personifying germination and fertility, watching over the harvest of corn, flax, grapes and olives.

King Josiah did away with those who sacrificed to Baal, the sun, moon and stars . . . and burned the sacred grove in the valley of Kidron.

Josiah, whose reign corresponded with the decline of Assyria, occupied the throne of Judah from 640–609 B.C. On the death of Assur-bani-pal in 633 a Chaldean prince, Nabopolassar, seized Babylonia and Cyaxares, King of the Medes, invaded Syria. The moment was propitious for the kingdom of Judah to win back a certain degree of autonomy. A series of reforms were to help in this. Josiah had two objectives: to repudiate the Assyrian gods, and to give back its vigour to the Jewish religion.

According to the account in the Book of Kings the moral reform of the religion had its origin in an incident. While repairs were being carried out in the Temple the book of the Torah was discovered. It was read to the king, who rent his clothes as a mark of sorrow at the impiety of his forefathers who had been guilty of forgetting the sacred teachings to such a degree. He decided to have the book recognised as the Law of the kingdom, summoned the people and made a covenant with them before Yahweh. He then took a series of measures to put the Law into execution.

The temple was purified, the altars of the astral gods, the *asherah*—or sacred groves— and a house set aside for the prostitutes was demolished.

The pagan sanctuaries disappeared: that of the satyrs, at one of the city gates, the altar of the Valley of Hinnom where children were burned, and the high places of the Mount of Olives which were consecrated to foreign gods. Josiah proscribed necromancers, Teraphim and idols. Jerusalem was given the exclusive right to the cult of Yahweh and the country priests were invited to come and

King Josiah has the Law of God read before his people and orders them to observe it from henceforth as the only law of the kingdom (seventeenth-century engraving).

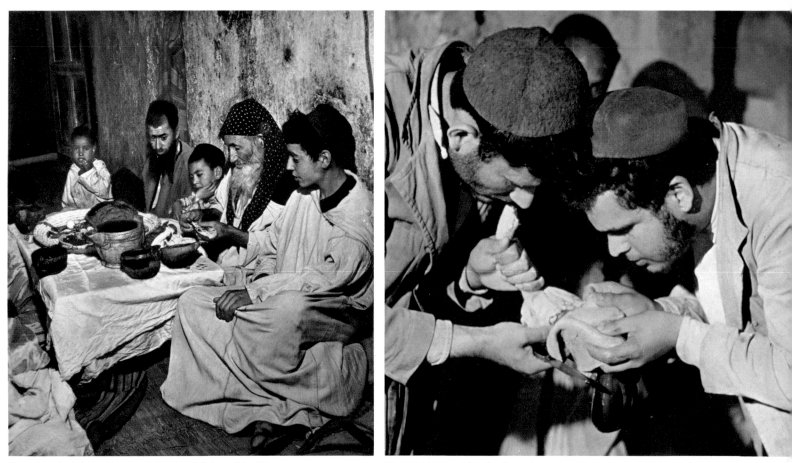

Moroccan Jewish family around the ritual dishes of the Passover.   Two rabbis examining the liver of an animal in order to verify its purity.

live there. He restored the Passover as it had been celebrated formerly, and as it had scarcely ever been celebrated since the days of the judges. This reform, which was in the name of national renewal and patriotism, clashed with numerous interests but was carried into effect in spite of the opposition it aroused. It introduced new developments into the history of Judaism. For the first time the authority of a written tradition was required in order to institute a reform and to bring the people together again around the cult.

The book discovered in the Temple was certainly not anterior to the previous century constituting, as it did, part of Deuteronomy, and may have been drafted at the time when differences had begun to make themselves felt concerning the meaning of the customary law. Up till then the use of writing was not indispensable either for the transmission of the customary law or for the teaching of the Torah which, by its very nature of a divine direction in reply to a particular case of dispute at law, was an oral, living answer which was never fixed.

The originators of the reform appear to have been the priests of Jerusalem who were, moreover, its principal beneficiaries. But their reform was an attempt to put into practice the aspirations of the great prophets: ancient customs and magical practices were spiritualised and

given a meaning more in keeping with the requirements of Yahweh. The hand of the priests is glimpsed, however, in the preservation of a form of worhip which the prophets had frequently denounced as an abuse; in the maintenance, for example, of the practice of sacrifice which they had already said was not really required by Yahweh. Deuteronomy gave back its pre-eminence to the Temple of Jerusalem. By amalgamating the prophetic elements and the rites of popular religion, Josiah's reform gave a new aspect to Yahvism. Its code was the first foundation of the Torah, in the sense of a written formula held to be the definitive expression of the will of Yahweh, and the authority of the written word marked the decline of prophecy. The death of Josiah, killed at Megiddo in 609 in a battle against the Egyptians who had come to the aid of the Assyrians, marked the end of the newly recovered independence of Judah. The victorious Pharaoh, Necho, carried off Josiah's chosen successor into Egypt, where he died, and installed in his place his brother Jehoiakim who had to pay a prohibitive tribute and whose destiny was to be even more turbulent, as was already announced by the mighty voice of the new prophet, Jeremiah:

'Can the Ethiopian change his skin, or the leopard his spots? Then also you can do good who are accustomed to do evil.

'I will scatter you like chaff driven by the wind from the desert . . .
'Woe to you, O Jerusalem!'

In the zoological garden at Jerusalem.

King Nebuchadnezzar
puts out the eyes of
the King of Jerusalem,
throws him in irons,
and carries him off
to Babylon. He calls
for the burning of
the whole town.

In the reign of Zedekiah, Nebuchadnezzar, King of Babylon, comes to besiege Jerusalem with his whole army.

The pitiless Assyrian conquerors (bas-relief found at Nimrud, British Museum, London).

Execution of Zedekiah's sons (nineteenth-century engraving by Gustave Doré).

Already in 605 B.C. Nebuchadnezzar had gained the victory of Carchemish over the Pharaoh Necho (609–594) which opened up the road to Palestine for him. Made king on the death of his father, he advanced into Philistine territory and Jehoiakim of Judah, Josiah's son, was compelled to accept neo-Babylonian suzerainty. However, he revolted in 601 and tried to treat with Egypt. Nebuchadnezzar was at that moment engaged in fighting on other fronts but in 598 he launched a punitive expedition. Three months after the death of Jehoiakim, when Joachim was king, Jerusalem capitulated. The king, the queen mother, the staff-officers and the notables were carried off to Babylon with a huge amount of booty.

Zedekiah ascended the throne. His reign was chaotic, the economic situation was unstable and a large part of the population disappeared. Several thousand people were deported. In 594 a

After eighteen months the assailants succeed in opening up a breach in the walls (seventeenth-century engraving).

rebellion broke out at Babylon in which some of the deported Judaeans seem to have taken part. Nebuchadnezzar had their prophets, who had predicted the downfall of Babylon, executed. An attempt at a Palestinian coalition came to nothing, but an insurrectionary movement sprang up at Jerusalem with the support of the Egyptians.

Nebuchadnezzar reacted vigorously. About the year 588 his troops embarked on the siege of the city and seized all the fortified places of Judah with the exceptions of Lachish. The siege was interrupted during the summer when Nebuchadnezzar learned that an Egyptian army was marching against him, but once the Egyptians had been repulsed the siege was resumed and continued until July of 587 when provisions ran out. The Babylonian soldiers then breached the walls and entered the city. During the night Zedekiah, who hoped to find refuge with the Ammonites, escaped to the Jordan but was recaptured near Jericho. His sons were executed in his presence, his eyes were put out and he was taken prisoner to Babylon where he died. Thus was fulfilled the prophecy which Jeremiah had made to him: 'Behold, I am giving this city into the hand of the king of Babylon, and he shall burn it with fire . . . You shall see the king of Babylon eye to eye and speak with him face to face; and you shall go to Babylon'.

After the capture of the city the Temple is set on fire and most of the population is led away into captivity (seventeenth-century engraving).

Nebuchadnezzar deported the Jews to Babylon where they remained until the creation of the kingdom of Persia (Assyrian bas-relief, British Museum, London).

'Then they will know that I am the Lord, when I have made the land a desolation and a waste because of all their abominations which they have committed.' (Ezekiel XXXIII. 29)

Jerusalem was burned and the Temple razed. Its inhabitants were led captive to Babylon in pitiful columns. The cities were destroyed, the land laid waste and the population decimated by famine and epidemics. About 20,000 Judaeans resisted and clung to their soil. Part of Judah was quickly occupied by the Edomites, while the north was annexed to Samaria.

For those who remained, the site of the Temple became a place of pilgrimage. But Jerusalem was to live more now in people's memories than in reality: 'If I forget you, O Jerusalem, let my right hand wither. Let my tongue cleave to the roof of my mouth if I do not set Jerusalem above my highest joy'. The exiles repeated these psalms and came together in the process. At first imprisoned or used as labour for Nebuchadnezzars's great building works, the Judaeans soon enjoyed the right to build houses and cultivate land. Some of them led a community life. They engaged in trade and within a few decades of their arrival the Israelite villages of the Middle Euphrates were thriving. At Babylon the Judaeans were admitted to the court and sometimes held high office. The great city was full of temptations and some of the Jews allowed themselves to become completely assimilated.

Religion became the most solid support of the exiled people which had regrouped itself around its prophets. The rites were followed, circumcision, for example, becoming a really distinctive sign. The Sabbath and the commemoration of the Passover brought the community together. Bereft of the Temple, the faithful started the habit of gathering in houses of prayer which were to turn into the synagogues. In order to maintain the Law and pass on the tradition a regular caste of scribes was constituted. The teaching of the prophets and their sense of the universal beyond historical contingencies enriched this new life. Jeremiah and Ezekiel proclaimed the purifying character of the exile and declared that Yahweh had not abandoned His people. Instead of glorifying the national dynasty and creed, they were to keep the Law and the Covenant.

With Ezekial the concept of a personal faith, which gave an essential place to responsibility, took a step forward. He was a visionary and made many symbolic gestures, like cutting off a third of his hair with a sword, burning another third

Jeremiah weeping over Jerusalem (Rembrandt).

and scattering the rest in order to convey the image of Israel. As the interpreter of the Torah he also became law giver and jurist. The last part of the Book of Ezekiel presents a detailed plan for religious and political reconstruction. Striving to adapt the old laws to the new conditions of the Jewish people, he formulated a number of reforms which had for long been suggested and desired, and endowed nascent Judaism with a charter that was to form the basis of all future attempts.

Some of the Jews had taken refuge in Egypt, where they were to remain until the Persian period, one of the most important colonies being that at Elephantine. It is probable that other Judaeans had found shelter among the neigh-

Interior of a synagogue (Djerba).

bouring Moabites, Edomites and Ammonites. The Diaspora did not yet cover the whole world, but Israel had already begun its dispersion among the nations. At Babylon the hope of returning grew as the difficultues of the empire increased. In 562 B.C. the death of Nebuchadnezzar precipitated the Assyrian decline; there were three different rulers in seven years, several of his sons succeeding one another. Nabonidus was on the throne when a petty king from southern Iran started to show the first signs of a mighty destiny as a conqueror. A strange figure, a mystic who gave himself up to lunar cults, Nabonidus held aloof from political affairs and was incapable of withstanding the danger looming on the horizon.

'Again I will build you, and you shall be built, O virgin

The cylinder of Cyrus' decree.

In 550 B.C. a new phase in the history of Asia began in a petty kingdom of southern Iran. Cyrus, a vassal of the Medes, rebelled against his sovereign, whom he deposed, seized his empire and created a state stretching from Lydia to Afghanistan more vast than any of those that had preceded it. In 539 Babylon came into the orbit of the new kingdom and Persian domination was established for two centuries.

Among the Babylonian crowds welcoming the new emperor were groups of exiled Jews who observed Cyrus, heralded by the prophet Isaiah as a hope of the Jewish people. The sovereign was to follow a different policy from that of the Assyrians. He practised neither systematic destruction nor the deportation of the defeated and organised his empire administratively while respecting foreign religions. In 538, the first year of his reign, Cyrus published a decree which, though in accordance with his policy, was astonishing in that it concerned, in that vast empire, a mere

handful of men. He authorised the restoration of the Jewish community and cult in Palestine. The Jews in exile could choose to remain or to return home while the Temple was to be rebuilt at the expense of the treasury. The sacred vessels removed by Nebuchadnezzar were to be returned.

The news spread like wildfire to the Jewish quarters: Jerusalem could rise again. Many of them preferred not to face the desert crossing again, but the first group left Babylon as early as 537 under the leadership of Sheshbazzar, a 'prince of Judah' and a descendant of David. The sacred vessels were entrusted to him. A small group of men, an infinitesimal detail in a vast historical fresco, were about to attempt to bring a tradition back to life again on the hill of Jerusalem.

They had only a relative degree of administrative autonomy and formed part of the fifth satrapy which was enclosed between the great bend of the Euphrates and the Egyptian frontier. Damascus

On the orders of Cyrus, in 538 B.C., the Temple is rebuilt at the king's expense and the Jewish community restored (seventeenth-century engraving).

Israel. Again you shall adorn yourself with timbrels, and shall go forth in the dance of the merrymakers.' (Jeremiah XXXI. 4)

was their capital and Samaria ranked before Jerusalem. They formed a religious community under the direction of Zerubbabel, the nephew and successor of Sheshbazzar, assisted by the high priest Joshua. Difficulties were legion. The country had remained poverty-stricken since the ravages of the Assyrians; part of it had been occupied by Edomites and Moabites while the Judaeans who had stayed behind wished to keep their lands, with the result that the influx of immigrants was disliked by all. Samaria, for its part, was not anxious to see a rival live again.

The work of reconstruction began nevertheless. The money brought back from Babylon made possible the ordering of materials; Joshua and Zerubbabel laid the foundation stone of a new place of worship. Within a very short space of time, however, the returned exiles and the Judaeans who had not left the city came into opposition. The latter had built sacrificial altars on the ruins of the Temple. To the newcomers, fortified by a religion strengthened in exile, these cults were suspect. A split occurred in the community between those who wished to preserve themselves from contact with foreigners and the Judaeans who had been 'contaminated' by them, and those who did not feel that orthodoxy was of such importance. These difficulties, to which was soon added a lack of money, paralysed the labour force and interrupted the reconstruction of the Temple.

In 520, during the difficult beginning of the reign of Darius, work was resumed under the impetus of nationalist sentiments inflamed by the prophets Haggai and Zachariah. In spite of the intrigues of the apprehensive Samaritan satraps, the great king took his stand on Cyrus' decree and allowed the work to be completed.

In 515 the Feast of Dedication was the occasion for an outburst of popular joy. The new Temple did not have the sumptuousness of the old, however: the Holy of Holies was empty, since the missing Ark had not been replaced. Only a stone slab preserved its memory. In the *hekal* were placed the altar of incense, the table for the shewbread, and a single seven-branched candlestick which symbolised the ten former candlesticks of the Temple of Solomon. In spite of the opposition of many Israelites, the building became a rallying-point for the former exiles.

During the crossing of the desert, nomadic Bedouin make a brief halt round a well.

'Then rose up . . . every one whose spirit God had stirred . . . to rebuild the house of the Lord.

Two wise men take the destiny of the new Jerusalem in hand: one rebuilds the ruined walls, the other prescribes obedience to the Law.

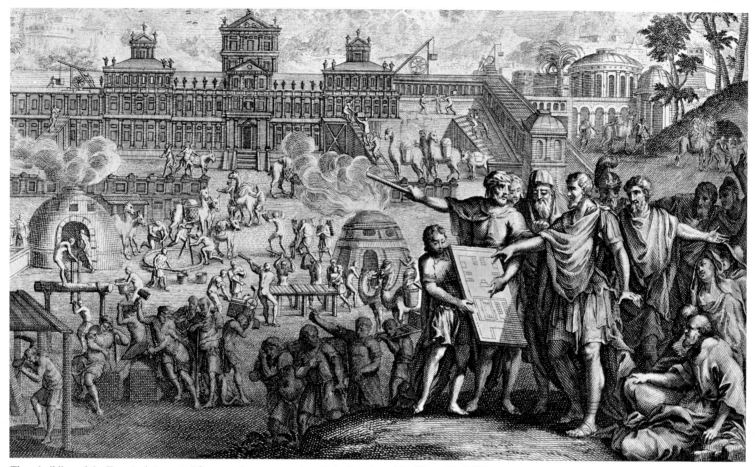

The rebuilding of the Temple, interrupted for several years, started again in the reign of Darius and lasted five years (seventeenth-century engraving).

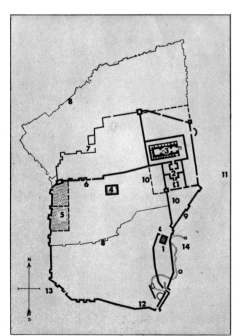

(1) Palace of David. (2) Palace of Solomon.
(3) The Temple. (4) Palace of the
Hasmonaeans. (5) Palace of Herod. (6–12) Wall
constructed from Solomon to Hezekiah.
(7) constructed from Hezekiah to Herod.
(8) present wall (twelfth-sixteenth centuries).
(9) Jebusites. (10) Ophel. (11) Mount of Olives.
(13) Valley of Gehenna. (14) Fountain of Siloam.

For the first half of the fifth century Jerusalem was under the control of the high priest and in administrative subjection to Samaria. Only a very few documents have survived concerning these years between the inauguration of the Temple and the appearance on the scene of Nehemiah and Ezra, the two great reformers of the middle of the century. The Jews were exposed not only to hostile interference from Samaritan officials, but also to Edomite attacks. When the territorial ambitions of the Edomites forced the Jews to rebuild the walls of the city, Samaria protested, appealed to the Persian court and managed to have the work stopped. It was then that Nehemiah, who held the office of cup-bearer at the court, took up the interests of his brethren. He was appointed 'Governor of Judah' and the new district was separated from Samaria.

When he arrived at Jerusalem Nehemiah announced his mission and, bearing in mind the numerous enemies that surrounded the Israelites, started the work cautiously. All the inhabitants contributed to it, divided into two groups: one keeping watch, their arms in their hands, while the other worked. When he had rebuilt the walls and the Temple Nehemiah organised Judaea, took measures to check abuses, and acted as a just and intelligent administrator.

After a two-year stay in Persia he found Jerusalem in a far less brilliant state than at his departure: the high priests were indulging in activities that were hardly in accordance with the sanctity of the Temple and Tobiah the Ammonite was trying to interfere in the country's affairs. Nehemiah purified the sanctuary and forbad mixed marriages.

The reorganisation of spiritual life was the work of another eminent Israelite, Ezra, whom Jewish tradition has turned into a second Moses. The legendary figure of the scribe reconstituting the whole of the Scriptures which were believed to have been destroyed, sprang, as do all legends, from a reality. An official envoy to Jerusalem, it was he who succeeded in regrouping the Jewish community around the Law.

Ezra working at the drafting of the Bible (early eighth-century miniature, Florence).

Ezra, priest and scribe of the Law, holds sway: the 'people of God' reflect on their past and fix in writing the 'Sefer Torah'.

It is to Ezra (fifth century B.C.) that the square shape of Hebrew letters is attributed, but historians favour the second century (engraving by Luycken).

Prior to Babylon the essentials of the Jewish religion were sacrifice and worship at the Temple; the growing importance of the written word marked a new stage in its development. Ezra arrived at Jerusalem with the official title of 'scribe of the law of the God of heaven' and full powers in religious matters. He brought with him a copy of Jewish literary texts from various sources and periods, and ordered an official reading of the Law to the assembled community. These texts were written in Hebrew, however, which in spite of Nehemiah's efforts to stop its disappearance was no longer a spoken language. Ezra had them translated into Aramaean, the current language with square-shaped letters which had replaced the round letters of early Hebrew. The Aramaean script consisted of twenty-two consonants—vowels, which were unknown in the Semitic languages, being excluded. Henceforth accessible, these texts were to compose the Torah, according to a plan devised by Ezra and which distinguished three parts, the Law, the Prophets and the Writings. The Law, or in the words of the Hebrews, the five fifths of the Law, corresponds to the first five books, known in English as the Pentateuch. Written on scrolls kept in metal caskets, the Pentateuch, or Sefer Torah, is elevated before the congregation during certain services.

The elevation of the Torah during a service.

You shall make a lampstand of pure gold . . . six branches going out of its sides, three . . . out of one side . . . and three . . . out of the other side.' (Hebrew MS)

The absence of documents casts a veil over life at Jerusalem in the fourth century. We only know that the high priests succeeded one another and upheld degrees of strictness. They were probably authorised to mint money and collect the Temple taxes. Coins have been found dating from this period with the inscription *Yehud*: Judah. The relations between the Jews and Samaritans grew more acrimonious and a temple was built on Mount Gerizim, in Samaria, to compete with that of Jerusalem. The Hebrew tongue was gradually replaced by the Aramaean, spoken throughout the Persian Empire.

A new element was the arrival of the Greeks, many of whom were travelling in Asia: merchants, mercenaries, adventurers and scholars, they brought with them something of the widely differing civilisation which had flowered over the sea. In 334 B.C. Alexander reached Asia and the Persian Empire collapsed with astonishing rapidity. The battle of Issus delivered it into the hands of the Macedonian conqueror in 333. Alexander headed for Egypt, through Palestine, probably following the coast. A legend has it, however, that he passed close to Jerusalem: the high priest went out to meet him dressed in his vestments and saluted him as the destroyer of Persian might foretold by the prophets. In a mood of benevolence Alexander then guaranteed to Israel the practice of her Laws, and offered up a sacrifice in the Temple of Yahweh. Alexander's conquest ushered in a new era in the ancient Orient. Hellenism constituted a grave danger for Judah: if the Jews allowed themselves to be seduced and forsook the Law, the Jewish nation would disappear.

The Hellenistic world was one of the most brilliant, accessible and seductive that had ever been proposed to them. Alexander's reign saw the blossoming of a multitude of Greek cities, endowed with every refinement. Thanks to the academies, museums, libraries, theatres and gymnasiums, critical intelligence and philosophical thought flowered, in pursuit of a humanist ideal. This dynamism threatened to carry away in its impetus the Jewish way of life, which until then had been founded on faith and not on science, on obedience to the Law and not on freedom of criticism. In addition the Greek world enjoyed an unprecedented economic prosperity. Greek ships supplied Asia with all the products of the Mediterranean and the markets overflowed with every kind of international merchandise. Would Jerusalem turn into a Greek city or take her stand around the Temple in faithful prayer?

Two parties were formed which were to oppose one another until the last days of Hellenism, one fully prepared to enter into the new world offered it, and consisting of the rich classes, the other attached to its traditions and religion and consisting of the peasants and the poor classes. On the death of Alexander in 323 his empire was rapidly divided between two Macedonian generals. Ptolemy was given control of Egypt, while Seleucus extended his sway from Babylon to Syria on the west and to Iran on the east. Both cast greedy eyes on Palestine and Phoenicia. In 301 Ptolemy defeated Seleucus at the battle of Ipsus: Palestine was to remain in the hands of the Ptolemies for over a hundred years.

Very little is known about the history of the Jews during this period. The Persian administrative system was retained and the Jews kept the same status. The high priest, however, who was surrounded by a priestly aristocracy, the Sanhedrin, who composed a kind of senate, came more and more to resemble a secular prince. Jerusalem enjoyed peace and prosperity. Only a garrison recalled the presence of the Ptolemies. But it was probable, if one judges by the history of the surrounding peoples, that despite the rigid protection of the Law, the little Jewish community did not escape from cosmopolitanism. No Jew could leave the territory of Judaea without immediately finding himself in Hellenistic centres where Greek was spoken. Furthermore, exchanges took place spontaneously at this period. Many Jews left for Egypt, and in particular for Alexandria where the Bible was translated into Greek, while numerous immigrants arrived from over-populated Greece. A mixing of the population, encouraged by the marriages between Greek soldiers and foreign women, blended the two cultures, but the star of David continued to leave its mark on objects as well as on hearts; only the monuments kept a completely characteristic form, copied from the Hellenistic East.

Seal with the inscription *Yehud*: Judah.

The tombs of the Hellenistic period.

are gymnasiums and Athenian learning if the God of Moses is flouted in His capital?

Alexander the Great (357–323 B.C.).

Ptolemy VI Philometer, King of Egypt.

Inscription bearing: 'Jerusalem' (second century).

Proud of their prestige, the Greeks acted by intimidation, but Yahweh drove from the Temple the idolator who attempted to seize its treasure.

At the beginning of the second century B.C., Egypt of the Ptolemies was at grips with serious internal difficulties: rebellions, strikes and inflation. Its power began to wane just when that of the successors of Seleucus I, the King of Syria, began to regain strength with the arrival on the throne in 223 of Antiochus III. The new king reorganised the kingdom and the army, won back the provinces that had broken away from Seleucia and re-established his influence as far as the frontiers of India. He then embarked on a campaign against the Ptolemies. Initially he was held in check, but in 198 he gained the victory of Panium over Scopas, one of the Ptolemies' generals, which gave him Palestine. At Jerusalem the news was greeted with joy, at least by part of the population. The Jews took up arms against Ptolemy's garrison and enthusiastically opened the gates to Antiochus.

The real penetration of Hellenism now began, encouraged by the skilful diplomacy of Antiochus. Well disposed towards Jerusalem, he officially recognised the theocratic state and permitted the return of exiles and the freeing of Jews who had been reduced to slavery. He authorised the Jews to rebuild their fortifications and restore the Temple, granted them financial aid and exempted them from taxes for a period of three years.

Coin bearing the head of Seleucus I.

This liberal policy naturally brought him supporters. A strong pro-Hellenic party adopted the way of life proposed by the Greeks and in the new stadiums the young Israelites acquired a taste for games and physical strength. Greek thought was adopted and circumcision neglected. The pious Jews reacted against this propaganda and formed a party themselves in opposition to their compatriots. Jerusalem was becoming more and more sharply divided

At the end of his reign Antiochus decided to attack Rome, a rising power in the Mediterranean world which had just crushed Carthage. Defeated in his turn, he lost the whole of Asia Minor—

with the exception of Cilicia—his fleet and his elephants. He surrendered twenty hostages to Rome, including his son, and had to pay an enormous tribute which he managed to collect by plundering temples. He was killed in 187 while despoiling an Elamite sanctuary.

His successor, Seleucus IV, was to follow his example. At the same time as he was confirming the privileges given to the Jews by Antiochus he sent his minister Heliodorus to Jerusalem to appropriate the Temple treasures. This action was the result, it must be added, of intrigues conducted from Jerusalem by a powerful faction hostile to the high priest, Onias III, whom they accused of

Antiochus III the Great (223-187 B.C.), who in 198 recaptured Palestine from the Ptolemies.

Heliodorus, the minister of Seleucus IV Philometer, attempts to seize the Temple treasures and is driven out by a divine apparition.

diverting Temple finances to his own profit. Heliodorus was given a bad reception at Jerusalem and the high priest forbad him to enter the Holy Place. He forced his way in though. 'And holding up their hands to heaven, they all made entreaty. There was something pitiable in the prostration of the whole populace and the anxiety of the high priest in his great anguish. While they were calling upon the Almighty Lord that he would keep what had been entrusted safe and secure for those who had entrusted it, Heliodorus went on with what had been decided.' But he was driven back from the Temple by an 'apparition': three angels, one on horseback, bore down upon him and prevented the theft. Terrified, Heliodorus left Jerusalem. After assassinating Seleucus, he made a vain attempt to assume power, but Antiochus IV, Seleucus' brother, returned from exile and ascended the throne.

Antiochus IV Epiphanes, King of Syria.

'A man could neither keep the sabbath . . . nor . . . confess himself to be a Jew.'

Antiochus Epiphanes: 'God manifest.'

The accession of Antiochus IV completely changed the relations between Jews and Hellenes. The new emperor's policy provoked a brutal confrontation and the first great religious persecution in history. Antiochus had grown up as a hostage in Rome, but after being released by the Romans he had become a fervent champion of Hellenism in the course of a lengthy voyage in Greece. He ascended the throne in 175 with the avowed ideal of unifying the eastern world by Hellenising it. He set up the worship of the Greek gods, including that of Zeus and his own person considered as a manifestation of Zeus, whence his title of 'Epiphanes' ('manifest'). He had no respect for the God of the Jews.

Nevertheless he found supporters for his policy at Jerusalem. The office of high priest, long hereditary, was then vacant, but henceforth was to be purchased and given by Antiochus to the highest bidder. During the absence of Onias III, the rightful high priest, his brother Joshua (Jason, in Greek) made an offer and obtained the sacerdotal office. He immediately set to work to Hellenise Jerusalem. A kind of club, 'the Antiochians', spread the Greek fashion for athletics. Membership of a gymnasium involved the worship of Hercules, Hermes or the dynasty. The orthodox Jews vehemently denounced Antiochus, this 'forsaker of the Laws'.

Jason was succeeded by a certain

Looting of the Temple: the Jews forsake the cult and the Law. 'God punished their impiousness by means of Antiochus' (seventeenth-century engraving).

(2 Macc. VI. 6).

Persecution under Antiochus IV: Eleazar, compelled to eat pork, prefers to die.

The Seleucids erect a fortress in the City of David: the Acra (seventeenth-century engraving).

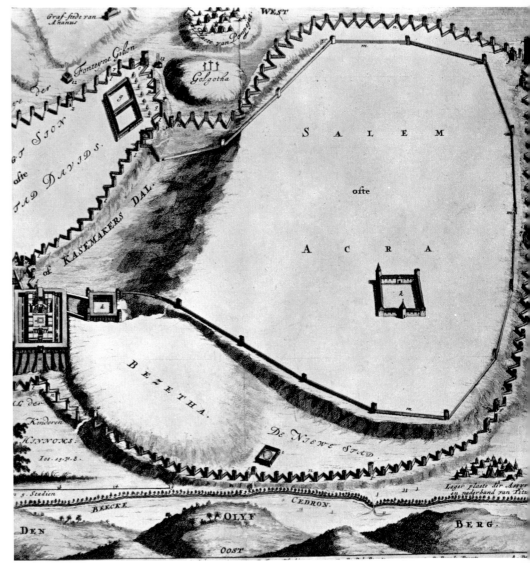

Menelaus, who offered a larger sum to Antiochus and, in órder to pay him, stole holy vessels from the sanctuary. Onias protested and was assassinated. The atmosphere at Jerusalem was now extremely troubled. Made confident by his victories in Egypt, Antiochus ordered the looting of the Temple and took away the gold-leaf decoration of the facade, the sacred ornaments, the remaining vessels and the seven-branched candlestick. A Royal commissioner was especially appointed to organise a campaign of compulsory Hellenisation.

The order was given to sacrifice to the Greek cult under pain of death, and to participate in the Dionysia. The Jewish religion was proscribed: it was forbidden to observe the sabbath, to practise circumcision or to take part in the traditional feasts. In December 167 the statue of Olympian Zeus was set up in the Temple; this was 'the abomination of desolation'. In the face of such excesses compromise was no longer possible. The sacerdotal caste and the propertied aristocracy chose alliance with the Greeks out of self-interest. The Hasidim, the pious Jews who remained faithful to their ancestral religion, organised the resistance. Persecutions began: families who had had their children circumcised were slaughtered, Jews who refused to eat pork were tortured and groups who celebrated the sabbath in secret were executed. But the author of the Book of Maccabees who records these atrocities urged 'those who read this book not to be depressed by such calamities, but to recognise that these punishments were designed not to destroy but to discipline our people'.

From this time on the Seleucid garrison was no longer able to control the mounting tension. Antiochus sent an imposing army to Jerusalem commanded by Apollonius, the leader of the mercenaries. The population were treated as enemies, put in chains and butchered; the fortifications were destroyed.

A fortress, the Acra, was erected inside the City of David in which the renegade Jews and the Hellenised pagans took refuge, and from which the Seleucid garrison terrorised the city. 'Because of them the residents of Jerusalem fled; she became a dwelling of strangers; she became strange to her offspring and her children forsook her. Her sanctuary became desolate as a desert; her feasts were turned into mourning, her sabbaths into a reproach . . .'

'Then Mattathias cried out in the city with a loud voice, saying, Let every one who is zealous for the law and supports the covenant come out with me.'
(1 Macc. II. 27)

The seven brothers (Boskovice Bible).

The Jews resisted religious persecution and Hellenistic propaganda by underhand methods and moving accounts of courage bear witness to this. Six brothers had just been put to death before their mother by order of the king for having refused to eat pork, a thing which was forbidden by the Law. When it was the turn of the last son, 'she spoke in their native tongue as follows, deriding the cruel tyrant: My son, have pity upon me. I carried you nine months in my womb . . . and have reared you and brought you up to this point in your life . . . I beseech you, my child . . . Do not fear this butcher, but prove worthy of your brothers. Accept death, so that in God's mercy I may get you back again.' But it was the priest Mattathias who gave the signal for open opposition in 167. Overwhelmed by the misfortunes of their nation, Mattathias and his five sons fled from Jerusalem to a nearby village and from there, after killing the king's commissioner who tried to compel them to sacrifice to the Greek gods, they escaped to the mountains. Followers flocked to join them and they organised themselves for resistance.

Apollonius, the governor of Samaria, decided to crush this centre of insurrection immediately. He was defeated by one of Mattathias' sons, Judas 'Maccabeus' (i.e. 'the hammer' in Hebrew), who had placed himself at their head. His men were badly armed and had to match themselves against increasingly heavy forces, but they were fighting both for an ideal and for their land; they had a thorough knowledge of the terrain and the support of the entire population.

After his victory over Apollonius, Judas managed to defeat the governor of Coele-Syria. When he was informed

Before the impiety of Jerusalem 'Mattathias and his sons rent their clothes, put on sackcloth, and mourned greatly' (seventeenth-century engraving).

After their victory, Judas Maccabeus and his brothers offer up a sacrifice on the rebuilt altar of burnt-offering (seventeenth-century engraving).

of this Antiochus instructed his general Lysias to put down the rebellion. The latter assembled 40,000 infantry men and 7,000 horsemen under the command of Nicanor and Gorgias, two of Antiochus' best military leaders. In the course of their victories the guerillas had managed to provide themselves with arms by taking the weapons of the defeated and were henceforth sufficiently formidable to warrant such a deployment of forces. Lysias' army pitched camp near Emmaus. Reinforcements flocked to join him from all sides while the merchants awaited the moment when they could acquire the Jewish prisoners as slaves. Gorgias left camp with the major part of the army and marched towards Judas, intending to attack during the night. Warned in advance, Judas and his troops abandoned their position but left their camp fires lit, and, while Gorgias was vainly searching for them, fell on Nicanor's camp. The Macedonians were taken by surprise and fled, while Gorgias' soldiers were seized with panic and did the same. Judas was left master of the field. Emmaus was a great victory for the Jews. They were to gain others all round Jerusalem, which remained their principal objective.

They entered the city in December of 165 and occupied it without, however, being able to gain the citadel of Acra which remained in the hands of the forces of Antiochus. Judas found the Temple 'desolate . . . the gates burned. In the courts they saw bushes sprung up . . .'

He undertook the purification of the Holy Place, replaced the sacred objects, set up the gates, pulled down the altar of sacrifices and built a new one from rough stones. The candlestick was solemnly relit, an empty oil phial burned miraculously for eight days, the shewbread was replaced on the table and a burnt-offering blazed upon the new altar. The festivities lasted for a week and, in their joy at regaining their religion, the people proposed that the restoration of the temple should be celebrated obligatorily each year: this would be the *Hanukkah*, 'the Feast of Lights'.

Judas surrounded the city with ramparts, built towers, on which he placed watchmen, and fortified Beth-sura a few miles away to act as a line of defence.

When he heard of the military successes of Judas Maccabeus, Antiochus took to his bed and became sick from grief . . . 'thus he who had just been thinking that he could command the waves of the sea, in his superhuman arrogance, and imagining that he could weigh the high mountains in a balance, was brought down to earth and carried in a litter, making the power of God manifest to all. And so the ungodly man's body swarmed with worms, and while he was still living in anguish and pain, his flesh rotted away, and because of his stench the whole army felt revulsion at his decay.' Thus died Antiochus Epiphanes the blasphemer, who had said in his pride when he arrived at Jerusalem that he would make of it 'a cemetery'.

Death of Antiochus (Boskovice Bible).

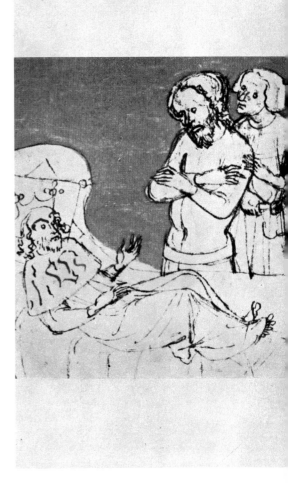

The forces of Judas Maccabeus face the army of Antiochus V: more than a hundred and twenty thousand soldiers and thirty-two elephants (engraving by G. Doré).

The Hasidim, the pious Jews and pioneers of religious resistance against the

Commemorative statue in the Negeb.

The death of Antiochus and the dissentions which followed it enabled Judas Maccabeus to regroup his forces. He won a final victory over 'Nicanor, who had been master of the elephants', but met his death in this heroic battle whose memory is still preserved in Israel. 'Then Jonathan and Simon took Judas their brother and buried him in the tomb of their fathers at Modein, and wept for him. And all Israel made great lamentation for him.' His brothers continued the struggle for political independence. Despite their military superiority, the Seleucids had to leave the Acra in 143 and recognise Jewish independence. Simon Maccabeus was made ethnarch of Judah. Although he was never crowned king, he is regarded as the founder of the Maccabean dynasty, also known as the Hasmonaean dynasty, which was to remain in power right up to the disappearance of the Jewish state.

United for a time in opposition, the Jews were to divide once again when confronted with the vital problem of participation or non-participation in the

Hellenistic world. The Hasidim, the 'pious Jews', who had been the pioneers of the religious revolt and had managed to assemble supporters from every class and sect, very quickly split into three parties: Essenes, Pharisees and Sadducees. The Essenes withdrew from political life and were to play a spiritual role, the importance of which was not to be understood until after the sensational Dead Sea discoveries *(see following pages)*. The Pharisees and Sadducees were to come into bitter opposition. The Pharisees represented the anti-Hellenistic group of the Hasidim party. They were recruited from the popular class, which remained attached to its own culture and refused to see Hellenisation as an advance. Liberal in religious and political matters, they were prepared to let manners, beliefs and institutions evolve along a path of their own and preached a new, oral interpretation of the Mosaic Law, while as supporters of prayer, the synagogue and rabbis, they were opposed to the Temple, the high priest and sacrifices. The Sadducees, on

Antiochus VII Sidetes (139–129), King of Syria, takes up the struggle against the Jews again and comes to besiege Jerusalem (seventeenth-century engraving).

Seleucids, divide into three groups; Pharisees, Sadducees and Essenes.

the other hand, were recruited from among the aristocrats and priests. Their particular form of Judaism dated from the period before the prophets. Highly conservative, they remained attached to the unity of a centralised cult in the Temple and the ceremonial of sacrifices. To them Hellenism seemed harmless both spiritually and where faith was concerned, and all the more harmless in that it was a source of considerable profit. The Sadducees were not opposed to the cosmopolitanism of the propertied classes who traded with the Orient.

The struggle between the two parties was set in motion by the murder of Simon. His son, John Hyrcanus, who belonged to the Pharisee party, was anointed king and high priest in 135. But the king was unable to ward off the Seleucid danger which was once again pressing. He had to submit to Antiochus VII Sidetes, and Jerusalem paid a heavy tribute. When the death of their conqueror enabled the Jews to regain their independence a long era of prosperity began which was further encouraged by

the daring and lack of religious scruples of the king. Although he posed as the champion of Judaism, Hyrcanus shocked the tradionalist Jews by minting money in his own name and by having recourse to foreign mercenaries, whom he paid with money stolen from the tomb of David. Having set his own party against him, he relied on the Sadducean party and followed them along the path of Hellenisation.

Within a few years Hyrcanus' kingdom surpassed that of David. This impetus and apparent strength did not prevent Jerusalem from being divided into two factions which opposed each other with increasing violence and were to bring about her ruin. The Jews had already called for help against the Seleucids on several occasions from a new power to whom the whole Mediterranean world would soon be subject.

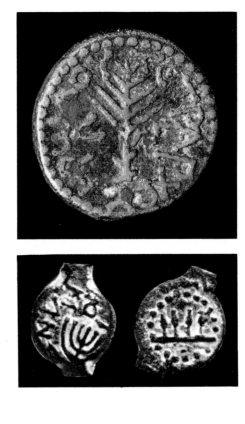

Coin struck by John Hyrcanus.

Coins of the Hasmonaeans or Maccabees.

General view of Qumran taken from the rocky cliff in which the caves of the scrolls are located. In the distance is the Dead Sea.

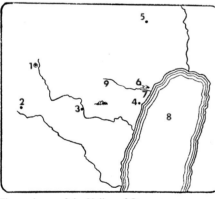

The environs of the Valley of Qumran:
(1) Jerusalem. (2) Bethlehem. (3) Mar Saba.
(4) Ain Feshkha. (5) Jericho. (6–7) Caves of the
Scrolls. (8) Dead Sea. (9) The Qumran wadi.

The careful unwinding of a scroll.

Around the Teacher of Righteousness the Essenes devote themselves to a new understanding of the Law.

In the middle of the twentieth century the discoveries made by Bedouin shepherds scaling the rocks in the region of the Dead Sea have thrown a vivid light upon a sect which was less conspicuously involved in the economic prosperity and the history of Jerusalem in the first century B.C., but whose intellectual and spiritual role must have been extremely important in the history of the city.

Neither the Old Testament nor the New Testament mentions the Essenes, who were situated at the junction of the two worlds. They are known from the texts of the historians Flavius Josephus, Philo the Greek and Pliny the Elder. The discoveries made at Qumran have made it possible to re-examine the theories formed about them, since it has been established, after some preliminary hesitation, that Qumran was an Essene 'monastery'. In the light of the documents and texts which have been discovered and saved from final destruction thanks to the painstaking processes of modern techniques, it is now thought that the Essenes were priests who had left the Temple of Jerusalem after Antiochus' edict of persecution to form small communities of ten or a dozen members each. Qumran, near the Dead Sea, would appear to be one of these 'monasteries', but the Essenes must have been found in large numbers in a great many cities of Judaea.

They led a conventual life, something which had never existed among the Jews before. Among the Dead Sea scrolls is a *Manual of Discipline* which gives the essentials of the rule of the sect which called itself 'the New Covenant'. The members of the community were priests to begin with, who were joined by disciples and volunteers. The bodies of women have been discovered in the cemetery but it is thought that the Essenes practised celibacy.

The sect intended itself as a community forming an everlasting covenant with God, and an authentic and more spiritual sanctuary than the Temple of Jerusalem. With them it was less a question of sacrifice than of virtue. They were a secret society: it was laid down that the doctrine and practices of the holy community should be concealed from those outside. Permission to participate in the life of the convent was granted after serving as a postulant and a novice for two years. First-year novices did not participate in the ritual ablutions nor in the sacred meals. They retained sole personal use of their belongings until the end of the second year of their novitiate. A ceremony marked their entry into the Covenant. The most important part of life in the monastery was dedicated to the study and interpretation of the Law. The Essenes attached a sacred value to the prophetic writings and sought a basis for their interpretation in the Torah. The Teacher of Righteousness, the leading figure of the sect, who appears in the manuscript of the *Habakkuk Commentary* but whose historical identification remains very difficult, had been given supernatural powers by virtue of which he was able to interpret the Law. The words of the Teacher of Righteousness came from the mouth of God Himself and he was the custodian of his secrets and the builder of His Church, as he proclaims in the *Hymns*. 'And thou hast built my dwelling upon the rock, and everlasting foundations serve as my support and all my walls have become a trusty rampart which cannot be shaken.'

The traitors to the Covenant and its adversaries were plotting against him and the community. Among these adversaries were the Man of Untruth and the Wicked Priest. The life of the Essenes becomes involved here with current events and incidents, the precise details of which are obscured by symbols. Although they remained faithful to Judaism, the Essenes had assimilated features derived from the Iranian religion as reformed by Zoroaster and which had spread at the time of the Persian domination. A dualism completely unknown in Judaism prompted the 'War of the Sons of Light against the Sons of Darkness' and uncompromisingly opposed Good and Evil.

Ideas were borrowed from the Persians as they were from Pythagoras, but were completely recast in the light of the Mosaic Law. 'The Qumran documents refer continually to authentic sources of the Jewish faith. Moreover this sect, with Judaism itself, was the most fervent inheritor of both the ancient sacerdotal spirit and the ancient prophetic spirit; it preserved the whole mystical legacy of Israel's past.' (M. Dupont-Sommer).

Specialist reconstituting a Dead Sea Scroll, fragment by fragment.

The rule of the Congregation, one of the Dead Sea Scrolls; on the right is an inkwell.

THE JERUSALEM OF CHRIST

from the Visitation to the Ascension

Now you are walled about with a wall;
siege is laid against us; with a rod they
strike upon the cheek the ruler of Israel.

But you, O Bethlehem Ephrathah, who are little
to be among the clans of Judah, from you shall
come forth for me one who is to be ruler in Israel,
whose origin is from of old, from ancient days.

Micah V. 1-2

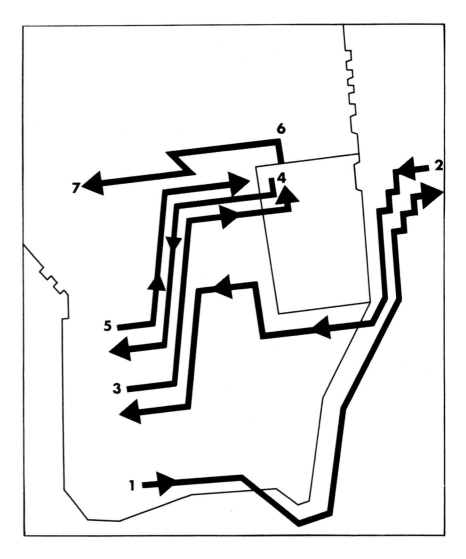

Christ's itinèrary during His Passion:
1. Cenaculum (Last Supper). 2. Gethsemane (the arrest). 3. Palace of the High Priest (appearance before the Sanhedrin). 4. Palace of Pilate (Roman trial). 5. Palace of Herod (appearance before the tetrarch). 6. Palace of Pilate (Ecce Homo).
7. Golgotha (Crucifixion).

Under Roman domination: taking advantage of the quarrels between estranged brothers, Pompey enters Jerusalem and Judaea becomes a Roman province for several hundred years.

Alexander Jannaeus Maccabeus (104–78 B.C.) puts down a revolt by having eight hundred people executed by his mercenaries (seventeenth-century engraving).

Pompey the Great (106–48 B.C.).

The Maccabees (or Hasmonaeans), the heroes of the revolt against the Seleucids, continued to control affairs at Jerusalem. Jonathan, Simon Maccabaeus and John Hyrcanus succeeded one another in turn as high priest. After the brief and bloody reign of Aristobulus, it was soon John Hyrcanus' third son who received the office of high priest and added to this function the title of king. He was an energetic ruler and pursued the expansionist policy initiated by his father. But as high priest he was reproached with the actions of the king, and as king he was regarded as a usurper because he was not descended from David.

In the name of the purity of Judaism, the Pharisees had no hesitation in calling on the worst enemies of the Israelites, the Seleucids, who were only too happy to invade the country. Realising their folly, however, the Pharisees quickly rallied to the side of Alexander Jannaeus in order to repel the invaders. Once the danger had been averted the king took his revenge and had 800 prisoners crucified on Mount Golgotha in his presence. He had, however, understood that the offices of king and high priest were not com-

patible and bequeathed his kingdom to his wife Alexandra and the Temple to his eldest son John Hyrcanus II. But at the death of Alexandra his two sons, Hyrcanus II and Aristobulus, began fighting over the throne.

The struggle between the two brothers seemed unlikely to be resolved, when a third party decided to appeal to Roman arbitration and chose Pompey who, with his legions, had just completed the conquest of Syria. After months of agitation and confusion the victor decided to intervene in favour of Hyrcanus, who was less of a danger to Roman authority than his brother. In 63 he marched on Jerusalem where part of the population awaited him as a peacemaker. Aristobulus, who had taken refuge within the walls of the Temple, had to surrender after a three months' resistance. Curious to learn the secrets of the Jewish religion, Pompey entered the Holy of Holies, his naked sword in his hand, and was amazed to find it empty of any prodigious idol. As governor of Judah he appointed Hyrcanus ethnarch under an adviser, Antipater; Judaea became a Roman province.

Pompey's entry into the Temple (Fouquet, miniature from *The Jewish Antiquities* of Fl. Josephus).

King of Judaea by the will of the Roman Senate, Herod the Great, the Idumaean, has to spend three years conquering his kingdom by force of arms.

In the foreground the fourteenth-century citadel on the site of the three towers built in the days of Herod. In the background, the dome of the Mosque of El-Aksa.

Hyrcanus had managed to hold on to the office of high priest. At the death of Antipater, in 43 B.C., the latter's two sons shared the kingdom, Phasael taking Jerusalem, and Herod, Galilee. But once again a descendant of the Hasmonaean house revolted. Antigonus, the son of Aristobulus, recaptured Jerusalem from the Romans, proclaimed himself king and high priest, and declared Palestine independent once more. Inside the city the rulers of Judaea offered a vain resistance. Phasael was defeated and committed suicide while John Hyrcanus was mutilated to render him unfit for the priesthood.

Herod set sail for Rome where he was given a highly sympathetic welcome. Octavius and Antony saw in him, despite his twenty-nine years, the man capable of restoring Roman order in Judaea and had him appointed king of the province by the Senate. But his kingdom would have to be conquered.

The enormous preparations for the battle of Jerusalem took more than a year. In 37, siege engines attacked the walls. Antigonus defenced the city stone by stone with the support of the entire population. But Herod commanded eleven legions and 6,000 horsemen. Three years after receiving the title of king, he entered the capital.

He reigned over the Jews from 37 to 4 B.C. and left behind a memory for implacable cruelty. Yet he was also known as Herod the Great. Intelligent and strange, he tried to reconcile his personal ambition with both the Jewish and Roman interests in his government. His sole support was his garrisons and his first concern was to build a fortress (the Antonia, as a mark of esteem for Antony), from the top of which he had a watch kept on the Temple, the city and its surroundings. The Antonia occupied a privileged strategic position which was preserved for several hundred years.

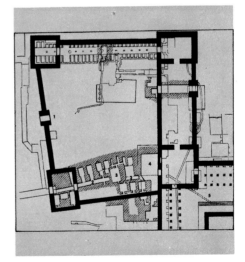

Plan of the Antonia after the descriptions of Flavius Josephus: the fortress, flanked by four stout towers, kept watch on the Temple (below right), which could be reached by means of a secret passage. The Antonia was destroyed in 70 A.D. by the armies of Titus.

The city from the walls of the Antonia.

Under Herod's brilliant reign a theatre, race-course, gardens, colonnades and

Jerusalem attained her greatest expansion in the days of Herod. The upper hill was completely built over and the Bezetha suburbs rose in tiers on the northern side. Situated as it was, however, on rising ground, the city did not have the open, carefully planned appearance of its Hellenistic rivals, Caesarea or Alexandria. It radiated out on different planes on either side of the filled-in trench of the Tyropoean, and could not extend beyond the bounds imposed on it by the gorges of the Kidron and the Hinnom (Gehenna).

For Herod the necessity of defending his capital was bound up with his concern to protect his throne and his authority from internal risks. Stronger walls than ever before encircled the entire city for almost three miles, interrupted only by fortified gates. Even inside the city, fortresses turned each zone and each large ward into a fresh stronghold. On the south the City of David could shut itself off and defend itself unaided. To the north of Mount Moriah the Temple was under observation from the Antonia, in that area of Jerusalem in peril from the rising ground of Bezetha, and which had always been fortified. The original tower, which had already been enlarged under the Hasmonaeans, was strengthened a little more each day. It communicated

by means of stairs with the Temple court, which was a public meeting place and a possible starting point for attempted revolts. Reservoirs were prepared beneath the flagged courtyard, while subterranean passages led into the heart of the city connected to the fortress by a single bridge. Three square towers christened Phasael, Hippicus and Mariamne (the brother, friend and wife of the king) protected the upper city, the aristocratic quarter in which stood the palaces of Herod and the high priest. They assured the defence of the royal and sacerdotal quarter. Known today as the Tower of David, Phasael still stands as part of the citadel built later by the Turks. The palace was of marble, and contained about a hundred rooms and banqueting halls large enough to accommodate a hundred couches for guests.

But it was above all the gardens which excited admiration, the only ones in the city to offer the spectacle of magnificent fountains and ornamental lakes fed by aqueducts. One of the few broad thoroughfares in Jerusalem connected this palace with the Temple. Close to the former palace of the Hasmonaeans a square was laid out, the Xystus or 'terrace'. A theatre and a race-course were constructed, in spite of the opposition of the pious Jews, as well as several swimming pools fed by the pool of Siloam. The ordinary inhabitants filled the various districts around the official buildings with the picturesque bustle of artisanal life, each guild giving its name to a small square around which clustered the houses. Each little group of dwellings had its own synagogue, of which there were 480 at this period.

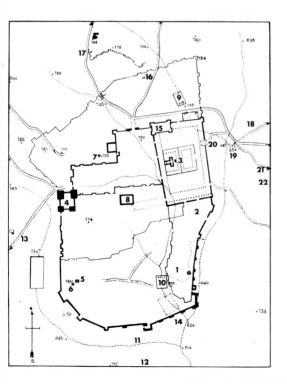

Jerusalem in the days of Herod:
(1) City of David. (2) The Ophel. (3) The Temple. (4) Palace of Herod. (5) Palace of Caiaphas. (6) Cenaculum. (7) Golgotha. (8) Palace of the Hasmonaeans. (9) Pool of Bethesda. (10) Pool of Siloam. (11) Valley of Gehenna. (12) Aceldama. (13) Tomb of the Herods. (14) Old pool. (15) Antonia. (16) Galilee road. (17) Caesarea Road. (18) Towards Jericho. (19) Garden of Gethsemane. (20) Golden Gate. (21) Towards Bethany. (22) Mount of Olives.

Reconstruction of the city: in the foreground the Temple watched over by the fortress of the Antonia; in the background, the towers and porticos of the palace of Herod; on the left, the Valley of Gehenna; in the foreground, on the right, the Mount of Olives.

a palace transform the Temple city into a great Hellenistic city.

Herod the Idumaean builds the second Temple to appease the Chosen People.

A Hellenistic prince with a sceptical mind, Herod had reasons which had nothing to do with the Jewish religion for setting on hand the adornment and enlargement of the Temple, which had been rebuilt in rather a simple manner after the return from exile. As well as being an attempt at rapprochement with a people hostile to their foreign king, this mighty undertaking was to add to the sovereign's prestige and bear witness, like the first Temple of Solomon, to the brilliance of his reign. Nevertheless he respected the fundamental concepts of Yahvism.

The project was a grandiose one. Ten thousand workmen toiled for ten years on the site. The court of the former Temple was doubled in size and it was necessary to cut into hill and rock and build stout supporting walls in order to obtain an esplanade almost a mile around the perimeter, which rose in tiers to form various courts. Both Jews and foreigners mingled in the Court of the Gentiles, which acted as a square and thoroughfare. All around it were colonnades, and on the south was the royal porch, whose four rows of Corinthian columns of white marble supported a rich, carved ceiling.

This public area was separated from three courts reserved for the Jews by a balustrade bearing the following inscription in Greek and Latin: 'It is forbidden for any foreigner to cross the barrier and enter the precinct of the sanctuary. Whoever is caught will himself be responsible for his ensuing death.' The sacred precinct, which began on the other side of this boundary, rose in two squares, one above the other. On the lower level the Court of the Women (who were not allowed to go any farther) gave access to the reserves of wood, oil and wine and also to the offertory boxes, while on a second level, ten feet higher, a huge bronze gate, the Gate of Nicanor, led to the Court of the Israelites, which was separated by several steps from the final enclosure, the Court of the Priests, which was 195 feet by 260 feet. Here at last were the outbuildings of the Temple: the hall of carved stone where the Sanhedrin met and that of the fountain or pool where the water for the ritual purifications was drawn; the storehouses for wood and incense and stables for the sacrificial beasts. In the court stood a dais from which the high priest gave his blessing, and next to the sacred accessories of the cult, the basins for ablution, there also stood the altar of burnt-offerings, a block of unpolished stone forty-five-and-a-half feet by thirteen feet with horns on the corners. The Temple

Coin of the second revolt showing the Temple with, in the furthermost part, the Holy of Holies with the scrolls of the Law.

Lapidary inscription at the entrance to the court of the Jews prohibiting access of the Temple to Gentiles.

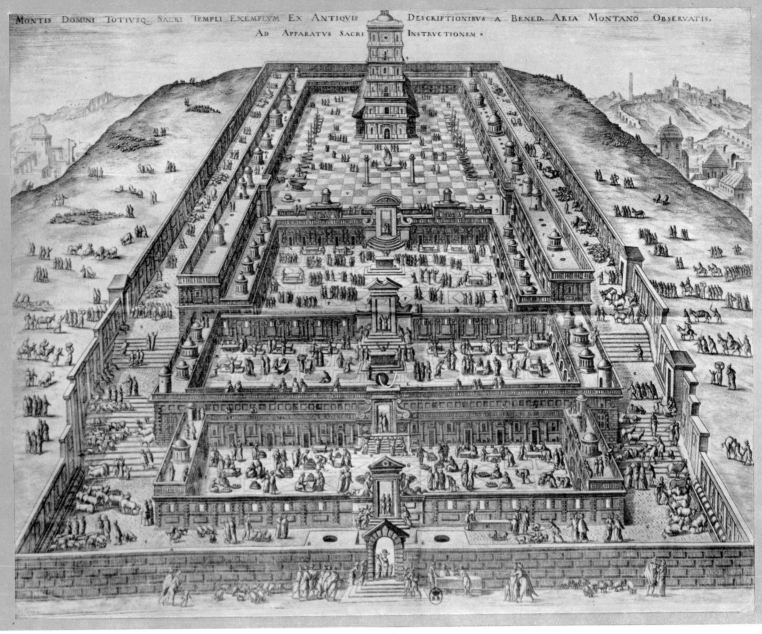

A seventeenth-century reconstruction from historical texts gives the Temple a classical style.

itself, which stood on twelve steps, was divided into three parts: the porch, the Holy Place and the Holy of Holies. The door of the sanctuary, which was made of cedar-wood covered with gold, was surmounted by a gilded ornamental vine branch, the symbol of creation, and always stood open. In contrast an embroidered curtain hid the entrance of the Holy Place, and only the priests had the right to draw it aside. This part was divided into two rooms: the *hekal* with the table for the shewbread, the seven-branched candlestick and the altar of incense, and the *debir*, the Holy of Holies, which was completely empty and only entered once a year by the high priest on the Day of Atonement.

'Do you see these great buildings? There will not be left here one stone upon another, that will not be thrown down.'

Christ's prophetic words were to be realised only a few months after the completion of the building operations. Only contemporary descriptions enable us to picture this stupendous edifice.

Plan of the Temple of Herod: (1) Antonia. (2) Court of the Gentiles. (3) Court of the Women. (4) Altar. (5) Holy of Holies (6) Royal Porch. (7) Solomon's Porch.

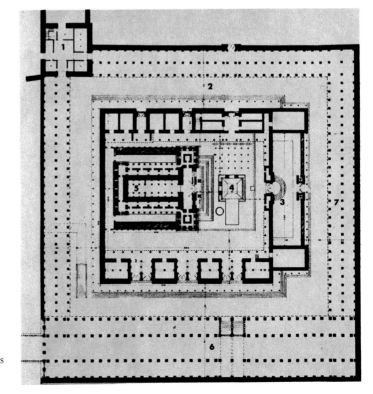

'... a narrative of the things which have been accomplished among us, just as they were delivered to us by those who from the beginning were eye-witnesses and ministers of the word.' (Luke I. 1-2)

Behind this dazzling facade Jerusalem and Judaea were living in a state of great agitation. Sects were being formed and groups were announcing the coming of a Messiah who would save Israel. From the midst of this ferment sprang the story of Jesus. A small group of witnesses collected the events of His life which were soberly recorded in four 'gospels'. As Christianity developed popular imagination seized hold of these in order to embellish them with legends and anecdotes which the artists of the East and West drew upon to create a new Jerusalem. In the setting of the Temple and its courts, and the streets of the Holy City, Christ, His family, His disciples and the common people were the protagonists of this extraordinary drama.

An aging couple were childless. The wife was called Anne, which means 'grace', and her husband Joachim, 'preparation to the Lord'. Their sterility weighed upon them like a curse: the high priest rejected the offering which Joachim wished to make to the Temple. Humiliated, Joachim fled from the city and sought refuge with a band of shepherds, leaving Anne alone at Jerusalem. In despair his barren wife could only weep and pray. God heard her and she had a dream which foretold that she would give birth to a daughter. Also informed of this grace from heaven, Joachim returned to the city; Anne ran to meet him and they met at the Golden Gate. This marvellous meeting was the prelude to the birth of the Virgin Mary. The Golden Gate, which was on the east of the precinct, gave direct access to the Temple. A few shafts and capitals set in the wall of the old city still show its position. It has a symbolic significance: an emblem of the gate of Paradise, Israelite tradition claims that the Messiah will use it at the Last Judgment when it will open to let him pass through in glory, while Moslem tradition claims that Mohammed will also come there to judge the world, seated on one of the pillars of the wall.

When her time was accomplished, Anne gave birth to the promised child. In the absence of a detailed account artists have pictured this scene differently in different centuries. In some paintings one finds an attendant midwife and the newborn baby's bath, details which were too realistic and disappeared later on. It is known that Jewish women were at this time assisted by midwives, who employed 'delivery stools'. Childbirth was so sacred that it was lawful to help a woman in labour even on the Sabbath. The father was never allowed to be present at the birth. According to tradition, the Virgin was born in September on the day of the great Jewish festival of Succoth, 'the Feast of Tabernacles'. She was given the name of Mary, a common one, the etymology of which is still disputed: (?) 'Star of the Sea', (?) 'Lady'. Where was she born? In a crypt near Jerusalem, near the pool of Bethesda, the birth of Mary is traditionally venerated. Above it rises one of the most beautiful churches in the city, the Church of St. Anne, which was built in the first half of the twelfth century and is one of the best-preserved monuments of Frankish Jerusalem. Almost entirely restored, in fact, under Baldwin I, this Romanesque building gives an impression of austere beauty.

Annunciation to Anne (Giotto, thirteenth-century fresco in Arena Chapel, Padua). The meeting of Anne and Joachim at the Golden Gate. (T. Gaddi, fresco).

The birth of the Virgin, which a second-century tradition situates at Jerusalem on 8th September (Giovanni da Milano, 1366, fresco in S. Croce, Florence).

Jerusalem in 1877. In the foreground is the Church of St Anne, one of the most beautiful in the city, erected on the crypt of the birth of Mary in the twelfth century.

The young Mary climbs the fifteen steps leading up to the Temple alone and offers herself to the Lord of her own accord (Titian, 1538, Accademia, Venice).

'Behold, a young woman shall conceive, and bear a son . . .' (Isaiah VII. 14)

In the court of the Temple, a symbolic ceremony had replaced the ritual sacrifice. Anne and Joachim took Mary there to dedicate her to God by presenting her at the altar of burnt-offerings. A few years later the candidates for Mary's hand were assembled around the same altar. She was fourteen years old, the age of marriage for the daughters of Israel. To the sound of trumpets the high priest had summoned together all the bachelors and widowers who were descended from David. It was the aged Joseph, a carpenter, who was chosen by God.

Jewish marriage took place in two parts, which were considered as one in the eyes of the Law but were separate in practice, since the young wife only went to live with her husband after a lengthy period which was given over to drawing up the contract, and during which she was subject to legal guarantees. Mary and Joseph had not yet lived together when the angel Gabriel announced to Mary the birth of a child conceived of the Holy Ghost, and explained to Joseph that he should not fear to take into his house his wife, Mary, whom he could have thought unfaithful. After the material details of the contract had been settled, the deed was signed on a Tuesday in the case of a young girl and on a Wednesday in the case of a widow—always at the time of the full moon which was considered lucky. On the eve of the wedding day the fiancé set off with his friends to fetch his fiancée from her father's house. The young bride was borne in a litter in her wedding dress with her head veiled and her forehead covered with golden discs. At the fiancé's door, decorated with myrtle and laurel, the father pronounced the set formulas of blessing and words of welcome. The guests and the families of the friends started playing games and dancing, but the fiancée took no part in these. At the official feast seeds and pomegranates were thrown before the couple in accordance with an ancient fertility rite, and a vase of perfume was broken.

At this point there was no actual religious ceremony, marriage was not a sacrament, and it was by adapting the scene to Western customs that artists represented the marriage of Mary and Joseph as a nuptial blessing given by the high priest within the Temple.

Mary's bridal procession before the house of Joseph (Giotto, fresco in the Arena Chapel, Padua).

Marriage of the Virgin. The high priest joins the hands of the kneeling betrothed couple (Pinakothek, Munich).

'He has helped his servant Israel, in remembrance of his mercy, as he spoke to our fathers.' (Luke I. 54–55)

The village of Ain Karim, a few miles southwest of Jerusalem, where John the Baptist was born.

John the Baptist and Jesus (Pintoricchio, detail).

Mary was at Nazareth when the angel Gabriel appeared and announced that she would be the mother of God. As a proof of the genuineness of his message he added that Elizabeth, an aging barren cousin of Mary's, was going to give birth to a son. Mary set off across Palestine for Ain Karim, where Elizabeth and Zacharias lived.

Ain Karim (in Arabic 'the spring of the vineyards') is a picturesque village about five miles south of Jerusalem. On its hills, scattered among the cypresses, are a number of religious houses, the most important of which is the monastery of St. John which belongs to the Franciscans. It was there that the Church of St. John the Baptist was built on the traditional site of the house of Elizabeth and Zacharias.

An angel in human form had appeared to Zacharias in the Temple of Jerusalem while he was performing one of the most sacred rites of the liturgy, the offering of the incense. He had been selected by lot that morning from among the twenty-four priests who, each week in rotation, carried out the Temple duties, and had

been designated for the offering. The two assistants who had helped him prepare the fire and the incense had just withdrawn and the priest was alone in the Holy Place, when Gabriel declared: '. . . your wife Elizabeth will bear you a son, and you shall call his name John.' Zacharias did not believe that his wife was capable of bearing a son as she was too old. He was immediately struck dumb for his lack of faith.

Elizabeth had been pregnant for several months when Mary arrived at the mountain village of Ain Karim. As soon as she entered Elizabeth's house, her cousin was filled with the Holy Ghost and cried: 'Blessed are you among women, and blessed is the fruit of your womb.' Mary's joy then burst forth in the *Magnificat*, which she sang when she saw that she had been recognised and that her secret had been shared. She stayed about three months at Ain Karim and assisted at the birth of Elizabeth's child, who was circumcised eight days later. The Law was categorical, every male had to be circumcised: to be uncircumcised was to 'belong not to the

sons of the Covenant but to the children of destruction'.

The operation which was originally performed by the father, or exceptionally by the mother in emergencies (this had happened in the days of the Maccabees), was performed at the time of Herod by a specialist, the *mohel*. During this ceremony the child was given its name. The choice was very important as the Jews ascribed to the name a power capable of affecting an entire life. This is why the privilege of choosing it belonged to the father. Unable to speak, Zacharias wrote his son's name on a tablet, and immediately recovered his speech. The name of John astonished the assembled company because it was not borne by anyone in the family. Associated with Christ from the moment of his birth, John was often portrayed as a child with the Saviour.

In one of these scenes (*see above*), in which the future role of both is already indicated, the child Jesus, on the right, is carrying His books while the infant John, in his sheepskin, bears on his shoulder a cross with a pennant and in his hand, the baptismal ewer.

The visitation of Mary to her cousin Elizabeth: the one expecting Christ, the other, John the Baptist (Fra Angelico).

'And Joseph also went up from Galilee, from the city of Nazareth, to Judaea, to the city of David, which is called Bethlehem.' (Luke II. 4)

'In those days a decree went out from Caesar Augustus that all the world should be enrolled. This was the first enrolment, when Quirinius was governor of Syria. And all went to be enrolled, each to his own city.' (Luke II. 1–3). There is no trace of Caesar's edict, Latin historians do not mention it and no record has come down to us, so that it is consequently impossible to know its exact date. It would have provided us at the same time with the date of Jesus' birth, since He came into the world at the end of the journey undertaken by Joseph and Mary in obedience to the emperor's command. The mention of Quirinius, however, an imperial legate whose stays in the East are recorded, enables us to place the census order around about the year 10 B.C. The time required to set up all the necessary administrative machinery would put back the actual census, which was not of the whole world (this would have left more traces), but of Palestine, to c. 7 B.C. If these hypotheses are correct, our reckoning of time is seven years out. This census was the first of a series imposed by the Roman administration upon the Jews for purposes of taxation. Despite the habitual flexibility of its administration, Rome was compelled, in the face of the Parthian danger, to impose upon both Judah and Galilee these authoritarian measures which were the marks of a dominion which was to weigh increasingly heavily upon them.

Already overburdened with taxes from the policy of grandeur which Herod had imposed upon them for forty years, the Jews objected strongly to this new form of fiscal regulation which, in addition to being a threat to their possessions, was a symbol of foreign domination. The first manifestations of hostility against the regime were already beginning to appear. Round about the year 7 B.C., then, Mary and Joseph left Nazareth where they were living, since it was not their town of origin. Enrolment on the official registers had, in fact, to be done at the family's place of origin, in accordance with the tradition evolved from patriarchal customs. Joseph, like Mary, was descended from David, whose house had originated in Bethlehem in Judaea. The

couple travelled for several days, Joseph leading the donkey which carried Mary. The distance between Nazareth and Bethlehem was a long one, over ninety miles, and the roads, which the Romans had not yet had time to repair, were poor. They journeyed through the Plain of Esdraelon and the mountains of Samaria before reaching Judaea.

The road to Bethlehem passed through Jerusalem where, after a short rest, the travellers took the Hebron road to the south through the mountains of Judah,

joining the long procession of people going to the city of David for the census.

Before long the travellers reached Bethlehem, 'the house of bread'. The town rose in terraces up the sides of twin hills, the whiteness of the houses standing out against the orchards and olive groves. Beyond, the desert fell away towards the Dead Sea. Bethlehem still exists today, a little town of 9,000 inhabitants with twisting streets, which the prophets had destined for fame.

The road from Jerusalem to Bethlehem. In the background the white town rises in tiers on the hills of Judaea.

Caesar Augustus issuing the decree for the census (miniature, Munich).

Bethlehem in 1877, photographed by Bonfils.

Entrance to the narthex of the basilica of the Nativity at Bethlehem (remodelled under Justinian), one of the rare Byzantine monuments still in existence.

'And this will be a sign for you: you will find a babe wrapped in swaddling cloths and lying in a manger.' (Luke II. 12)

In 325 A.D. the Emperor Constantine ordered the erection of a basilica at Bethlehem in honour of the Nativity. The flagstones of the original atrium, in which cisterns collected rain water for the ritual ablutions, have survived the ages. The nave was saved from destruction in 614, at the time of the Persian invasion, thanks to the mosaic portraying the three Magi. The invaders recognised their own priests in these kings who, in order to emphasise their eastern origin, were dressed as servants of Mithra. The stout Crusader walls have preserved this monument for us, one of the few Constantinian edifices still in existence.

'And she gave birth to her first-born son and wrapped him in swaddling cloths, and laid him in a manger, because there was no place for them in the inn.' In spite of the restraint of the gospel text, the birth of Jesus in the grotto of Bethlehem has fired peoples' imaginations, and within a very short time the ox and the ass made their appearance in the grotto as a result of a text of Isaiah wrongly interpreted in apocryphal writings: 'The ox knows its owner, and the ass its master's crib.' The

Virgin's attitude is also a reflection of the controversies of theologians throughout the centuries: did the Virgin give birth in pain or painlessly? For long depicted as a scene of child-birth, the travail of the Virgin became, from the fourteenth century onwards, a scene of adoration. The gospels give contradictory information about Christ's birthplace: Matthew and Luke state that He was born at Bethlehem, Mark and John Nazareth. But since the second century the tradition in Palestine has it that Jesus was born in one of the grottoes around Bethlehem. In the crypt of the basilica of the Nativity there is a silver-gilt star with the inscription: 'Hic de Virgine Maria Jesus Christus natus est.'

Like the place and year, the day and month of Christ's birth have also given rise to controversy. The liturgical date of 25th December is not based upon any historical information and none of the evangelists thought to state it precisely. Originally celebrated on 6th January, the nativity was moved, in the fourth century, to 25th December, the date of the winter solstice. According to certain Christian exegetes the rebirth of the sun was

preferred for the birth of Him who has been called the 'true sun'. In point of fact, it was obviously in the Church's interests to substitute a Christian festival for the celebration of the solar god Mithra and for that of the Roman Saturnalia which were important nature festivals of paganism. Its fixing on that date automatically regulated those of the festivals that depended on it: the Annunciation (25th March) and the Circumcision (1st January), while 6th January was preserved, with its typically oriental name of Epiphany, or apparition, of the divinity.

Jesus Christ is the Greek translation of 'Joshua the Messiah'. In Hebrew, the word Messiah means 'anointed' and Joshua 'Yahweh saves'. It was the explanation of this name that the angel Gabriel had given to Joseph: '. . . you shall call his name Jesus, for he will save his people from their sins.'

Grottos near Bethlehem which still shelter nomads.

The silver-gilt star on the altar of the birth of Christ in the basilica of the Nativity.

The adoration of the Child, with the ox and the ass, which a late tradition introduced into the stable (Hieronymus Bosch, fifteenth century, Cologne).

'And in that region there were shepherds out in the field, keeping watch over their flock by night.' Herdsmen in present-day Palestine.

The Three Wise Men journey towards Bethlehem guided by the star (S. di Giovanni Sassetta, Metropolitan Museum, New York).

The adoration of the shepherds and the Magi: the humble and mighty of the earth come to offer homage.

Work ceased at Jerusalem when the sound of trumpets announced the end of the day. But all round the city, in the fields and mountains of Judaea, for a large part of the population the night had been divided from very ancient times into watches in which each man kept watch in turn. Watch was kept over the crops, but above all over the herds. A bandit's calling for some, for others the calling of shepherd was that of their ancestors, the nomadic patriarchs and the prophets.

To a band of shepherds keeping watch like this near Bethlehem one night, an angel announced the birth of the Saviour. Luke is the only evangelist to relate the adoration of the shepherds, which he does very briefly: 'And they went with haste, and found Mary and Joseph, and the babe lying in a manger.'

The tidings to the shepherds is one of the most popular themes of the Nativity.

Other watchers learned the news that night; scholars from a country at once both close at hand and far away— Persia, perhaps, or Arabia or Babylon— who were scanning the heavens and who discovered a star which was the sign announcing the birth of the King of the Jews. How was it that the wise men from the East thought to derive this portent from an unknown star? The settlements of the Diaspora were influential in the regions of Babylonia, where Aramaean was spoken as in Judaea. The Messianic prophecies had spread there: '. . . a Star shall come forth out of Jacob, and a Sceptre shall rise out of Israel'. Guided by a star or a comet, the wise men set out. Before the grotto, kneeling down or standing up, their

hands veiled in accordance with the oriental custom, the pilgrims offered their gold, fankincense and myrrh.

St. Matthew is the only one of the canonical gospels to mention these wise men, but does not give either their names or their number. As time went on these astronomer-astrologers were turned into kings, sometimes two or four, then twelve, and finally three, a sacred number. Around the ninth century they were given names: Caspar, Melchior and Balthazar. In the twelfth century the last one became an African and was portrayed as a negro. After the salutation of the humble of this world they symbolised the universe doing homage to God, and their offerings showed the threefold quality of His son: gold, the token of His kingship, frankincense of His divinity and myrrh of His death.

The Wise Men kneeling before the Child bring as their offerings gold, frankincense and myrrh (school of Botticelli, National Gallery, London).

'And when the time came . . . they brought him up to Jerusalem to present him to the Lord (as it is written in the law of the Lord . . .)' (Luke II. 22–23)

At His circumcision the Child received the name which the angel dictated: Jesus—Yahweh saves (Giovanni Bellini, fifteenth century, National Gallery, London).

The various ceremonies which followed the birth of an Israelite child took place in the Court of the Priests. Only circumcision was practised under the paternal roof, among witnesses and friends, without the presence of a priest being compulsory. The *mohel* was also present as specialist of the operation.

Ignorance of Jewish customs has led to Jesus' circumcision being set in the Temple, by an assimilation with baptism. In this way it loses its original social character of an entry into a family community. Representations in which the twelve witnesses and the vacant seat of Elijah are omitted, reducing it to three participants, the Virgin, the *mohel* and the Child, deprive it of its reality. Performed after eight days, the circumcision could not have taken place in the sanctuary from which the mother was excluded for a period of forty days. The first ceremony which took place in the Temple was, as it happened, that of her purification. Childbirth was, in fact,

regarded as unclean by the Law, the remains of the old taboo concerning the shedding of blood which was anterior to Moses but had been ratified by the Law. For seven days the woman was unclean and for thirty-three days she was barred from the Holy Place. After forty days she would present herself there afresh and bring a turtle-dove or a pigeon as a sin offering. Mary and Joseph went to the Temple to perform this lustral rite and to obey a second precept of the Law: all the firstborn belonged to Yahweh and had to be 'redeemed' with an offering.

When they arrived at the Temple, Mary and Joseph were greeted by the aged Simeon. He was not a priest, but simply one of those pious people who came to pray in the court. He took Jesus in his arms, held Him over the altar with his hands covered by a veil as a sign of respect and foretold His destiny of glory and suffering: '. . . this child is set for the fall and rising again of many in Israel, and for a sign that is spoken

against.' (Luke II. 34).

While Simeon in the house of God was acknowledging the ruler awaited by Israel, Jerusalem was protesting against her tyrant. In spite of the peace and prosperity which he brought them, the Jews did not forgive Herod, who was king by the will of Rome, for being an 'ill-circumcised Idumaean' and for levying heavy taxes to finance his schemes for urbanisation. Herod replied to the general hostility by police methods and the bloody repression of all real or supposed plots. The last Hasmonaeans were done away with; the handsome, young Aristobulus whom Herod himself had appointed high priest was drowned. At Jerusalem Mariamne the Jewess, his favourite wife, was executed on a mere suspicion. Several hundred Pharisees were executed. A score of youths were burned alive for having torn down the golden Imperial eagle suspended over the gate of the Temple. Such was the climate that reigned in the capital.

The presentation in the Temple (The Master of Liesborn, National Gallery, London).

'... go to the land of Israel, for those who sought the child's life are dead.' (Matthew II. 20)

The Sanhedrin, at once the tribunal, religious and political council of the Jews, which increased its authority under the Roman procurators (seventeenth-century engraving).

The Massacre of the Innocents forms part of this web of violence. According to Matthew, embroidered by the Golden Legend, Herod ordered the killing of all male children of two years old and under in order to be certain that the future King of the Jews would not escape him. Lovingly depicted by the iconography of the Middle Ages and the Renaissance, this slaughter must be adjusted to the proportions of the little village of Bethlehem. Out of its then 2,000 inhabitants the number of male children under the age of two years could not be more than thirty. Mentioned by only one evangelist and passed over by the Roman annalists, everything inclines to the belief that the account of the drama contains a good measure of fable. The theme of the predestined child threatening the reigning king is a universal theme of folklore and is inspired by the popular hatred of tyranny. Be that as it may, Jesus escaped the tyrant's cruelty. On the advice of an angel Joseph and Mary had left for Egypt. They were to remain there until the death of Herod in the year 750 of the Romans, or 4 B.C. Three of his sons subsequently shared the kingdom among themselves. Philip received the region of Gennesaret; Herod Antipas, Galilee; Archelaus, Judaea, Idumaea and Samaria—the best part of the territory of Palestine—together with the capital, Jerusalem. In spite of the favour of Augustus, Archelaus was only to govern Jerusalem for a period of ten years. He wearied the Jews by his arbitrary and violent policy. When a delegation came to Rome for the second time to demand his deposition, Augustus finally made up his mind to send Archelaus into exile. His kingdom became a Roman province and was put into the hands of procurators.

Recruited from among former soldiers, these highly-placed Roman officials were ill-equipped to understand Jewish society, completely ignorant of diplomacy and generally imposed their authority by force. However, under the Roman procurators the Sanhedrin acquired a greater authority than ever before. This aristocratic senate came to constitute a kind of permanent commission for civil and religious affairs. Its seventy members, under the direction of a president, appeared as the higher native authority. It played the role, at one and the same time, of supreme tribunal (before which Jesus was to appear), political council, which intervened in the relations between the population and the Roman occupiers, and, above all, of a religious council. For the orthodox Jews the Sanhedrin and the high priest were Yahweh's sole representatives on earth and were entrusted with upholding His Law.

During a ceremony on the tomb of David a rabbi sounds the shofar, a ram's horn used in Jewish ritual from the most ancient times.

The massacre of the Innocents (Giotto, thirteenth-century fresco in the Arena Chapel, Padua).

At the age of twelve the young boy becomes a 'son of the Law'. On the banks of the Jordan John the Baptist sees Jesus approaching in the midst of the throng of Judaea.

Rabbi Gamaliel, Rabbi Johanan Ben Zakkai, Rabbi Eleazar Ben Azariah and many other 'doctors of the Law' kept a school beneath the temple colonnades for young Israelites who wished to dedicate themselves to religious studies. A secular education was unthinkable at Jerusalem. It was at the synagogue school and in the Bible that children learned to read and know their language. If, at the age of twelve, a child wished to continue his studies, he would enrol himself at the *Beth-ha-midrash* and become the disciple of a rabbi until such time as the latter decided that he was qualified to become a teacher himself. The 'doctors of the Law' formed a distinct caste of the sacerdotal class; they were not descended from either Levi or Aaron and did not wear a ritual costume or play any part in the cult. Nevertheless their whole life was devoted to the study of the Law.

This intellectual and pious aristocracy played an increasingly important role in Jewish life. It maintained the dogma against first Greek, and then Roman paganism, formulated Hebraic thought, quickened intellectual life, took charge of higher education and gave the commentaries on the Law in the synagogues. Their teaching formed the substance of the Talmud which was drawn up later, and incorporated the Mishnah, which was written in the second century, and its Aramaean commentary, the Gemara, of the fourth century.

We come across Jesus again at the age of twelve (the age at which the child became a 'son of the Law' and commenced his higher education), engaged in disputation in the midst of a group of doctors. Mary and Joseph had come to Jerusalem for the Passover. It was 14th Nisan (March–April) of the year 6 or 7. The feast had gone on for eight days, during which the ceremonies had continued without a break in the court. The lambs had been brought to the sacrificers who waited in front of the Priests' Court. Trumpets had sounded for each sacrifice, the blood had flowed before the altar, the fat and entrails had been burnt and the lambs had been returned to their donors for the Passover meal. The clergy busied themselves with the cult while, further off, the doctors assembled the crowd of those who had questions to put to them so that they might scrupulously obey Yahweh.

An opposing conception, although claiming equally energetically the Law as its authority, led one group of Israelites to flee Jerusalem and collective life. They returned to the desert and broke with the community and the Temple priesthood. These were the Essene sects who migrated to the desolate shores *(see* p. 102) of the Dead Sea. Besides them, and still more ascetic, were the solitaries of the desert who wore only loin-cloths.

It was only a short distance from the Essene monastery of Qumran, on the banks of the Jordan at the ford of Bethabara that John, the son of Elizabeth and Zacharias, baptised all those who came to him from Jerusalem and Judaea and the surrounding region. He baptised by immersion, that is to say in accordance with an Essene rite. Was he for all that an Essene himself? 'He was fairly well acquainted with the congregation at Qumran and felt a certain sympathy for its ideas, but differed from them on important points, at least by his hostility towards esoterism.' (Millar Burrows).

The first act of Jesus' public life was this baptism performed by the Precursor on the banks of the Jordan.

The eastern bank of the Jordan at Bethabara, near Jericho, where John baptised Jesus.

Baptism of Jesus (Barna, fourteenth-century fresco at San Gimignano).

Leaving Galilee, Jesus

Jesus on the highest point of the Temple being tempted by the Devil (Botticelli, Sistine Chapel, detail).

After tempting Christ in the wilderness, Satan conveyed Him to Jerusalem to subject Him to a second trial, that of pride. They conversed like rabbis, with the aid of Biblical quotations: 'If you are the Son of God, throw yourself down; for it is written, He will give his angels charge of you . . .' Jesus replied: '. . . it is written you shall not tempt the Lord your God.' How should this tempting demon be represented? Some people imagine the devil as repulsive and fearful, with horns, bats and cloven hoofs; others give him a more reassuring, and hence more deceptive appearance, as an angel or even a Franciscan monk *(see left)*—a naively anachronistic disguise which, to a fifteenth-century Florentine, best expressed the devil's cunning. Tradition has located this scene on the 'Pinnacle' of the Temple, that is to say not on the roof, but at the steepest point of the esplanade. To the east Solomon's Porch opened onto the panorama of the Mount of Olives and the Valley of Kidron. A tower occupied the southern angle of the porch and its terrace some 470 feet sheer above the ravine; this was the 'Pinnacle'. The theme of a temptation exists in most Eastern religions; Zarathustra, too, was tempted by the Evil One who offered him dominion over the whole world in order to divert him from his projects. These trials generally took place in the desert where popular belief situated the dwelling of demons, while high places were the abode of the gods. Christ's temptation offers in addition parallels and correspondences with the Old Testament. He suffered in the wilderness for forty days, as did the children of Israel for forty years, His trials began after a baptism of purification in the Jordan, as did those of the Hebrews after the crossing of the Red Sea.

After overcoming Satan, Jesus began His ministry and went into Galilee to preach His gospel to the multitudes. He collected His first disciples and for two years lived with them in poverty, teaching them the gospel ideals of justice, tolerance, compassion and love. He preached respect of the Mosaic Law and His words in no way contradicted the tradition of the prophets and rabbis. The people listened to Him, drawing from His words the courage which helped them bear Roman domination in the hope of better days. Opposition was already coming from authority, however. The tetrarch of Galilee had put John

The Pinnacle, south-eastern angle of the esplanade.

enters the city by the Golden Gate to celebrate the Passover.

Jesus casting the merchants out of the Temple on the eve of the Passover (school of Quentin Massys).

the Baptist to death and was not anxious to have any agitators in his area capable of creating difficulties with the Romans. Jesus left Galilee and made His way to Jerusalem where He arrived on the eve of the Passover. He was still unknown there and had not revealed to anyone that He was the Son of God, so that His first action gave rise to stupefaction. He entered the city by one of the gates, that of the fountains or the Golden Gate, which gave direct access to the Temple when arriving from Bethany. There was the usual excitement in the court. For a long time now Judaism had presented two aspects: that of the synagogues or houses of prayer, and the official one of the Temple, which was involved in public life and required a considerable administrative apparatus accommodated on the spot. The ritual of sacrifice, for example, involved the sale of animals (turtle-doves and lambs) which the pilgrims came to offer up. They arrived bearing the various Greek and Roman currencies which were in circulation in Palestine and which they had to change for their purchases and offerings into silver shekels.

In the tradition of the reformers who had been trying for centuries to rescue the cult from everything which ran the risk of disfiguring it, Jesus, armed with a whip, cast out the sellers and merchants, and in the name of respect for the house of God, drove them down the steps of the sanctuary: '. . . he overturned the tables of the money-changers, and the seats of those who sold pigeons; and he would not allow any one to carry anything through the temple. And he taught, and said to them, Is it not written, My house shall be called a house of prayer for all the nations? But you have made it a den of robbers.'

The evangelists do not agree on the date of this episode. John even situates it right at the beginning of Jesus' ministry. Medieval exegesis saw in Christ's gesture the fulfilment of the prophecy of Zechariah XIV. 21: 'And there shall no longer be a trader in the house of the Lord of hosts . . .' This scene, which is regarded as apocryphal by rationalist critics, is hard to explain (above all if it is true), as the Talmud asserts that the merchants were only installed around the Temple, in the court, which would give the picturesque appearance of the Jewish markets still found all round the Mediterranean basin on holidays.

Jewish merchants on a feast day.

133

The fourth day of Succoth, or Feast of Tabernacles, which commemorates the crossing of the wilderness and the expectation of the Promised Land (seventeenth-century engraving).

Orthodox Israelis choosing branches for the huts of the Feast of Succoth.

The adultress saved by Jesus (Poussin, Louvre, Paris, detail).

Succoth: water and light are celebrated, but the Pharisees are uneasy.

The joyful liturgy of Succoth, which assembled the faithful beneath huts made of branches, celebrated water and light, the two forces which give life to the earth. The high priest would go, with pitchers of gold, to draw water from the pool of Siloam, followed by the people in procession, and then come back to offer a libation west of the altar. The festival of light began at nightfall, Levite musicians were installed with their lutes and cymbals on the fifteen steps which led to the men's court. At a trumpet signal a torch dance would wind its way in incandescent circles while the people chanted: 'Our fathers worshipped the sun in this place but we turn our faces towards the Only One.' It was on the occasion of Succoth that Jesus came to Jerusalem in secret. But He soon began to teach in the court, returning every evening to the Mount of Olives where many pilgrims spent the night.

The Pharisees put Jesus to the test by bringing to Him a woman taken in adultery. From the outset Jewish Law had protected the family and adultery was forbidden. A woman taken in *flagrante delicto* was condemned to death and stoned (according to Deuteronomy) if she was engaged, and if not, strangled. The Law dated from Mosaic times, and the Pharisees hoped to catch Jesus in flagrant contradiction of it. The reply, written in the dust, avoided the trap and condemned neither the Law nor the woman: 'Let him who is without sin among you be the first to throw a stone at her.' This answer saved Jesus, but did not reassure the Pharisees or Sadducees.

His actions and utterances continued to cause disquiet: they introduced symbols which were foreign to the Temple cult. Jesus cured a man who had been blind from birth by sending him, after covering his eyes with mud, to wash himself in the water of the pool of Siloam: the ritual water which gave life became the water which purified. Moreover He performed this miracle on a Sabbath, the day sacred to Yahweh.

'We must work the works of him who sent me, while it is day: night comes, when no one can work.'

In the same way the words recorded by John the Evengelist were grafted onto the liturgy of light: 'I am the light of the world; he who follows me will not walk in darkness, but will have the light of life.' Those entrusted with maintaining the Law in all its purity questioned themselves about this new prophet.

Shortly after, Jesus had to leave the city. He left to go to the bedside of a sick man about two miles away on the Jericho road in the village of Bethany. When He arrived there, Lazarus had been dead for three days. There was a crowd of people from Jerusalem with Mary and Martha, Lazarus' sisters. Jesus went to the tomb and, after praying, called to Lazarus in a loud voice: 'Lazarus, come out.' And the dead man immediately came out of the tomb, his hands and feet still swathed in his grave-clothes and his face covered by his shroud.

The healing of the blind man (ninth-century Constantinople Gospel).

The raising of Lazarus (sixth-century Byzantine mosaic. Ravenna)

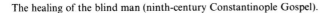

'Tell the daughter
of Zion, Behold,
your king is coming.'
(Matthew XXI. 5)

Children perched on a fig-tree.

Entry of Jesus into Jerusalem (thirteenth-century
mosaic, Palatine Chapel, Palermo).

Shortly before the Passover, Jesus, who
had taken refuge in the region of
Ephraim, went back to Bethany, had a
meal at the house of Martha and
Mary, took leave of His mother and
returned to Jerusalem via Gethsemane
and the Mount of Olives. When they
heard of His arrival the inhabitants of
the city cut palm branches and went to
meet Him, crying: 'Blessed is he who
comes in the name of the Lord.'
Riding an ass, in order to fulfil a
prophecy of Zechariah, and surrounded
by disciples, Jesus made His way along
a road covered with cloaks spread at
His feet like a carpet, in accordance
with the oriental custom. As soon as He
saw Jerusalem, He wept over the city:
'For the days shall come upon you when
your enemies will cast up a bank
about you and surround you, and hem
you in on every side, and dash you
to the ground, you and your children
within you, and they will not leave one
stone upon another in you . . .' The
crowd was so dense at the approaches
to the city that the children and
adolescents, and even the publican
Zacchaeus, had climbed the palm-trees
or fig-trees in order to get a better
view. It was in this way that, six days
before the Passover, Jesus entered the
city by the Golden Gate. From henceforth He would not leave it again.

HBAH

'Let the people of Israel keep the Passover at its appointed time . . . according to all its statutes and all its ordinances shall you keep it.' (Numbers IX. 2–3)

In the days of Christ the Passover rites were still the same as those that Moses had revealed to his people to bring them out of Egypt: a lamb was sacrificed, the door-lintels were sprinkled with its blood and its flesh was eaten with unleavened bread. Only the practice of eating standing up with a traveller's staff in the hand had disappeared. The Passover meal took place in the upper chamber of the house (in Latin, *cenaculum*). Its ceremonial was detailed. When the lamb was cooked to a turn, unleavened bread was dipped into a red sauce, the *hasoreth*, and a first cup of wine was taken while a blessing was said and the psalm which recounted the coming out of Egypt was recited. After drinking a few drops of salt water, the lamb was eaten accompanied by bitter herbs and then, to the singing of the Hallel (Psalms CXIII–CXVIII), the cup passed from hand to hand twice more.

At nightfall Jesus and His followers were assembled to celebrate the feast, but also to take part in a farewell meal. Jesus began this meal with a significant lesson of humility. Leaving the table, He knotted an apron round Him and approached the first of the disciples, Peter, in order to wash his feet. The washing of guests' feet before serving a meal was an Eastern custom, but this office was reserved for slaves. Perhaps this episode should be seen as a vivid putting into action of the saying: 'I am among you as one who serves.'

During the meal Jesus introduced a rite which did not form part of the Passover ceremonial of the ancient Law. He 'took bread, and when he had given thanks he broke it and gave it to them, saying, This is my body which is given for you. Do this in remembrance of me.' In the same way he offered the ritual cup, saying: 'Drink of it, all of you; for this is my blood of the new covenant, which is poured out for many for the forgiveness of sins.' An ancient tradition locates the scene of this last Passover on the summit of Mount Zion, on the present demarcation line. It is in a Gothic hall dating from the time of the Crusades and then turned by the Moslems into a hall of prayer, that today pilgrims come to meditate the Last Supper.

Before the Last Supper Jesus washes the feet of the disciples, an office reserved for slaves (Giotto, fresco in the Arena Chapel, Padua).

The Last Supper: Christ and apostles. In the foreground, Judas Iscariot (tenth-century Fulda Sacramentary).

The Cenaculum, on Mount Zion, the upper room set aside for the Last Supper and rebuilt by the Crusaders.

'. . . let the greatest among you become as the youngest, and the leader as one who serves.' (Luke XXII. 26),

Gathered together around Jesus in the upper chamber were the twelve apostles chosen from among the crowd that followed Him. Almost all of them were Galileans, six of them being fishermen or peasants, and another a publican, or civil servant. There was Peter, the leader, Philip, Jude, Andrew, James the Elder and John, Bartholomew, Thomas, Matthew, James the Less, Simon the Zealot and Judas, the treasurer of the group. For two years they had been preaching in the name of Jesus. After the Paschal meal custom demanded that the participants should stay on for some time, eating and drinking or talking. Christ was the only one to know the events about to take place and spoke to His disciples, who listened attentively to Him without always completely understanding the meaning of what they heard. '. . . some of his disciples said to one another, What is this that he says to us. A little while, and you will not see me, and again a little while, and you will see me.'

Jesus announced His departure. 'Lord, where are you going?' Peter asked Him. 'Where I am going you cannot follow me now; but you shall follow afterward.' 'Lord, why cannot I follow you now? I will lay down my life for you.'— 'Will you lay down your life for me? Truly, truly, I say to you, the cock will not crow, till you have denied me three times.' It was not the first time that Jesus had foretold the perfidy of one of His followers. 'Truly, truly, I say to you, one of you will betray me', He had already predicted, and He returned to the subject again. 'Lord, who is it?' asked John. 'It is he to whom I shall give this morsel when I have dipped it.' And He gave it to Judas. 'Then after the morsel Satan entered into him. Jesus said to him, 'What you are going to do, do quickly,' Judas, called the Iscariot, though the precise meaning of this name is not known, is one of the least known of the disciples and is always cited last with the indication of his treachery. He went out of the room. Judas betrayed Jesus for thirty shekels of silver (the Temple currency)—the price of a slave. The members of the Sanhedrin and the Pharisees had, in fact, made up their minds to put Him to death by arresting Him at a propitious moment without provoking riots or popular disturbances. It was for this reason that they had to bribe a familiar acquainted with Jesus' behaviour. Some contemporary exegetes have studied Judas' betrayal and seen in it a reminiscence of the Old Testament in the selling of Joseph by his brothers and descried in the expulsion of Judas the necessity to make room for Paul in the college of the twelve Apostles.

At the close of the Paschal evening Jesus and His faithful followers left the upper chamber. Jerusalem was bathed in the full moon of Nisan. They were in the upper room. Silhouetted around them were Herod's palace and that of the high priests; the mass of their towers hid Golgotha from sight. Opposite, on the other side of the Tyropoean, the Antonia was keeping watch. The shortest route from the upper room to the Mount of Olives went via the Temple esplanade to the Golden Gate. But only the priests could use the sacred precinct at night. Jesus and His disciples had to go down into the lower quarters by the wide-stepped streets which led to the gates. They then crossed the Valley of Kidron to get back to the Mount of Olives.

'. . . the cock will not crow, till you have denied me three times', Christ says to Peter in the course of the last meal taken with the apostles (mosaic, Ravenna).

Judas receives the reward for his betrayal; thirty silver shekels (the Temple currency), the price of a slave (bas-relief from the rood-screen of Naumburg Cathedral).

To go down to the Valley of Kidron, Jesus and His companions probably took these stone steps which have been uncovered by excavation.

The Mount of Olives, opposite Jerusalem, as it was in 1877 before being covered with churches, monasteries and convents of all confessions.

The Mount of Olives today: below, the garden and basilica of Gethsemane; above, on the right, the Russian church of St Mary Magdalene.

'And he came out, and went, as was his custom, to the Mount of Olives.'
(Luke XXII. 39)

Today the Mount of Olives can only boast a few scattered clumps of trees. Apart, in an enclosure, eight very old trees with shaky trunks still grow in this earth which has been arid for centuries, but it is not possible to say with certainty that they witnessed Christ's agony. The literal meaning of agony in Greek was 'debate' and also 'contest'. Here it stands for Christ's last struggle against the fear of death, which gave rise to a far greater disquiet than did the hunger, ambition and covetousness upon which Satan had speculated.

Jesus had kept only three disciples by Him, Peter, James, and John. 'My soul is very sorrowful, even to death; remain here, and watch.' He withdrew a short distance and prayed: 'Father, if thou art willing, remove this cup from me; nevertheless not my will, but thine, be done.' Rising to His feet again, Jesus came to His disciples and found that they had fallen asleep, worn out by grief. He said to them: 'Why do you sleep? Rise and pray that you may not enter into temptation.'

All the representations of the agony of Christ are arranged according to these three moments in the gospel accounts. In the middle, Jesus, on His knees; above, an angel or angels with the instruments of the Passion (the cross, the spear with the sponge, and the column of the flagellation); below, the three sleeping disciples. The agony of Christ, who was more alone in this garden in which His followers were sleeping than He was in the wilderness, before the all-powerful city, with its walls, its Temple, its fortresses and its towers, is the most moving avowal of human weakness: the battle for the acceptance of death. 'Jesus', wrote Pascal, 'suffered in His Passion the torments which He imposed upon Himself.' 'Are you still sleeping and taking your rest? It is enough; the hour has come.' For the third and last time, Jesus came to wake His three favourite disciples, the sole witnesses of his suffering. A body of men was climbing towards Gethsemane: armed Roman soldiers, a crowd with staves, and Judas at their head.

The 'agony' in the Garden of Gethsemane. While His three favourite disciples sleep, Jesus watches and prays (Mantegna, fifteenth century, National Gallery, London).

The foot of the Mount of Olives. On the right is the Garden of Gethsemane with its ancient trees.

'... all this has taken place,

At the foot of the Mount of Olives today rises the basilica built on the ruins of a fifth-century church. From that period on, indeed, the sacred mount with which so many memories of Christ are associated has become covered with churches and monasteries, some of which go back to Byzantine times (see p.204) and the Crusades. Is it the exact location of the Garden of Gethsemane?

Judas knew it well from having often slept there in the open air with Jesus and the apostles. It was he who led the throng which Christ had caught sight of in the night. 'Now the betrayer had given them a sign, saying, The one I shall kiss is the man; seize him and lead him away safely. And when he came he went up to him at once, and said, Master! And he kissed him.'

This sign was agreed in order to avoid any mistake, the soldiers fearing to confuse Jesus with the apostle James the Less. Jewish custom required that the disciple should kiss the hand of his master and Judas probably performed this gesture, which was transformed by medieval tradition into a kiss on the cheek loaded with all the sentiments of hypocrisy and treachery of the disciple. Who were the men who accompanied Judas and who had ordered this arrest? Jerusalem had two legal authorities, the Jewish and the Roman. It seems probable that Roman soldiers took part in this operation, since there is mention of a cohort and tribune. But the responsibility of the procurator has not been proved. The troop sent by the chief priests and the Pharisees were armed with staves recalling those which the Talmud relates the former readily employed against the people. The account of the gospels has been vigorously contested, as has the role given by them to the Sanhedrin. Indeed, according to Jewish procedure of biblical times, no one could be arrested during the night. In addition, it did not fall within the province of the Sanhedrin to order an arrest. To doubt the intervention of this supreme tribunal in the arrest of Christ is to call in question the responsibility of the Jewish authorities in the condemnation of Jesus, and the debate is not closed.

The companions of Jesus asked: 'Lord, shall we strike with the sword?' Peter struck Malchus, the servant of the high priest, who was holding a lantern to light the soldiers. Jesus ordered him to put up his weapon and restored the

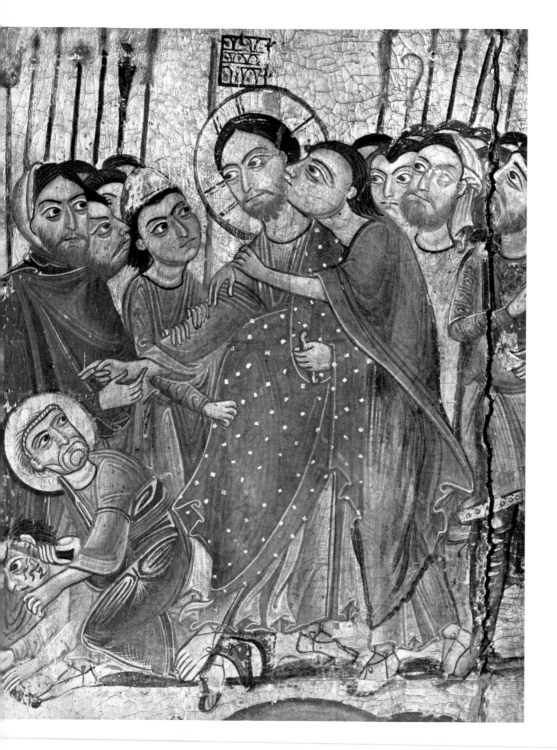

The kiss of Judas and Peter's violent attack on Malchus (twelfth century, Florence).

that the scriptures of the prophets might be fulfilled.
Then all the disciples forsook him . . .' (Matthew XXVI. 56)

The tree on the Mount of Olives from which Judas supposedly hanged himself.   The suicide of Judas (N. di Cione, fourteenth-century fresco, Badia, Florence).

victim's ear. Luke is the only one to relate this incident, one of the most popular of the arrest, which contrasts the gentleness of Christ with the instinctive reaction of the disciples. Less bellicose than Peter, the other disciples took flight without defending their master. Only one young man remained behind, Mark recounts, in whom many commentators have seen the evangelist himself: he had only 'a linen cloth about his body; and they seized him, but he left the linen cloth and ran away naked.'

Smitten with remorse, Judas took back to the high priest the thirty pieces of silver paid him for his betrayal and then went and hanged himself from a tree. To this account of Matthew's was grafted the following legend: 'His belly burst open, his entrails gushed out and his soul passed out of his anus, instead of his mouth, in the form of a black bird.' The image of Judas hanging satisfied the popular thirst for justice which could not endure that treachery should go unpunished.

Jesus before the Sanhedrin: 'When day came, the assembly of the elders of the people gathered together, both chief priests and scribes . . .' (Luke XXII. 66)

In the Valley of Kidron the funerary monuments saw Jesus retrace His steps along the path which He had climbed only a few hours earlier. He was first taken to the house of the high priest which stood on the esplanade of the upper city and appears to have been one of the finest palaces in the aristocratic quarter. Since 7 B.C. a family known for its skill in its relations with the Romans had lived there. Annas, the head of this dynasty, had held the office of high priest until the accession of Tiberius in 14. Although deprived of his office he first obtained the appointment in his stead of his own son Eleazar, then that of his son-in-law, Caiaphas, who maintained himself in the sovereign pontificate for eighteen years, until 36.

At the period when Jesus caused an upheaval in life at Jerusalem Caiaphas was high priest, but the strong personality of Annas still dominated sacerdotal life. Since the time of Herod, and since the scribes had taken upon themselves the interpretation of the Law, the office of high priest had lost much of its importance. The Romans turned it into a political weapon, and intrigues, bribery, threats and extreme cunning presided at the appointments.

Nevertheless in the eyes of the people, the high priest, being the head of the sacerdotal college, still retained a large measure of prestige. His palace, his style of living, his special consecration which was infinitely more awe-inspiring than that of an ordinary priest, his costume ornaments with pomegranates and gold bells intended to remove both demons and crowds from his path as he approached, surrounded him with a liturgical respect which was increased by his magnificent appearance at the Temple on the days of important ceremonies. On these occasions he wore the diadem, the gold ephod secured by precious stones, and the pectoral containing the *urim* and the *thummim,* sacred objects the significance of which is unknown. Thanks to this peculiar, awe-inspiring distinction and to his personal adroitness the high priest was still able to rouse the people and calm or inflame popular feeling. As a result the relations between him and the occupying power were subtle and based on a mutual interest in maintaining an order profitable to both. By His teaching, which tended towards an upset of the social hierarchy, Jesus was one of those who risked disturbing that order, and it was reasons of state that Caiaphas invoked to sway the council which had met the same night. 'It was Caiaphas who had given counsel to the Jews that it was expedient that one man should die for the people.'

Peter had followed Jesus at a distance and awaited events in the courtyard of the house. A maidservant caught sight of him and asked him whether he was one of the disciples. Peter denied it. 'I neither know nor understand what you mean.' He stayed there warming himself in the company of the guards who thought they recognised him; indeed, twice more before cock-crow Peter, as it had been foretold, was to deny Jesus . . .

In the early hours of the morning, still in the house of Caiaphas, Jesus was led, His hands bound, before the high priest who was presiding over the Sanhedrin. Caiaphas asked the accused whether He was the son of God. 'I am', Jesus answered, 'and you will see the Son of Man sitting at the right hand of Power, and coming with the clouds of heaven.' The high priest then rent his clothes, as it was laid down in the Law for those who heard sacrilegious words, crying: 'You have heard his blasphemy.'

After it had been consulted, the Sanhedrin rallied to the side of Caiaphas and pronounced the penalty prescribed for all crimes against religion: that of death. Jesus' way of sorrows was about to commence.

Tombs in the Valley of Kidron which separates the city from the Mount of Olives.   The denial of Peter at the door of the high priest (mosaic, Ravenna).

The Via Dolorosa, Christ's traditional route from the Antonia to Golgotha.

The Via Dolorosa, the path of Christ from the Antonia to Golgotha and the path of Christianity from the Middle Ages to the present day.

The ideal Jerusalem, or rather the Jerusalem of the imagination, surpasses by the abundance of her testimony the Jerusalem of archaeology. Parallel with the strictly historical life of the town, a whole legendary life has grown up throughout the ages nourished by thousands of stories, and the historian of the city is even less able to pass over this as the tourist or the pilgrim finds 'proofs' of it at every step.

More than any other books of the Bible, the gospels, even at the relatively late period of the Middle Ages, continued to inspire people's imaginations. By fitting the whole of Christ's Passion into a single picture, Memling succeeded in doing what had been attempted by all. But pity and piety combined efforts to make of Christ's Passion—from the moment when He appeared, pitiable, on threshold of Pilate's tribune up to the Resurrection—the main theme to which everyone sought to add precise details savouring more of naivety than erudition. In depicting this final episode artists have displayed all sorts of beliefs; serene, grave or morbid feelings according to their periods or temperaments; literary, theatrical, exegetical and (more rarely) archaeological allusions, and even a touch of anti-Semitism. Often they thought to give more liveliness or veracity by reinstating the present and the faces, architectural setting and customs of their own time, adding sometimes an oriental detail, a touch of exoticism, again equally imaginary. What does it matter if time has modified and transformed the face of the city to the extent where nothing can restore the narrative of the Passion with precision any more.

Every Friday at 3 p.m. the old quarter is filled with a devout crowd which follows a route similar to the one Jesus must have taken from the judgment-hall to Golgotha, proceeding along one of the small-stepped streets which still descend towards the Tyropoean to climb up again opposite, towards the north-east of the city. This custom springs from a devotion to the 'way of the cross' instituted by the Franciscans who had been given the guardianship of the holy places. It was they who named this route the 'Via Dolorosa'. It was imagined that, worn out by his scourging, Christ must have fallen several times beneath the weight of the cross. These falls and halts became the 'stations' which have since marked out the naves of Catholic churches. Their ordering bears no relation to the very brief accounts of the gospels. The fourteen halts of the way of the cross are now located in the following manner in the streets of Jerusalem: beneath the playground of the Arab school (the first station) Jesus is condemned to death. At the foot of the slope of the Antonia (the second station) Jesus takes up the cross. At the crossroads of the Austrian hospice (the third station) Jesus falls for the first time. Near the arch of the Ecce Homo (the fourth station) the meeting with Mary. At the corner of the street (the fifth station) Simon of Cyrene helps Jesus. Halfway up the slope (the sixth station) the meeting with Veronica. At the crossroads of the bazaar (the seventh station) Jesus falls for the second time. At the wall of the Johannite hospice (the eighth station) the holy women. At the entrance to the Coptic convent (the ninth station) Jesus falls for the third time. The Via Dolorosa used to end at the Judicial Gate, but further episodes were added, and it is at the altar of the Holy Sepulchre itself that is located the fourteenth station: the entombment.

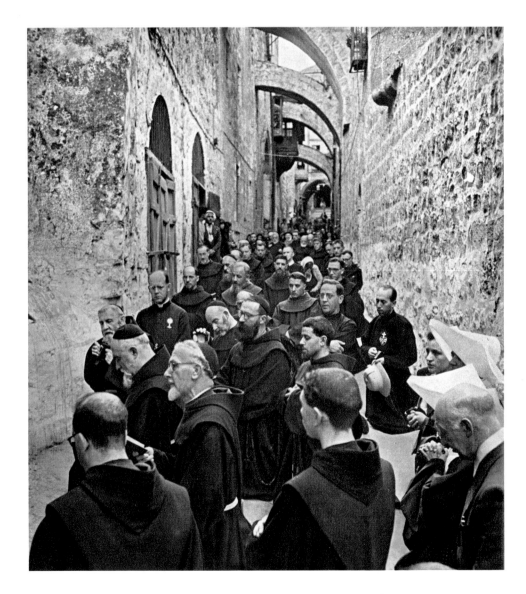

Preceding pages: the Passion of Jesus (Memling, Pinocoteca, Turin).

Ecce Homo. Jesus appears wearing the crown of thorns and the purple robe. Pilate says to them: 'Here is the man.' (Hieronymus Bosch, Frankfurt).

Pilgrims kneeling before a 'station' of the Via Dolorosa.

Twice Jesus appears before Pontius Pilate, the representative of Roman authority and the only holder of the *jus gladii*.

Condemned to death by the Sanhedrin, Jesus would only be executed if the Roman authority confirmed the sentence. Since the deposition of Archelaus, the procurator had been given the *jus gladii* by Rome which assured him full powers where criminal jurisdiction was concerned and real autonomy. Ill-prepared for the role of governor of an occupied country by the military life which he had led until then, he generally made fairly bad use of it. Undiplomatic and inclined to enforce his authority by violent means, he committed mistake after mistake in Judaea.

The fifth official to occupy this post, Pontius Pilate, had been appointed procurator in A.D.6. For the Passover, as he did for all other popular festivals, he left the seat of the Roman administration at Caesarea and went to Jerusalem. The opening of Christ's trial was a bad piece of news for him. He had already found himself in difficult situations with the population of Jerusalem on several occasions. He had excited indignation by placing votive shields on the emperor's effigy in the Temple, where all human representations were forbidden by the Law, and had provoked a riot by taking money from the sacred treasury which ended in carnage.

Seated on the dais set up in the middle of the inner paved courtyard of the Antonia which acted as a judgment-hall, Pilate saw coming towards him the man who called Himself the King of the Jews. The crowd stayed at the entrance so as not to defile themselves by entering the house of a pagan. After a brief interrogation Pilate went out and announced to the crowd that he found no fault in Jesus. When he learned of his Galilean extraction he tried to withdraw from the trial and sent the accused to Herod Antipas, King of Galilee, who was at Jerusalem for the festival. Herod was delighted at first since he hoped that Jesus would perform a miracle for him. Disappointed in his expectation, he sent Jesus back to the judgment-hall. The disturbance continued to gain in strength and the uproar became increasingly violent. 'Away with this man, and release to us Barabbas.' Three times Pilate tried to save the accused, then he gave in. He washed his hands saying: 'I am innocent of this man's blood.'

Christ before Pilate. Only the Roman procurator had the right to pass judgment (The Master of Nuremberg, Berlin).

Traces on the flagstones of the Antonia of the game played by the soldiers of the guard.

'I am innocent of this man's blood . . .' (fifteenth-century Book of Hours of Marguerite d'Orléans).

'So Jesus came out, wearing the crown of thorns and the purple robe.'
(John XIX. 5)

Jesus had been sentenced to be crucified. Crucifixion, however, was not laid down by Jewish Law, which prescribed death by stoning or strangling. Invented by the Persians so that the condemned should not defile the earth which was sacred, this mode of execution had spread throughout the Hellenistic and Roman world: some of the Hasmonaeans made wide use of it, but legally it was reserved as an ignominious death for fugitive slaves or those who had rebelled against their masters. A torture aimed at inducing the condemned to make a confession preceded the execution: the flagellation. Frequently employed, it was strictly regulated to avoid killing the condemned man under the blows. The Jews had therefore set precise limits to the number of strokes of the birch: there were to be a maximum of forty, with the advice to stop at the thirty-ninth in case the following one should prove fatal. This scourging took place in private; the condemned man used to stand for the Romans and lie down for the Jews. Two executioners with birches struck in turn.

Iconographical tradition was to add an element which does not exist in the gospel account: a column to which the condemned man was attached, similar to those preserved as relics at Rome and in the Franciscan chapel of the Holy Sepulchre at Jerusalem. Pilate had only ordered the scourging. It was of their own accord that the soldiery on guard inflicted a second torture on the condemned man: the humiliating 'mocking' of Jesus who had proclaimed Himself King of the Jews. The soldiers dragged the prisoner inside the palace, dressed Him in a purple robe, then, after placing on His head a crown of thorns, they 'began to salute him, Hail, King of the Jews! And they struck his head with a reed, and spat upon him, and they knelt down in homage to him.'

The origin of this scene has been sought in the games carved on some of the flagstones of the Antonia. In fact it is still possible to make out a circle and the letter B, the first letter of *Basileus*: king *(see* p. 153). Was a game with a king played there? Although this crown was primarily a symbol of humiliation, in the brutal, tortured imagination of the Middle Ages it became an instrument of torture, which an iron-gloved hand or two long crossed staves forced down upon the head of Christ. Bought for a huge sum by St. Louis, this crown (the

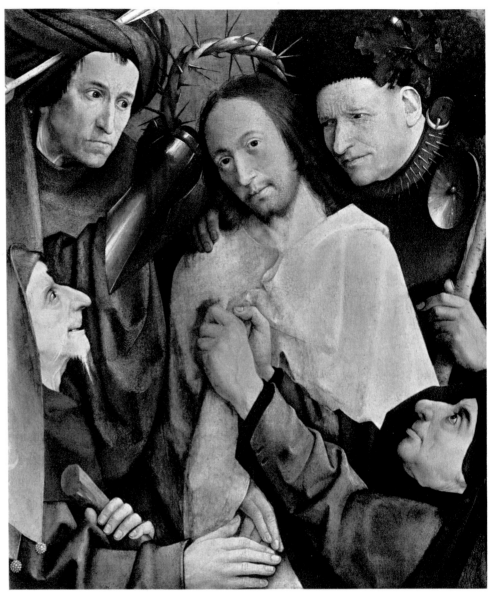

The crowning with thorns of the 'King of the Jews' (Hieronymus Bosch, National Gallery, London).

fragments of which are today preserved in Notre Dame in Paris) was probably woven from the spiny branches of a tree very common in Judaea, the jujube tree. Crowned with thorns, dressed in a purple cloak and holding a reed sceptre, it was in this derisive attire that Pilate showed Jesus to the crowd gathered together before the judgment-hall, saying: 'Here is the man!' *(Ecce Homo) (see* p. 150). At the beginning of the Via Dolorosa, a Roman arch spans the street and has borne, since the end of the fifteenth century, the name of the 'arch of the Ecce Homo'.

The scourging of the Lord (Fra Angelico).

Arch of the Ecce Homo in the Via Dolorosa.

Roman Law requires the condemned man to carry his cross to the place of execution.

On Friday 15th Nisan, between eleven o'clock and noon, at the sixth hour of the Jewish day, Jesus, condemned to death, came out of the Antonia. The procession which was to escort Him to Golgotha, the place where executions were carried out, moved off. Golgotha, the place 'of the skull', was the name given to a whole area in the shape of a mound at the foot of the hill of Gareb, beneath the northern rampart of the city, and formed part of the lands of Joseph of Arimathaea. In the midst of the tombs rose the gibbets for the executions. An exposed promontory was ideal for these since Mosaic Law wanted them as public as possible in order to make them an example. A ceremonial, described by the Talmud but doubtless already employed at the time of Jesus, regulated them. The condemned man had to be led to his execution in daylight, the crime of which he was accused being written on a placard or proclaimed aloud by a herald. Representatives of the Sanhedrin assisted at the execution and in order to enable a pardon to stay the execution up till the last minute, a man followed the pro-procession walking backwards to watch for the white flag which would give the reprieve. A system of horse-guards with despatch-riders and relay-stations was ready to transmit the order of pardon to the place of execution.

A crowd gathered, attracted by the publicity given to the execution. From the Antonia to Golgotha, the path still taken by pilgrims is not very long. The procession went out by the Ephraim Gate and climbed the hill of Calvary. It seems that no voice was raised from the crowd on behalf of the condemned man. Only a few women were wailing and, turning towards them, Jesus prophesied: 'Daughters of Jerusalem, do not weep for me, but weep for yourselves and for your children. For behold, the days are coming when they will say, Blessed are the barren, and the wombs that never bore, and the breasts that never gave suck. . . . For if they do this when the wood is green, what will happen when it is dry?'

At the present cross-roads of the Austrian hospice, Jesus fell for the first time. The soldiers stopped Simon of Cyrene, and ordered him to help Christ.

Good Friday procession along the Via Dolorisa. It is here that Jesus fell for the first time.

The bearing of the cross (Simone Martini, fourteenth century, Louvre, Paris).

Simon of Cyrene helping Christ to bear His cross (Piero della Francesca).

The tree of knowledge of the earthly paradise becomes the redeeming cross of the world.

Veronica wipes Christ's face at the sixth station of the way of the Cross (Ghirlandaio, fifteenth century).

The True Image (Master of Saint Veronica).

The sixth station of the way of the Cross.

Halfway along the Via Dolorosa occurred the incident of Veronica, born in the fifteenth century in a stage production anxious to show the audiences of the mystery plays how well God reveals Himself to those who love Him. In the crowd which followed the procession a woman had the courage to wipe the sweat and dust from the face of the condemned man. The features of Christ were imprinted on the cloth. *Vera icona*, the true image, gave its name to Veronica; this was the sixth station of the way of the cross.

Other portraits were to materialise miraculously. After the death of Christ, Luke had been praying and fasting for three days before painting the face of Christ so that he would not forget it, when the Holy Face appeared on the

empty panel, miraculously represented . . . legends such as these were inscribed at a later date in the history of Jerusalem where, since the Mosaic commandments, Yahweh had forbidden all human representations. For a long time the early Church also contented itself with symbols to signify Jesus: the fish, the lamb, the vine, and the ear of wheat. It was from pagans (the Greeks) that were borrowed the models for the first human representations, in particular for the Good Shepherd, which was related to the Calf-bearer of the Acropolis, and the votive effigies of Mediterranean shepherds.

The earliest effigies represented Christ as young, vigorous and beardless, like Moses, Abraham and Noah in the paintings of the catacombs, since youth was the attribute of the gods. It was only in the fifth century, under Byzantine influence, that a Christ 'in majesty' would prevail, an hieratic pantocrator

The soldiers escort Christ and the two malefactors to the place called 'of a skull', in Aramaic: Golgotha, a bare hill on the north of the city (Tintoretto).

with a bony face, long nose and forked beard. The representations of the ascent to Calvary varied greatly. The bearing of the cross, particularly at the end of the Middle Ages, took on an allegorical significance, developing Christ's saying: 'If any man would come after me, let him . . . take up his cross and follow me', all the outcasts of the world came to help Christ bear His cross which was heavier than their own.

There is another highly romantic legend invented in the Middle Ages about the cross borne by Jesus. Before coming into the world, Adam had torn off a branch from the tree of knowledge, which had been the cause of his transgression. At the time of her visit to Jerusalem, the Queen of Sheba refused to tread on a plank made from its wood, which had been thrown across a stream as a bridge, seeing all of a sudden

the Saviour fastened to the wood. Solomon had this plank buried, but it was rediscovered floating in the pool of Bethesda, where it used to perform miracles. It was there that the executioners went to seek it, and they gave it to Jesus to carry. In this way, the new cult of the cross was substituted for the old pagan cult of the tree, and Jesus atoned for Adam's transgression with the very wood of sin.

'They gave me poison for food, and for my thirst they gave me vinegar to drink.' (Ps. LXIX. 21)

Almost at the end of the road, Christ fell to the ground for the third time. In some representations, which bear the mark of a somewhat aggravated sense of pathos, He does not get to his feet again but seems to crawl along under the weight. When the procession reached the top of Golgotha, the executioners started their preparations. According to the descriptions left by Greek and Latin historians the condemned man was nailed by the hands to the beam which he had borne on his shoulders, and this was hoisted by a system of pulleys, or a simple rope, up the long vertical post erected at the place of execution.

The account given in the gospels is of a striking restraint. Let it speak for itself. Once they had arrived at the place called Golgotha which, because of its shape and its smooth appearance like a skull was called 'the place of the skull (Calvary)', the four Roman soldiers stripped Jesus of His clothes, only leaving Him a loin-cloth, and gave Him wine mixed with myrrh to drink which composed an opiate as bitter as gall, in order that He might lose consciousness of pain. But, after sipping a little, so as not to offend the women who had prepared it for Him, He was unwilling to drink any more as He wished to suffer all the pains of crucifixion. The Roman soldiers then laid Him on the ground and stretched His arms across the transverse beam of the cross, set down there by the Cyrenian. They nailed His hands and then His feet. Finally they placed above His head the reason for His condemnation, written on a tablet as follows: 'This is the King of the Jews.'

The two thieves were then crucified with Him in the same way, one on His right and the other on His left, so that His disgrace might be increased. Pilate had caused to be written and placed on the cross the inscription: 'Jesus of Nazareth, the King of the Jews.' Many of the Jews read this inscription, since the place where Jesus was crucified was close to the town, and it was written in Hebrew, Latin and Greek. So the Jewish pontiffs said to Pilate: Do not write, The King of the Jews, but This man said, I am King of the Jews.' Pilate replied: 'What I have written I have written.'

The evangelists record in detail the

Jesus is nailed to the cross which rests against a rock (fifteenth century, Wallraf-Richartz Museum, Cologne).

Christ falls beneath the weight of the cross (The Master of Cologne, fifteenth century, detail).

Detail of the cricifix (Church of St Mary im Kapitol, Cologne).

insulting remarks of the observers: 'You who would destroy the temple and build it in three days, save yourself! If you are the Son of God, come down from the cross.' Likewise, the pontiffs said in mocking tones together with the doctors of the Law and the elders of the people: 'He saved others; he cannot save himself.' '. . . let him save himself, if he is the Christ of God, his Chosen One.' 'He is the King of Israel; let him come down now from the cross, and we will believe in him. He trusts in God. Let God deliver him now, if he desires him: for he said, I am the Son of God.' Only one of the malefactors crucified with Him rebuked his companion who was joining in the general raillery: 'we are receiving the due reward of our deeds; but this man has done nothing wrong . . . Jesus, remember me when you come in your kingly powers.'

'Behold the vinegar, the gall, the reed, the spittle, the nails and spear of the

The executioners hoist the cross into an upright position after inserting its foot into a hole in the ground (Lerambert, seventeenth-century cartoon for a Saint Merri tapestry,

From the sixth hour, that is to say from noon, the time when Jesus was placed upon the cross set up on the top of Golgotha, the clouds became so thick that it was dark throughout the whole of Judaea. About the ninth hour Jesus cried out in a loud voice: '*Eli, Eli, lama sabachthani?*' that is, 'My God, my God, why hast thou forsaken me?' And some of the onlookers, hearing Christ cry: '*Eli, Eli*', said 'This man is calling Elijah.' After this, so that the holy

Scriptures which foretold that the Messiah was to die parched with thirst and slaked with vinegar might be fulfilled, Jesus said: 'I thirst.' Now there was lying on the ground there a vessel full of a drink made of water and vinegar which the soldiers used to quench their thirst. Immediately one of them ran to take a sponge soaked in water and vinegar and, placing it on the end of a reed, gave it to Him to drink. When Jesus had taken the water mixed with

vinegar, He said: 'It is finished.' And crying again in a loud voice, Jesus said: 'Father, into thy hands I commend my spirit.' And as He said this, He bowed His head to show that He was abandoning Himself voluntarily to death.

According to St. John the Jews, fearing that the bodies might remain upon the cross during the Sabbath, which would have been a serious defilement for the city, asked Pilate to have their legs broken in order to kill them at once.

noble triumph, that of the Redeemer of the world,
when sacrificed, he conquered.' (Hymn)

National Library, Paris).

Interior of the Basilica of the Holy Sepulchre: the site of Golgotha where the cross was erected.

Christ's side is pierced by the spear-bearer. On the right, the sponge-bearer (tenth century, Aachen).

The soldiers therefore broke the legs of the two felons. When they came to Jesus, seeing that He was already dead, they did not break His legs 'that the scripture might be fulfilled, Not a bone of him shall be broken'—the ritual specification for the Paschal lamb. But one of the soldiers pierced His side with his spear and immediately there came out of it blood and water (a symbol of redemption and baptism, exegetes were to say).

The holy women (Mantegna, detail).

One of the most beautiful traditional interpretations of Calvary (Mantegna, Louvre, Paris).

The Roman soldiers throwing dice for Christ's tunic (Mantegna, detail).

The city, behind the hill of Golgotha (Mantegna, detail).

'. . . he bowed his head and gave up his spirit.' (John XIX. 30)

Without departing from a long iconographical tradition, Mantegna has given one of the finest representations of Calvary. Avoiding confused or grandiloquent crowd effects, he gives a prominent position to the group of women with John, and the group of Roman soldiers at the foot of the triple execution. Mary, the mother of Christ, and many other women who had come from Galilee with Jesus had assisted at His last moments. When He had seen His mother beneath the cross and, beside her, John, the disciple whom He particularly loved, Jesus said to her: 'Woman, behold your son!' Then He said to the disciple: 'Behold, your mother!' The soldiers who had placed Jesus on the cross had shared out His garments among themselves, then coming to the tunic which had no seam, being woven in one piece from top to bottom, they said to one another: 'Let us not tear it, but cast lots for it to see whose it shall be.' Then with the centurion who commanded them they stayed there to mount guard. Opposite Golgotha, Jerusalem was joyfully celebrating the Passover.

'They took the body of Jesus, and bound it in linen cloths with the spices, as is the burial custom of the Jews.' (John XIX. 40)

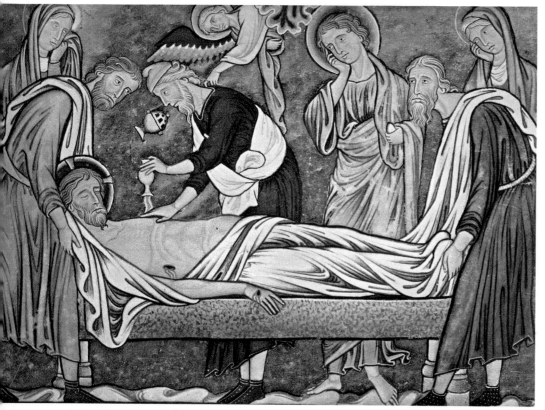

The anointing of Christ in accordance with Jewish funeral custom (twelfth-century Ingeborg Psalter, Condé Museum, Chantilly, France).

When Jesus expired the great veil which divided the sanctuary of the Temple tore in two, from top to bottom, the earth trembled, and the rocks split open. The Roman centurion and his soldiers were seized with terror and said: 'Certainly this man was innocent.' 'Truly this was the Son of God.' When the crowd saw these amazing sights they returned to the city beating their breasts.

At Jerusalem, as in all Jewish communities, there was a profound respect for death. The body of a man created by God, even that of a criminal, had the right to a sepulchre. It was Joseph of Arimathaea who went to ask Pilate for the authorisation to remove the body of the executed man and who, with Nicodemus, unnailed Jesus from the cross. They were both members of the Sanhedrin and were people of influence at Jerusalem. Held back until then by fear, they paid Christ the last respects. Jesus was taken down from the cross before night fell and the trumpets for the Passover sounded, as otherwise the city would have been polluted. The rites of the funeral toilet were begun. The eyes of the dead man were closed, He was washed, and then rubbed with spices and perfumes, spikenard, myrrh and powdered aloes.

A slab of red limestone, surrounded by tall candlesticks marks the spot within the precinct of the Holy Sepulchre where, according to the Latin Church, Christ was embalmed, and, according to the Greeks, He was wept by His mother.

The cremation practised by the Romans appeared sacrilegious to the Israelites. Each family purchased a site where it constructed a tomb, but it was tradition only that gathered them together in one or another part of the city. There was no actual cemetery, except for those disqualified by the Law. At the foot of Golgotha Joseph of Arimathaea owned a tomb in which no corpse had ever been buried. It was there that Jesus was buried.

The descent from the cross, the deposition, the lamentation and the entombment made up a funeral tetralogy which was illustrated by Byzantine art before the mystery plays took it over, and the Crusades, which were devoted to the Holy Sepulchre, made it the favourite theme of mystics and primitive painters.

The stone of the Unction in the Holy Sepulchre.

The Crucifixion (fifteenth-century miniature, Boussu Book of Hours, Arsenal Library, Paris).

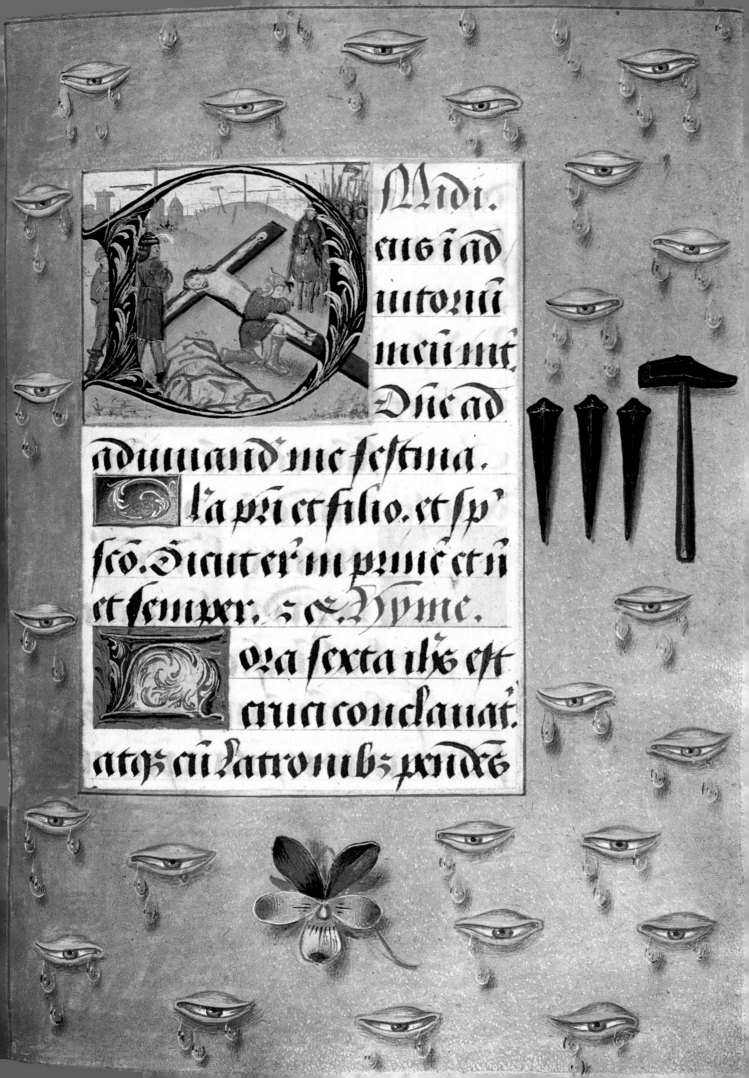

OREMVS.
DEVS QVI NOBIS IN SANCTA SINDONE, QVA CORPVS TVVM SACRATISSIMV
È CRVCE DEPOSITVM À IOSEPH INVOLVTVM FVIT, PASSIONIS TVÆ VESTIGIA
RELIQVISTI; CONCEDE PROPITIVS, VT PER MORTEM, ET SEPVLTVRAM TVAM AD
RESVRRECTIONIS GLORIAM PERDVCAMVR, QVI VIVIS, ET C.

'Thus says the Lord God: Come from the four winds, O breath, and breathe upon these slain, that they may live.' (Ezekiel XXXVII. 9)

The so-called tombs of Herod still give the pattern of the sepulchres of the first century. Connecting vaults were hollowed out of the rock and their walls were faced with a white stone which probably came from the quarries of Solomon. A circular stone, fifty inches in diameter and a foot thick, seals the entrance to these catacombs. This method of sealing, which was current at the time, was used for the tomb of Christ. As a precaution the priests and Pharisees asked Pilate to have it guarded. But he left them to see to its surveillance, and men were posted.

After the sacred meal of the Sabbath, on 'the first day of the week', at daybreak, some women climbed, as was the custom, three days after the shrouding of the corpse, to pour spices at the entrance to the tomb: Mary Magdalene (from the village of Magdala), Mary, the mother of Christ, Mary, the mother of James, Salome and Joanna. They found the tomb open; the stone had been rolled away from the sepulchre. They went in but could not see the body of Jesus. His wrappings were lying on the ground and His shroud was thrown down a little farther off. Still not understanding that the Scriptures were fulfilled, the apostles looked at the empty tomb.

How did Jerusalem receive such a piece of news? For the second time a man had risen again, following Lazarus, who had come out of the tomb at Christ's command. In its most ancient beliefs Israel makes no mention of resurrection. 'The angel of Death placed the drop of bitter gall' upon the lips of the deceased, seized his soul and carried it off. The breath of life went away and the body returned to clay. A shade remained, the *repha,* and the *rephaim* dwelt in a mysterious place, *sheol,* which was nothingness. But since the exile, beliefs had altered and these are found formulated in the most recent texts of the Bible. The idea of a judgment had appeared. The soul was conducted before a tribunal and rewarded if it was good and punished if it had led a bad life. The wicked were cast into *sheol,* while a paradise awaited the righteous: 'thou dost not give me up to sheol', states Psalm XVI. This paradise was sometimes referred to as 'Abraham's bosom' *(see* p. 11) while it was also compared to the Eden of the first man. Another doctrine, which was taught by some of the doctors of the Law who had taken it from the prophets, is also found in several Essene manuscripts which announced an actual resurrection. 'Thy dead shall live', cried Isaiah, 'their bodies shall rise.' And Daniel says: 'And many of those who sleep in the dust of the earth shall awake, some to everlasting life, and some to shame and everlasting contempt.'

Although their religion, which was so precise in other respects, left each Jew complete liberty in this matter, it appears that the idea of a resurrection was very widespread among the people. 'Your brother will rise again,' Jesus said to Lazarus' sister, and Martha replied: 'I know that he will rise again in the resurrection at the last day.' This conception of everlasting life was to become one of the foundations of the Christian faith.

So-called tomb of Herod hollowed out of the rock, the entrance of which could be closed by a heavy circular stone which was rolled along on rails.

The shrouding (Giulio Clovio, sixteenth-century aquatint composed in honour of the Holy Shroud of Turin, with scenes from the life of Christ set in medallions).

'So you have sorrow now, but I will see you again and your hearts will rejoice, and no one will take your joy from you.' (John XVI. 22)

Jesus showed Himself several times to His scattered disciples at Jerusalem, on the very day of His resurrection. Mary Magdalene was weeping beside the empty tomb. She turned and saw Christ beside her, without recognising Him. 'Jesus said to her, Woman, why are you weeping? Whom do you seek? Supposing Him to be the gardener, she said to him, Sir, if you have carried him away, tell me where you have laid him, and I will take him away.' Jesus made Himself known and replied: 'Do not hold me ... but go to my brethren and say to them, I am ascending to my Father ...'

On the same day two disciples who did not belong to the twelve were making their way to Emmaus, a little village some seven miles from Jerusalem. While they were walking along Jesus joined them and made the journey with them. 'But their eyes were kept from recognising him. And he said to them, What is this conversation which you are holding with each other, as you walk?' One of them, Cleopas, told Him that they hoped that Jesus would deliver Israel, as some women had found His tomb empty. As evening was falling the two travelling companions proposed to the newcomer that He should share their meal. Jesus took bread and broke it and gave it to them. They then realised the identity of their guest, but He vanished immediately. Jesus had appeared as a gardener to Mary Magdalene; He has been represented with the disciples of Emmaus as a pilgrim, wearing a goatskin tunic and with a staff in His hand. This is a naive illustration of a passage from Luke which was imperfectly understood in the Middle Ages. 'Are you the only visitor to Jerusalem who does not know the things that have happened there in these days?' In the Middle Ages, stranger was a synonym for pilgrim. Immediately after Christ's disappearance the two companions ran back to Jerusalem and went to the upper room, where a few of the disciples were gathered together behind locked doors for fear of the Jews. 'The Lord has risen indeed.'

They were still recounting their adventure when Jesus entered and, so that He should be recognised, showed them His

Noli me tangere (thirteenth century, Florence).

The village of Emmaus with archaeological remains in the foreground.

Christ and the pilgrims before the inn at Emmaus (Duccio, Siena).

hands and feet. But since the disciples still doubted that it was really He, fearing that they were the victims of an apparition or a delusion of their senses, He asked for a piece of broiled fish and ate it in front of them. Then, in that room where they had gathered so many times, He spoke to His disciples at length and expounded the Scriptures to them. He left them, telling them to wait for Him at Jerusalem, 'until you are clothed with power from on high'.

Thomas was absent that day and refused to believe his companions' account. 'Unless I see in his hands the print of the nails . . . and place my hand in his side, I will not believe.' Eight days later the disciples were once again in the house, and Thomas with them. Jesus came, the doors being shut, and said to Thomas: 'Put your finger here, and see my hands; and put out your hand, and place it in my side; do not be faithless, but believing.' Thomas answered: 'My Lord and my God.' Jesus said to him: 'Have you believed because you have seen me? Blessed are those who have not seen and yet believe.'

Doubting Thomas (The Master of Bruges, Rijksmuseum, Amsterdam).

171

The mosque of the Mount of Olives perpetuates the sanctuaries that have commemorated the Ascension.

Luke is the only evangelist to relate the Ascension. 'Then he led them out as far as Bethany, and lifting up his hands, he blessed them. While he blessed them, he parted from them and was carried up into heaven.' In the Acts of the Apostles he added that a cloud hid Christ from the eyes of the disciples and the Virgin Mary. Artists drew their inspiration from these details and arranged their pictures on two planes: the group of onlookers, in an attitude of prayer, lift up their eyes towards the upper part where all that remains of Jesus' body are His feet disappearing into the clouds.

People wished to give the Ascension a date and location. The earliest tradition made it coincide with the Resurrection. Later on a conventional interval of forty days was introduced, during which delay Christ appeared on several occasions, forty days being a sacred figure which had already been the duration of Moses' sojourn at Sinai, and Christ's in the wilderness. The Ascension has been located on the top of the Mount of Olives, where the double imprint of Christ's passage on a rock is still shown to pilgrims. Luke mentions Bethany, close to Jerusalem, but it was from the Mount of Olives that Jesus saw the city for the first time. It was there,

furthermore, that He wept in the garden of Gethsemane while gazing upon it, and it was from there that He was to leave the earthly for the heavenly Jerusalem.

Round about 378 a wealthy Roman lady called Pomoenia built the first sanctuary commemorating the Ascension on the Mount of Olives. Until the latest excavations carried out by the Franciscan fathers, this church was only known from the testimony of a Gallic bishop, Arculf, who had travelled through Palestine around 670. According to his description and his drawings the church was a circular building. The excavations carried out in this part of the Mount of Olives in 1959 have shown that the Crusaders completely transformed the original circular edifice, which became octagonal. They constructed thick walls, using all the available old material, and these still exist inside the present structure. In this manner thay enclosed the holy place inside a veritable fortress in anticipation of a Saracen attack. 'It is well defended by towers and turrets, by advanced works, and night watches', wrote a pilgrim in 1172. Today the only part of the sanctuary that has been preserved has been turned into a mosque and covered with a Moslem dome, under which Christians are allowed to celebrate their rites.

The Ascension (Memling [right panel], Louvre, Paris).

Remains of the fortress built by the Crusaders to protect the basilica of the Ascension.

Basilica of the Ascension turned into a mosque. A Moslem dome now covers the octagonal edifice built by the Crusaders in the twelfth century.

4

CALAMITIES AND RENEWALS

from Titus to Constantine

May those who sow in tears reap with shouts of joy!
He that goes forth weeping, bearing the seed for sowing,
shall come home with shouts of joy, bringing his
sheaves with him.

Ps. CXXVI. 5-6

The epistle of Paul (miniature from the Bohemia Bible, library of Prague University).

'I do not pray for these only, but also for those who believe in me through their word.'
(John XVII. 20)

Pentecost (Bull of Our Lady of Zion).

Christ Himself had announced the coming of another 'Comforter', 'the Spirit of truth', to complete the teaching of the Word of God. At Pentecost, the fiftieth day after the Passover, the Holy Ghost descended upon the Apostles who, still twelve in number (Judas having been replaced by Matthias), were gathered around the Virgin Mary in the upper chamber of the house where they had continued to meet since the death of Christ. Suddenly a sound like a violent rushing wind came from heaven and filled the house. They saw tongues like fire appear, which divided and settled on each of them. 'And they were all filled with the Holy Spirit and began to speak in other tongues, as the Spirit gave them utterance.' Luke's account in the Acts of the Apostles was written long after Paul had committed the Church to breaking with the Jewish milieu and evangelising the pagan world with its multifarious languages.

In reality, in the period immediately after Christ's death, the little community at Jerusalem was still far from contemplating extending beyond Palestine. It numbered some hundred members, all of them Jews, and lived in accordance with the Law, in the shadow of the Temple. If they did break new ground it was in their conception of the community and their desire for fraternity. '. . . and no one said that any of the things which he possessed was his own, but they had everything in common . . . for as many as were possessors of lands or houses sold them, and brought the proceeds of what was sold and laid it at the apostles' feet . . .' This practice seems to have been general, but it was not obligatory. To enter the confraternity it was sufficient to receive baptism conferred in the name of Christ which had the power to wipe out original sin and bestow the Holy Ghost. The baptismal rite was generally accompanied by the laying on of hands, a very ancient Jewish custom which conferred a supernatural efficacy upon the recipient. For the Christian it implied a direct transmission of the gifts of Pentecost.

The most important act of the assembly was the meal taken together, which was always preceded by the eucharistic rite of the breaking of bread.

The Romans saw no distinction between this little group of Christians and the irreducible mass of the Jewish people who constantly created difficulties for the occupying power. In A.D. 36 Pontius Pilate left the city, after being deposed by the Eastern legate, following complaints from the population who were tired of massacres, thefts from the sacred treasury and the profanation of the Temple. He left only an aqueduct as a useful memorial of his mandate and would have had little chance of passing into history had he not been an unwilling witness and actor in events which were to make Jerusalem a city unlike any other.

The tomb of David and the Cenaculum, where, fifty days after the Passover, the Holy Ghost descended on the twelve apostles (photograph by Bonfils, 1877).

Pentecost (tenth-century Winchester Pontifical, Rouen, France).

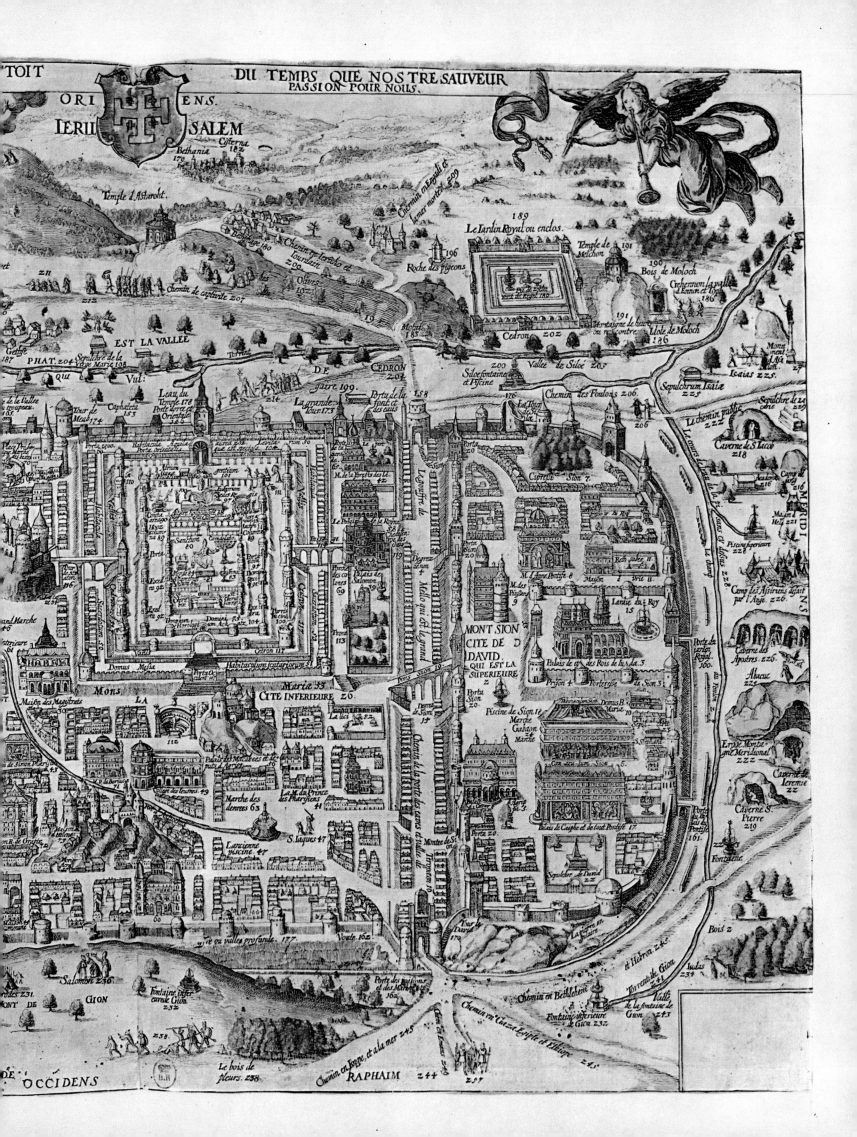

'I have given them thy word; and the world has hated them because they are not of the world, even as I am not of the world.' (John XVII. 14)

Every day the disciples addressed the crowd beneath the Temple colonnades. They tried to convince them that Jesus of Nazareth, who had died a few weeks earlier nailed to the cross, was indeed the Christ, the Messiah promised to Israel and foretold by David and the prophets. They were not lacking in arguments: the Resurrection? 'We are witnesses', said Peter. Their proofs? The miracles they performed in the name of Jesus: the cures—the paralytic walking and, above all, the raising of the dead (Tabitha, who had been dead for three days, sat up at Peter's command and stood in the midst of the mourners). Conversions multiplied until the day when, tired of hearing the resurrection of the dead in the person of Jesus announced in the Temple precinct, the priests and Sadducees arrested the apostles. The Sanhedrin assembled and was preparing to pass sentence when a very great rabbi upon whom Israel was even to bestow the title of *Rabban*, borne only by four or five doctors in the whole tradition, intervened. This was Gamaliel the Elder who was as celebrated for his gentleness as for his profound knowledge, the son of Hillel, who had laid the foundation of rabbinical teaching.

After sending out the accused he addressed the assembly: 'Men of Israel, take care what you do with these men ... keep away from these men and let them alone; for if this plan or this undertaking is of men, it will fail; but if it is of God, you will not be able to overthrow them. You might even be found opposing God.' The tribunal listened to Gamaliel's advice and, on their release, the apostles started their preaching again. The number of Christians grew. Two categories of Jew joined their ranks: the Jews of the Diaspora, who were called the 'Grecians' because they had special synagogues where the Bible was read in Greek, and the Jews of Jerusalem, the 'Hebrews', who spoke Aramaean but read the Bible in Hebrew in their synagogues. This division of tongues reflected a difference of spirit and, on becoming Christians, these two groups carried over their division into the early Church.

Peter, the leader of the apostles, used to address the crowd every day (Fra Angelico, Uffizi, Florence).

'Tabitha, arise', said Peter, and the dead woman opened her eyes (Masolino, early fifteenth century).

Preceding pages: The Jerusalem of the Gospels, as pictured in the seventeenth century.

Preaching of Stephen before the Temple (Carpaccio, sixteenth century).

'Men of Israel . . . listen . . . we bring you the good news that what God promised to the fathers, this he has fulfilled to us their children.' (Acts XIII. 16, 32–33)

When Peter spoke he confined himself to making Christ the fulfilment of the Jewish tradition, the successor of Moses and the descendant of David. It was another matter with Stephen, a young Grecian Jew from a town of the Diaspora and a reader of the Greek-speaking Jewish philosopher Philo, who was attempting a synthesis of the Old Testament and the works of Plato in Alexandria. Expressing the desire for renewal in advanced Jewish circles, he made a forceful frontal attack on the inhabitants of Jerusalem: 'As your fathers did, so do you,' he exclaimed. 'You stiffnecked people, uncircumcised in heart and ears, you always resist the Holy Spirit . . . Solomon . . . built a house for him. Yet the Most High does not dwell in houses made with hands . . .' Stephen spoke, debated and convinced. He was arrested on the pretext that he was attacking the Temple, which was true, and had suggested changing the customs bequeathed by Moses, which is probable. A lengthy discourse to the Sanhedrin roused his audience to such a pitch of exasperation that they 'stopped their ears and rushed together upon him. Then they cast him out of the city and stoned him'.

A young man called Saul was present at his execution, and approved it. He came from a background doubtless fairly similar to that of Stephen. He was a citizen of Tarsus and a Jew of the Diaspora. He had come to Jerusalem to pursue his studies, since he intended to become a rabbi; this was the future Paul. One might speculate as to what sort of rabbi he would have been, in view of the fact that when he became

Death of Mary (Bull of Our Lady of Zion).

a Christian he was the least Jewish and the least Judaising of the apostles. But in the days of Stephen, Saul was one of the most rabid participators in the persecution unleashed against the Christians, and in particular against the Grecian group. '. . . Saul laid waste the church, and entering house after house, he dragged off men and women and committed them to prison.' The Christians fled from Jerusalem in little groups of two or three and scattered throughout the country of Samaria and Judaea. For the first time since the death of Jesus the propagation of Christianity began, as the result of force, outside Jerusalem.

In every town or village which they came to the apostles first attempted to preach in the synagogues; they did not yet venture beyond the Jewish milieu. What became of Mary during these persecutions? All trace is lost of her in the Acts of the Apostles after Pentecost, at which she was present among the twelve. There is not even a reference to her death. When did she die, and where? According to some, two years after the Ascension. She would then have been about fifty, if we assume, as is probable, she was fifteen at the birth of Jesus.

All kinds of legends are associated with her last moments. Jesus descended 'in a bright light, surrounded by angels', to take her soul, which left her body in the form of a child while the apostles prayed . . . a legend still evoked by the worn silhouettes of the bull of Our Lady of Zion.

The apostles and Mary parting (fifteenth-century Book of Hours of Duke of Berry, Condé Museum, Chantilly).

Stoning of Stephen (Juanes, Prado Museum, Madrid).

Herod Agrippa sacrifices in the Temple; the apostles perform miracles.

'She offered thanks to the Lord and gave up the ghost.'

When Mary died her body was conveyed, at Christ's command, to the east of the city. 'It was laid on a stretcher and the procession of the apostles moved off with Peter and Paul carrying the bier and John at the head bearing the luminous palm. Above the corpse floated a crown of clouds, as gentle as the moon at its full; inside it the angels were singing and the whole earth resounded with harmony. Alerted by the lights and music, the people had come out of the city. A crowd fifteen thousand strong gazed upon the body surrounded with glory. When they had come to the valley of Josaphat, to the east of the city, the apostles laid the holy body upon a new sepulchre. They rolled the stone in place in order to seal it, sat down before it and awaited the promised coming of the Lord. And when Jesus descended again on the clouds accompanied by thousands of angels, they said to him: If it pleaseth thy all-powerful majesty, as thou hast conquered death and reignest in glory, restore this body to life also and

take it with thee to heaven. Let it be so, said Jesus . . . Mary immediately rose to her feet and ascended, borne aloft by the flight of angels, to be for ever glorified . . .'

Scholars have wondered whether the accounts in the apocryphal gospels were inspired by a tomb believed to be that of Mary, or whether they did not rather lead to the location and discovery of this tomb in the valley of Josaphat. It has been suggested that the cult of the Virgin was originally the cult of her tomb. It is in a modest edifice—the former crypt of an abbey built in the days of the Crusaders and destroyed after their domination—that it can be seen today. Near the Cenaculum or the upper room, another church was built to commemorate the place of Mary's death, the basilica of the Dormition.

The story of Christ's disciples became involved with political history. In 40 Judaea changed her regime. She was still subject to Rome, but the period of the procurators was at an end. Herod Agrippa I, the grandson of Herod and the son of Aristobulus, had the King-

dom of Palestine conferred upon him by the Roman emperors Claudius and Caligula. In spite of a stormy youth at the court of Rome he exhibited great religious zeal from the moment of his arrival at Jerusalem. His first action as king was to go to the Temple and offer a thanksgiving sacrifice, without forgetting a single prescription of the Law. In the sanctuary he deposited a gold chain given to him by Caligula, the weight of which equalled the iron chain with which Tiberius had loaded his royal hands. The Talmud recounts that while celebrating the Feast of Tabernacles one day, Herod Agrippa, who was half Idumaean, burst into tears when he read the passage in Deuteronomy: '. . . you may not put a foreigner over you, who is not your brother.'

He took the Jewish interests in hand with energy and built a third defence wall at Jerusalem. His religious zeal also led him to persecute the Christians. His first victim was James the Elder, the son of Zebedee and the brother of John the Evangelist, one of the apostles who had been present at the Transfiguration.

The sanctuary, near the Mount of Olives, of the tomb of the Virgin, the crypt of a Frankish abbey—Our Lady of Josaphat—partially destroyed in the twelfth century by Saladin.

On the strength of apocryphal accounts Christian pilgrims have come to this crypt since the fifth century to kneel before the tomb of the Virgin Mary.

James brought himself to the attention of the public in a spectacular manner by converting the magician Hermogenes, who had sent his disciple Philetus to him in order to work some of his spells against him. However, when he saw the miracles performed by James, Philetus was converted and attempted to convert Hermogenes also. In a fury the magician then paralysed him, but the apostle covered the disciple with his miraculous cloak and cured him. Hermogenes then called up demons and commanded them to deliver James to him in chains. Mastered by the apostle, the demons put Hermogenes in chains instead and brought him back bound hand and foot. Defeated, the magician threw himself at James' feet, burned his magic books and asked to be baptised.

Very little is known about the true activity of James the Elder, so that his life has consequently become the subject of legends. One tradition has him preaching the Gospel at the other end of the Mediterranean, thus making him into the national saint of Spain and the patron saint of pilgrims. He never went there, however, and died at Jerusalem about 44, a martyr of Herod Agrippa I.

Baptism of Hermogenes (the Magician), by James the Elder (Mantegna, Ovetari Chapel, Padua, but now destroyed).

Will the impassioned, violent Paul succeed in having the Mosaic Law abandoned? The schism between Jews and Christians slowly evolves.

The persecutions continued. James the Less, the head of the Church at Jerusalem, was cast down from the Temple and stoned. Arrested in his turn, Peter was only saved from death by the intervention of an angel.

Shortly afterwards, in 44, Herod Agrippa died, 'eaten of worms'. Judaea then became a procuratorial province again, but the Emperor Claudius extended the terms of occupation. He appointed the brother of Herod Agrippa inspector of the Temple with the right to choose the high priests. The Christian Church was undergoing difficulties as a result of its growth in pagan lands. In 49 it met in council at Jerusalem in order to settle a burning issue: Should the pagans who had been converted to Christianity be made to become Jews first with all the ritual that that implied—circumcision, dietary rites and the journey to Jerusalem for the Passover? The apostles were divided, as Jesus had never said that His followers should be exempt from the Law.

One group, the 'Hebrews', took its stand upon the words of Jesus and insisted upon the observance of the Jewish Law from the new adherents. They appear to have been in the majority at Jerusalem but did not prevail over Paul, who supported the contrary opinion. The convert of the Jerusalem-Damascus road occupied a position apart in the Church. He was the only one of the chief apostles not to have known Christ. He was a Pharisee, the 'son of a Pharisee' as he proclaimed forcefully, but also a Jew of the Diaspora, a citizen of Tarsus and Rome. From a well-to-do, if not wealthy, family he had come to Jerusalem to study and was from a background quite different from that of the Galilean fishermen whom Jesus had collected around Himself. For Paul Judaism was a barrier to the expansion of Christianity and he did not hesitate to demand a rupture. The council adopted a solution close to the one he advocated. A minimum of Jewish usage was required of pagans (such as abstaining from prohibited meats), while the observance of the Law remained valid for the Jewish Christians who had grown up with its customs.

Miraculous deliverance of St Peter from prison (Raphael's Stanze in the Vatican, detail).

Paul debating with the Greeks and Jews (twelfth-century enamel, Victoria and Albert Museum, London).

Martyrdom of James the Less (Mantegna, Ovetari Chapel, Padua, largely destroyed).

A whole century of Roman occupation. The revolt which was simmering

Although she benefitted from preferential treatment compared with other Roman colonies, Palestine had been living beneath the burden of occupation for a century. For a century too, part of the population (a minute one, it is true) refused to accept this situation. Some men had gone underground. The uncompromising Hasidim of the Maccabean revolt were the first, then Pharisees, Sadducees and Christians refused in turn to accept Roman coercion and violence. They formed armed bands throughout the country and were known as the Zealots.

During the Passover of 66 the insurrection which had been simmering broke out. The Zealots won over the people, occupied the palaces of Agrippa and the high priest, defeated the legate of Syria who tried to intervene and won the whole country over to the side of the insurrection. Rome appointed Vespasian to put it down. The inexorable patience and authority which can be seen on the face of the future emperor were to mark the campaign. For three years Vespasian took his time and methodically recaptured the country, isolating Jerusalem. He assembled huge forces; the Fifth, Tenth and Fifteenth Legions were massed in the north of Palestine. He recaptured Galilee stronghold by stronghold. John of Gischala, the leader of the Galilean

Zealots, then fell back upon Jerusalem. Vespasian marched down the length of the coast, secured the ports, left the reconquered littoral for the valley of Jordan and prepared to besiege Hebron Shechem. He held the whole country at the moment when the news of Nero's death reached him. In order to put an end to the crisis caused by the succession the legions proclaimed Vespasian emperor. The general left Judaea immediately, leaving to his son Titus the task of ending the war and taking Jerusalem. The resistance there had already held out for three years and, despite the enormous forces which Rome was able to put into the field, it took Titus another year to

On 1st April 70 the Roman legions, with thousands of battering-rams and ballistas at their disposal, besieged Jerusalem

Coin depicting Vespasian.

The future Emperor Titus, the son of Vespasian.

breaks out at last. With John of Gischala at their head, the Zealots repeat the exploits of the Maccabees.

capture the city.

For this final battle—one of the most fantastic sieges in history—Titus commanded 70,000 infantrymen, 10,000 horsemen and thousands of battering rams and siege engines. He displayed these forces beneath the gaze of the defenders of Jerusalem in a gigantic parade which lasted for three days, in the hope of making them capitulate before this deployment of strength. But to the complete stupefaction of those taking part, the Jews massed on the walls greeted this spectacle with acclamations and enthusiasm . . . The Fifth, Tenth and Fifteenth Roman Legions then delivered the first assault.

The seal of the Tenth Legion, responsible for the destruction of the Temple, and stationed in the city.

under the command of Titus. After a three months' siege, the assailants finally succeeded in taking the Antonia and the Temple by storm (seventeenth-century engraving).

The Jews resist for three long years, but finally, the city is taken and the Temple set on fire.

A moderate government was formed after the first Zealot revolt and was led at Jotapata in Galilee by Flavius Josephus and at Jerusalem by the high priest, Ananias. But as the Roman army invaded the country the moderates had to yield to the Zealots who, with the help of the Idumaeans, butchered the temporising elements likely to treat with the enemy.

This extremist government lacked unity, however, and several factions were fighting one another. Simon Bar Giora and his men held the upper city; John of Gischala, the leader of the Zealots, occupied the Temple court, while the Temple itself was under the command of the priest, Eleazar. These conflicts within the city weakened the parties and exhausted the reserves which neither side hesitated to set on fire at one point.

The city was in this state of anarchy when Titus began his siege. After the unsuccessful parade of his forces, Titus attacked on the north. Missiles were hurled from the ballistas. Perched on wooden towers overlooking the walls, the besiegers bombarded the defenders and stones were torn from the battlements. Protected by testudos (overlapping oblong shields raised above their heads), the Roman troops advanced to attack the towers. After two weeks of repeated assaults they made a breach in the northern wall. Titus entered and occupied the suburb of Bezetha. After fifteen days of desperate fighting, however, the Jews drove the Romans back outside the surrounding walls. Jerusalem was so well protected by her solid fortresses that Titus gave up trying to take the city by assault. He therefore decided to exhaust the contending forces by starvation. He patiently constructed an earthwork all round the city to the height of the walls. It was impossible for the besieged to go out without being captured.

'With the exception of the Roman soldiers, whoever was surprised in the act of scaling this rampart of beaten earth was crucified on top of the walls for the edification of the besieged. It was not unusual to see as many as five hundred unfortunates nailed to the cross in this way on a single day. The air was foul with the stench of rotting flesh and rent by the agonised cries of the crucified. Despite this, the Jews held out for another year, the fourth of the war, to

On 17th July for the first time since the return from exile, sacrifice ceased in the Temple. On 6th August, in spite of Titus'

the great shame of Titus. The end was inevitable. With the help of enormous battering rams and by throwing across foot-bridges, the Romans crossed the surrounding walls. They streamed through the city like ants, slaughtering the people, which were reduced to extreme weakness by starvation. By resisting for four years and inflicting defeat after defeat upon them, the Jews had dealt a severe blow to the reputation

for invincibility of the Roman soldiers and only carnage could soothe their wounded pride.' (Max Dimont: *Les Juifs, Dieu et l'histoire.*)

It is a fact that the repression was terrible. As soon as it was taken, the Antonia was demolished. The Temple held out for some time and then the colonnades fell. On 17th July 70, sacrifice ceased in the Temple for the first time since the return from exile. It was

190

prohibition, the sanctuary was completely burned down. Only a few pieces of furniture and cult objects were spared and carried away by the victors.

not to be resumed again. Tradition has it that Titus ordered the sanctuary to be spared, but in the course of the fighting a soldier threw a flaming brand. Although part of the furnishings were saved, the building was completely destroyed by fire. On the west, the last resistance held out until the beginning of September. Finally the whole town fell into the hands of Titus.

Only the towers of Phasael, Hippicus and Mariamne were spared to serve as quarters for the Tenth Legion which was stationed at Jerusalem. The greater part of the population had been butchered. Tacitus estimates the number of civilians killed as 600,000. The Romans had never earned with greater justice the lucid words of one of their historians: 'They cause desolation to reign and call it peace.' (Tacitus). Jerusalem had held the Roman legions in check for four years.

Only the numerical superiority of the Romans and the strength of their equipment had overcome the Jewish resistance. All the survivors were taken to Rome (among them John of Gischala and Simon Bar Giora), where they were to follow the trophies and piles of booty before being sold as slaves, thrown to the wild beasts in the arenas, or thrown from the Tarpeian Rock for the amusement of the crowds.

A Jew in the service of Rome, a Hellenist in defence of Judaism.

Coin depicting Judaea defeated and captive.

To celebrate such a costly victory the Romans minted coins commemorating the destruction of Jerusalem with a woman personifying Judaea weeping before the Roman trophy of victory. A spectacular triumph was organised at Rome. The victors marched past laden with the spoils of the city: the Temple furnishings saved from the flames, the seven-branched candlestick, and the table for the shewbread on which lay the sacred trumpets, as recorded on the arch of Titus.

A Jew appeared beside the victors, Joseph Ben Matthias, whose Latin name, Flavius Josephus, would at least have the merit of passing into literary history. His life had changed abruptly a few years earlier. Born at Jerusalem in 37–38, everything seemed to mark him out for a career as a doctor of the Law. On his father's side he came from the priestly aristocracy, while his mother claimed to be descended from the royal house of the Hasmonaeans. He had acquired a knowledge of Jewish Law at an early age and spent three years in the desert with the ascetic, Banus. On his return to Jerusalem he joined the Pharisee sect and carried out duties as a member of the Temple priesthood. Entrusted with a mission to Rome to obtain the release of the priests arrested by the governor Felix, it was possibly at that point that he became aware of the military strength of the Romans and the futility of the Jewish revolt. On his return to Palestine he found the country in a state of agitation. Whether he wished it or not, he was instructed by the Sanhedrin to prepare the defence of Galilee and took part in the revolt, but his lack of zeal aroused the mistrust of his compatriots.

On the arrival of Vespasian, Josephus and his troops withdrew into the fortress of Jotapata. After a siege of forty-seven days the survivors, who had taken refuge in a cistern, decided to kill themselves. Perhaps by cheating at the drawing of lots in order to remain the last survivor, Josephus escaped this collective suicide and surrendered to the army. Brought before Vespasian, the general-in-chief, he predicted his accession to the throne. From that moment onwards the fate of Josephus was linked with that of the conquerors of his country.

Attached to Titus' general staff, he was present at the siege of Jerusalem where all his family were trapped: 'When Jerusalem had already been taken by assault, Titus Caesar invited me several times to take whatever I wanted from the ruins of my fatherland . . . but after the fall of my native city having nothing dearer to preserve to console me for my misfortunes, I asked for the release of a certain number of prisoners and accepted a collection of sacred books . . .', he recounts with a certain lack of discernment in his autobiography. From then on he chose to live at Rome, became a Roman citizen and until his death enjoyed the favour of a dynasty of emperors who, among other titles to fame, prided themselves on the annihilation of Judaea.

It is hard to understand through his writings, even in his autobiography, the personality of this changeable, diverse

Candlestick of the last Temple of Jerusalem (bas-relief on the Arch of Titus, Rome, detail).

The last liturgical objects saved from the fire carried by the victors in Titus' spectacular triumph at Rome (bas-relief on the Arch of Titus).

being, a curious mixture of keen Jewish 'patriotism', Hellenic culture (all his books, in fact, were written in Greek) and guilty conscience. His first work, 'The Jewish War', endeavoured to prove that the war was brought about by the fanatical Zealots, while the people profoundly desired peace. Although his sources are reliable, since he relates events in which he had taken part himself, his glorification of the Flavians and his own justification give a tendentious character to the book. In view of the success of this work he undertook in a long account in twenty books, 'The Jewish Antiquities', to bring to the knowledge of the non-Jews the history of his people from their origins up to the disaster of 70, and then composed a veritable apology for Judaism, the 'Against Apion', in which he proclaimed the superiority of the moral and religious conceptions of the Hebrews over paganism, in reply to an anti-Jewish lampoon by the Alexandrian writer Apion. In order to defend himself against the accusations made against him concerning his conduct during the Jewish-Christian war, Flavius wrote an auto-biography, the famous *Testimonium Flavinium*, in which he explained and justified his attitude in a confused and naive manner. Disdained by the Jews, his books were collected by the Christians. In spite of his uncertainties, contradictions, exaggerations and a regrettable lack of historical objectivity, Flavius Josephus is the only writer to give detailed information about the last two centuries of the existence of the Jewish people as a nation and about the historical environment in which Christianity originated. St. Jerome had no hesitation in calling him the 'Greek Livy'.

Flavius Josephus offers a dedicatory copy of his book to Titus (eleventh-century Moissac Manuscript).

Under a barren exterior, the rock of Masada still bears witness to the desperate exploits of the last Zealot resistance.

Jerusalem was in ruins but the war was not yet over in Palestine, where desperate fighting was still taking place. In 71, three strongholds were holding out, Machaerus, Herodium and Masada, which was the last to fall and remains the symbol of of Jewish resistance. Masada is the name of a crag whose peak rises sheer in the wilderness of Judah beside the Dead Sea, some twenty-five miles from Jerusalem. Judas Maccabeus was the first to think of constructing a fort on the platform which towered almost 1,000 feet above sea-level and stood as a naturally-fortified castle surrounded by ravines.

Herod had also appreciated this eyrie and fitted it out so that he could take refuge there in case of trouble. The top of the rock was enclosed by a casemate wall and the platform, 650 yards long, was turned into a kind of city where huge reserves were stored. There were cisterns holding over seven million gallons of water and silos capable of furnishing provisions for a thousand men

for a year. At the highest point Herod built a palace on three levels which overhung the ravine. At the very top were the apartments of the king and his household, in which a black and white mosaic pavement has been found, the oldest in Israel. On the intermediate terrace, which was partly dug out of the rock, rose a circular tower with double concentric walls, the purpose of which remains obscure. The lower terrace served as a banqueting hall and was surrounded by columns and decorated with frescoes. This ensemble was built partly on the rock and partly on vaulted cellars. A huge retaining wall, almost one hundred feet high, supported the edifice on the north-eastern slope.

The Zealots occupied this Herodian fortress. There were less than a thousand of them, including women and children. Suddenly one day there were 15,000 soldiers advancing towards them. This was the Tenth Roman Legion which, under the command of Flavius Silva, had

been instructed to reduce the bastion. It had come from Jerusalem with thousands of prisoners detailed, in particular, for the water fatigues and who consequently witnessed the last episode of the war.

The Roman general considered it useless to attempt a direct attack; the only approach to Masada was a twisting path which made the use of war engines impossible. He surrounded the position with a double wall and set up eight camps to block all the exits. From the top of Herod's tower it is still possible to see the square outline of one of these fortified camps. The Zealots were prisoners. No one would come out and all that was required was to wait and wear down the strength and patience of the besieged.

On the western slope where the rock rose only 500 feet, the difference in level was filled in by an accumulation of stones and earth which was tirelessly heaped up by the soldiers. On this embankment they constructed a platform from which they could already see Herod's palace on their left: they erected an iron-clad tower one hundred feet high and reached the level of the besieged. A battering ram was brought into action and attacked the wall. After a few days a breach was opened up, but the besieged hastily improvised a second wall of two rows of beams, between which they packed earth. The battering ram became absorbed in the earth and only packed it tighter. Silva then gave the order to set fire to the beams. The wind, which was blowing from the south, at first drove the flames towards the Romans, but then drove the fire back onto the palisade. It was late and the assailants withdrew to their camp to prepare themselves for the final assault on the morrow.

There was to be no battle. The Zealots preferred to commit suicide. During the night they chose ten men to strangle the others. Once this task had been completed the ten chose one who was to kill the remaining nine and he committed suicide. Two women and five children appeared from a cave and told the soldiers of the night's drama which they had escaped by hiding. Flavius Josephus reports that the Romans were full of admiration for the heroism of the besieged. Their leader was called Eleazar, and archaeologists have found around the crag and in the rock itself the evidence of his exploits and his final sacrifice.

Terrace of the fortress of Masada, the square outline of a Roman camp can be seen in the distance.

After surrounding the fortress of Masada the Roman legions attacked it on its western face, which rose only 500 feet above the ravine.

On this rocky, barren platform jutting out over the plain less than a thousand Zealots held out for several months against the Tenth Roman Legion.

Simon Bar Kochba, 'the Son of the Star', proclaims himself the Messiah of Israel and summons the Jewish people to liberation.

Jerusalem was no longer the capital; the seat of the Roman administration was at Caesarea. The Jewish population of Palestine had temporarily lost its strength. The last pieces of evidence of the revolt, a few coins stamped with a cup or a fruit, were hidden among the souvenirs. Judaea abstained from participating in the movements which, under Trajan, were causing violent upheavals in the Diaspora, and in Egypt in particular.

Once the *pax Romana* had been re-established, Hadrian succeeded Trajan and ascended the throne with the intention of putting an end to wars and conquests and giving to the Roman sphere of influence (whose farthest limit he set at the Euphrates) a common Graeco-Roman legal system and culture. The emperor visited Jerusalem and took measure for the construction of a city and a temple of Zeus. Without bothering about Jewish particularism (which appeared to him to be broken), and con-

fusing castration and circumcision, or almost so, he forbad both practices in a single edict which struck indiscriminately at the Jews, the Samaritans and the Arab tribes. He continued his journey and went on to Egypt, Asia Minor and then Greece, where he learned that a revolt had broken out in Palestine.

At the summons of Rabbi Akiba, Simon Bar Kochba and the priest Eleazar the country had taken up arms. The resistance movement was organised this time in inaccessible caves. Rabbi Akiba had acquired an enormous influence over his compatriots. As a young shepherd he fell in love with a rich young girl from Jerusalem who married him on condition that he educated himself and, at the age of thirty, he went to school with his young son. Rapidly outstripping his teachers, he became an intellectual and moral leader for all those who were seeking in the Law a means of remaining Jewish without a Temple or political independence. For him, however, the Torah was

not a refuge. He refused to accept Roman occupation and when he thought that he had discovered the Messiah, he brought him all the weight of his authority.

This Messiah was Bar Koziba whose name Akiba changed to Bar Kochba which meant 'Son of the Star'. A product of the circle of doctors of the Law, Bar Kochba was the kind of leader of whom the people dreamed. His legendary bravery caught their imagination, he had the strength of Samson and proclaimed himself the Messiah and a descendant of King David. Letters discovered in the Dead Sea caves give proof of his authoritarian, hot-tempered, resolute character and of his fascinating personality which inspired absolute devotion in his followers and communicated to them his ardour in battle. 'O Eternal One, I ask only that thou shouldst not intervene against us!', he is said to have exclaimed. The Sanhedrin did not like Bar Kochba proclaiming himself Messiah, but Akiba's support gave him credit.

Coins of the first revolt.

The Emperor P. Aelius Hadrian (117–138) who founded Aelia Capitolina on the ruins of the city.

In these caves, close to the Dead Sea, Bar Kochba and his followers established their hide-outs.

The liberty of the land of the forefathers is ephemeral. The last partisans die in obscure caves.

In 132 the revolt broke out simultaneously at various points in the country. Surprised by these sudden multiple attacks, the Roman army lost control of the region. The Tenth Legion split up to deal with the different centres of insurrection, but the resisters avoided pitched battles, cut communications and harried the enemy with savage lightning attacks. In view of the extent of the revolt, which had Jerusalem as its principal objective, the Tenth Legion wanted to avoid being trapped and left the city. In the year 1 of national liberation Simon Bar Kochba entered Jerusalem. The Jews immediately minted coins (a privilege refused by the Romans to subject countries), decorated them with a cup, bunches of grapes or the cupboard of the Torah and stamped them with the name of 'Simon, prince of Israel' or of 'Eleazar, priest'. Worship was probably started again on the ruins of the Temple. Simon retained the structures of the Roman administration for the country, substituting himself for the emperor and collecting the dues of the tax-farmers in his place.

It was evident, however, at Jerusalem that a Roman riposte would be forthcoming and Simon was at fault, once he had liberated Palestine, in not carrying the war outside its frontiers among the Jews of the Diaspora or seeking alliances —with the Parthians for example. But his movement was only aimed at the liberation of the land of the forefathers. In these conditions the regrouping of the Roman forces was inevitable. The Jews tried to arm themselves, consolidated the walls and manned the strongholds in Judaea, but Rome's revenge was soon to end these days of independence. Far from underestimating the importance of the revolt, Hadrian called upon one of his best generals, Severus, who was transferred from Britain to Palestine. The emperor himself came to supervise the development of the counter-attack until such time as Jerusalem should be recaptured and the repression far enough advanced to ensure a definitive victory.

In 134, beset by the Romans towards the north, Bar Kochba had to withdraw all his forces into the most desolate regions of Judaea. Quarrels broke out there provoked by the provisioning, which became more and more defective. Bar Kochba intervened energetically, punished those responsible and managed to maintain the morale of his troops. One of his officers, who occupied a strategic position three miles from Hebron, was compelled to draw in his camp before the Roman advance to the shelter of the caves of Murabba'at, which were to become the last centre of resistance. Fragments of a Hebrew Bible, documents concerning the revolt, letters signed by Bar Kochba himself, a goatskin bag containing booty taken from the enemy and a bundle of papyrus have recently been discovered there.

Bar Kochba's lair remained hidden from the Romans for a long time. Practically inaccessible except along the line of crests which would have left the enemy exposed, these four caves were over 160 feet deep and could conceal a large number of soldiers. But Severus had also adopted guerilla tactics. He explored the region cave by cave and displayed great technical ability. The desert of Judah progressively lost its last defenders.

Coin of the second revolt.   A letter from Bar Kochba written on a fragment of papyrus.

A goatskin bag which contained a bundle of papyrus, booty and various female objects.

The Romans were forced to take the whole region of Murabba'at in the wilderness of Judah, from which the rebels harried the legions without respite, cave by cave.

Coin depicting Capitoline Jupiter and inscribed *col (onia) Ael (ia)*.　　　　A coin of Aelia depicting the plough which traced the sacred boundary of the city.

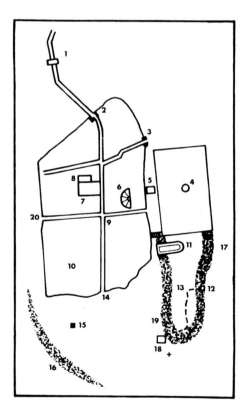

Aelia Capitolina on the old upper city:
(1) Commemorative arch. (2) Northern Gate.
(3) Eastern Gate. (4) Statue of Hadrian.
(5) Small thermae. (6) Theatre. (7) Forum.
(8) Capitol. (9) *Cardo Maximus*. (10) Roman camp. (11) Circus. ;12) Fountain of the Virgin. (13) Ophel. (14) South Gate. (15) Cenaculum. (16) Valley of Gehenna. (17) Valley of Kidron. (18) Large thermae. (19) Valley of Tyropoean. (20) Western Gate.

In 135 the Jewish army of resistance surrendered. According to some Bar Kochba capitulated, according to others he died in a final battle. Akiba was taken to Rome and flayed alive. According to the historian Dio Cassius, Israel's last rising was settled by the death of 580,000 fighting-men, the destruction of fifty fortified places and the ruin of 900 villages. The insurrection had gone beyond the limits of people's strength, the country was exhausted; this time the Romans were pitiless.

Jerusalem was reduced to the point where she completely lost her former inhabitants, the historian Eusebius informs us, and contained only foreigners. Scattered, sold as slaves, in flight throughout the entire Orient, the Jews could no longer return there without risking death. A new town was built on the ruins of the old. Its founder, Publius Aelius Hadrianus, gave it his name and that of the high place of Rome. Jerusalem became 'Aelia Capitolina', the city of Aelius and Capitoline Jupiter. Its first inhabitants were the soldiers of the Tenth Legion. Only the noises from their camp and the sound of their marching brought life to the ruins before the builders started work. Ignoring the previous street plan, the surveyors traced the straight line of the *cardo maximus*—the principal street with its double row of columns—from north to south, and from east to west the *decumanus maximus*. At the point of

intersection the augurs solemnly searched the entrails of pigeons to read the future of the new Roman colony. On the site arose an imposing gate with four openings, beneath which the two principal thoroughfares crossed.

Roman town-planning was ill-adapted to sloping ground and the southern part of the city, the ancient City of David, was abandoned. Aelia Capitolina occupied the former upper city, where the Roman camp had been set up. It was solemnly inaugurated, to the sound of the trumpets of the Tenth Legion, by the imperial legate Tineius Rufus and the legionaries in full dress. After this a plough harnessed to an ox on the right and a cow on the left was driven in procession by Tineius, his head half covered by his toga. When the procession came to the south of the city Tineius ploughed the sacred boundary. Four times he lifted his ploughshare to mark the positions of the future gates, and when the circuit was finished the builders began work.

A circus dating from the time of Herod was rebuilt; a forum was laid out on a former square which was enlarged and paved with great blocks of stone. A little further to the north the hill of Golgotha was the perfect site for the Capitol with the Temples of Jupiter, Juno and Venus. The remains of the old Herodian wall served as a sub-foundation for the forum, which was entered through a triple arch. A second thoroughfare

Jerusalem is no longer in Jerusalem. She has become Aelia Capitolina, by the will of Hadrian, a city at once Jewish, Greek, Roman and Christian.

crossed the *cardo maximus* and led to the Tyropoeon. A theatre was built, like the circus, with stones from the Temple. In order to construct the *thermae* the architects relocated the waters of Siloam. The baths were rather far away from the new city but a street linked them to the circus. The formidable Temple esplanade, which was virtually indestructible, was preserved; Hadrian ordered that his statue be set up there, while the ancient sacred Rock of Abraham was left free of any construction. Aelia did not have a fortified surrounding wall. Her gates were purely decorative, and an example of these still exists in the fragment of the arch of the Ecce Homo. On the northern gate, in front of which stood a large column, were inscribed the dedications of Antoninus and Hadrian.

Hadrian's edict banning Jews and Christians of Jewish extraction from Jerusalem did not affect Christians of other nationalities. A community was re-formed, its language and liturgy were Greek and it had no Jewish tradition. The first church, the first premises of the community, was built on the western hill on the present site of the Cenaculum, which perpetuates the memory of the meetings of the apostles. A Roman colony, Aelia would not have had a history of its own if the rapid spread within the Roman Empire of the Christian religion had not given it the privileged role of the city in which Christ lived and died, and guardian of the documents and traditions bearing witness to His message and His life.

Scholars and researchers then attempted syntheses between the Christian sources and Greek philosophy. They visited Jerusalem and worked in the holy places, where a library had been established since 212. Origen left his chair at Alexandria to come and see 'the traces of Jesus, his disciples and his prophets'. It was at Jerusalem that he published his 'Commentaries on the Old and New Testaments' and his book 'On the Fundamental Principles', the basis of the discussions which were about to open within the Church. Julius Africanus began at Jerusalem his erudite attempt to compare the Christian, Jewish and pagan stories in his 'History of the World', of which only a few fragments remain today. In this he wished to prove the superiority over the Indo-European race of the Semitic race whose age-old history had unfolded in accordance with a cyclical rhythm which bore a divine stamp. His pro-Semitic ideas must have been very widespread in Palestine, and show the importance of the syncretism of Jewish and Graeco-Roman elements. Eusebius of Caesarea sought in this work the sources of his 'History of the Church'.

However, this first golden age of the Christian Jerusalem was to be brief. In 250 the Emperor Decius demanded proofs from all his subjects of their adherence to the pagan cult. The bishop of Jerusalem, Alexander, died under torture. At the end of the third century external dangers were added. Once again Jerusalem almost succumbed to the threat of the Sassanid invaders. The arrival of Diocletian on the Eastern throne restored peace. Nevertheless it was under his rule that persecutions of an extreme violence broke out against the Christians. Refusing to accept the imperial cult, they were undermining the very principle of the emperor's authority. The influx into the holy city started again after Constantine granted religious liberty in 313. A few years later the announcement of the visit of the emperor's mother, Helena, roused the enthusiasm of the population of Aelia. It was the first time that an official personage of Rome who had received Christian baptism intervened personally in the life of the Church.

Born in Bithynia, Helena had married Constantius Chlorus before he became emperor. Repudiated then, because she was not Roman, she had her revenge when her son Constantine, in spite of his origin, was proclaimed emperor by the legions in Britain. Tradition has it that on the eve of the battle which was to decide whether he was to enter Rome, at the Milvian bridge, Constantine saw Christ in a dream, and that he won the victory thanks to the cross. This vision had determined Helena to go to Jerusalem to try to find the wood of the true cross.

Detail of a gold coin showing the head of Helena Augusta, mother of the Emperor Constantine I the Great.

The Empress Helena miraculously discovers the cross on Golgotha.

The discovery of the three crosses of Golgotha by the Empress Helena during her pilgrimage to the holy places (Church of St Quattro Coronati, Rome)

At her arrival Helena received a triumphal welcome from Macarius, the bishop of the city. According to the somewhat anti-Semitic tradition of the Middle Ages a certain Judas, who was said to be the sole repository of the secret, refused to give information. After being starved for six days Judas ended by pointing out the hiding-place where, indeed, the three crosses of Calvary were discovered. Which one was the cross of Christ? In a speech made at the funeral of Theodosius the Great, fifty years later, St. Ambrose relates that Helena identified it from the inscription on the cross in three languages condemning Jesus.

Rufinus of Aquileia gives a different version: 'Having come to the place which had been revealed to her in a vision . . . , she had the earth removed, and found three crosses of the same description . . . She was unable to recognise or distinguish which of the three was that of Our Lord. For that reason, seeing that human understanding was failing to recognise the said cross, she had recourse to divine grace. It happened that there was in that city a woman afflicted with such a grave illness that she was near to death . . . the bishop went into the house of the woman who had the illness and first brought up to her one of the crosses of the two thieves but nothing happened, and afterwards the other one also, but it was the same. Finally having laid upon her that of Our Lord, immediately she opened her eyes and at once stood up.' In the general rejoicing, Judas then became converted and exchanged his name of sorrowful memory for that of Cyriac, and it is said that later he even became a bishop.

Further searches on Golgotha brought to light the nails of the crucifixion 'which appeared at ground level shining like gold'. Helena had one of them melted down to serve as the bit of her son's horse and the other for his diadem. The rocky cavity where the cross was discovered (now a crypt beneath the church of the Martyrium) perpetuates for pilgrims Helena's discovery. Once again legend has expressed and embellished an historical reality, that of the triumph of Christianity in the Roman world after Constantine's edict, and the growing importance of Aelia—once again became Jerusalem—the guardian city of the relics of Christ.

Miracle of the raising of the dead woman revealing the cross of Christ (Marmion, fifteenth century, Louvre, Paris.)

The chapel of the Invention (discovery) of the True Cross inside the basilica of the Holy Sepulchre.

'Take off the garment of your sorrow and affliction, O Jerusalem, and put on for ever the beauty of the glory from God.' (Baruch V. 1)

Constantine devoted himself to reforming under his authority the unity of the Roman Empire. In 325 the emperor renewed Hadrian's edict forbidding the Jews to enter the holy city and furnished Macarius with sufficient means to give lustre to the new holy places. The bishop immediately undertook excavations beneath the forum and the temple of Venus, where the Christians traditionally located the tomb of Christ. The sacred tomb was rediscovered inside the new city and a group of monuments was immediately undertaken.

Although it was destroyed by the Persians 300 years later, this grandiose ensemble can be largely reconstituted through archaeological excavations and contemporary descriptions. First there was an atrium open to the sky, surrounded by a portico and, in the centre, a pool for ablutions. Next the church of the Martyrium, dedicated to the Passion of Christ, with three doors that opened onto a nave fifty yards by six-and-a-half. Near the choir, steps led to the crypt of the true cross. On either side of the apse two doors gave access to a second atrium similar to the preceding one; at its southern corner rose the rock of Calvary. At the far end stood the principal sanctuary, that of the Anastasis or Resurrection. The dome over Christ's tomb rested on columns and its rotunda was enclosed by an ambulatory with three apses.

On 13th September 335 three hundred bishops, assembled around the emperor's representative, inaugurated the basilica, the magnificence of which gave back to Jerusalem a brilliance lost since the destruction of the Temple. Two more basilicas were built in the fourth century to honour the mysteries of Christ, that of the Ascension and, next to it, and still unknown until recently, that of the Eleona which the excavations carried out on the Mount of Olives during the last few years have enabled us to reconstruct. Built over the cave where Christ gave His last teachings, this sanctuary was a vast edifice with three naves opening onto a portico facing the city. But only the nave of the basilica of the Nativity, which has managed to survive the storms of the centuries, recaptures today something of those Constantinian sanctuaries where, for more than 300 years, the Christian liturgies were enacted.

We know the details of their ceremonies from two works of the fourth century; the 'Catecheses' of St. Cyril of Jerusalem and, above all, the *Peregrinatio* of Eutheria. This Spanish nun, who had come on a pilgrimage, relates how the future Christians, the catechumens, were initiated into the religious mysteries. After two years of instruction baptism was performed on Easter Sunday.

'When Easter-tide comes round', she wrote in her *Peregrinatio*, 'people go to the Anastasis singing hymns, as soon as the repeat which ends the liturgy at the church of Golgotha has taken place. Then a prayer is said; the congregation is blessed and the bishop, standing behind the barrier which surrounds the cave of the Resurrection, explains everything that happens at baptism . . .' For the whole of the Easter week the neophytes (those who had just been baptised) wore a white garment until the following Sunday, when they became members of the Christian community.

However, if the crowd of pilgrims flocked to Jerusalem attracted by the splendour of its basilicas and the pomp of its liturgy, other more intransigent voices were raised: 'Do not imagine that something will be lacking from your faith because you have not seen Jerusalem, an overcrowded city where there is a curia, a garrison, prostitutes and buffoons just as in other cities.' It was St. Jerome who delivered this harsh judgment upon Jerusalem. The ascetic had arrived from Rome to stay in the Holy Land, but fleeing the opulent capital he retired to Bethlehem where he completed his translation of the Bible and founded a convent with the assistance of Paula, a rich Roman lady who was one of his disciples.

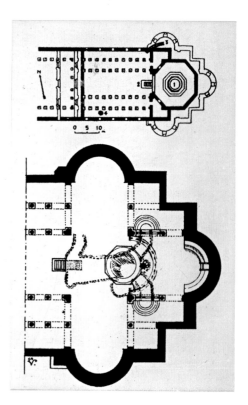

The basilica of the Nativity built in the reign of Constantine and restored by Justinian in the sixth century. Top: Constantine's plan shown by a broad line and Justinian's plan by a thin line. (1) Grotto. (2) Central stairs. (3) Adumbration of the future plan. (4) Baptistry. Bottom: transept and apse of Justinian's Basilica.

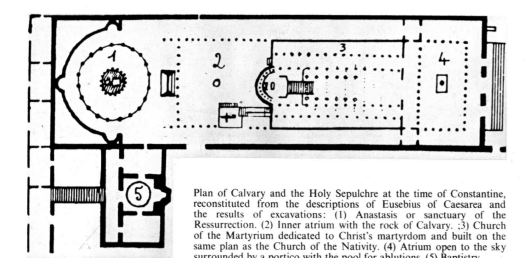

Plan of Calvary and the Holy Sepulchre at the time of Constantine, reconstituted from the descriptions of Eusebius of Caesarea and the results of excavations: (1) Anastasis or sanctuary of the Ressurection. (2) Inner atrium with the rock of Calvary. ;3) Church of the Martyrium dedicated to Christ's martyrdom and built on the same plan as the Church of the Nativity. (4) Atrium open to the sky surrounded by a portico with the pool for ablutions. (5) Baptistry.

From top to bottom: St Jerome leaving for Jerusalem; working on the Bible; distributing his translation (ninth-century Bible of Charles the Bald).

FIT HIERONIMUS ROMAE CUM DECCERAVERSA AT IERUSALEM MEMORIAE LEGIS HONORIFICA

IN STAGNO NICMON PAULE DIVINA SUB VITIO SUPRADAT ALE THRONO EVLTUS UBIQUE DO

Byzantine Jerusalem blossoms with churches. In spite of the storms and undercurrents in a Church seeking its identity, Christianity triumphs officially.

To the east of the Temple precinct the Golden Gate, which remains permanently blocked up, would appear to date from the beginning of the Moslem occupation. It is to the Empress Eudocia, however, that tradition attributes the erection of this monument, on the site of the former Susa Gate through which Christ's procession made its entry on Palm Sunday. According to tradition it will only open again on the day of the Last Judgment.

The story of the Empress Eudocia is intimately bound up with fifth-century Jerusalem. It shows the city's attraction, her complexity and her wealth. Since the fall of Rome in 410 beneath the shock of barbarian invaders, Jerusalem had passed into the orbit of the Byzantine Empire. Christianity was the official religion there under Theodosius I, and the association of throne and altar turned the emperor into the defender of the Christian Faith. The Holy Land benefitted from his generosity and churches with rich mosaics were built on every site that recalled some occurrence in the Old or New Testaments.

Jerusalem adorned herself, pilgrims flocked there and the wife of Theodosius II, Eudocia herself, a converted Greek, made a vow to go there. She arrived in 348, spent several months there, offered a gold cross to Calvary, made various other gifts and took the happiest memories of the city away with her at her departure. From a distance she encouraged the building of new churches. One of these was erected on the site of the future Mosque of el-Aksa; another followed, that of St. John the Baptist which later became the cradle of the order of the Hospitallers.

This first journey was only a prelude to the dramatic story of Eudocia. The empress was not happy at Constantinople. An intelligent, cultured young woman, the daughter of an Athenian professor of rhetoric, she was thrust aside from the affairs of state by her sisters-in-law who governed with Theodosius. Her confidant, Paulinos, was executed by Theodosius, who was jealous of him. Eudocia fled and sought shelter at Jerusalem. Theodosius had her pursued by Saturninus, a court official, who killed her councillors, the priest Severus

and the deacon John. The empress struck down the murderer herself and refused to return to Constantinople. Theodosius finally accepted the separation, Eudocia kept her title and revenues and remained at Jerusalem for twenty years where she was more or less governor, loving the city with passion and taking part in the quarrels which divided it.

At this time a theological conception was spreading throughout the entire Orient, the discussion of which was even more delicate in that it masked the political opposition of the various nationalisms to the government of Constantinople. A Greek monk called Eutyches asserted that the son of God had only a single nature—whence the name monophysitism for this heresy—which was completely divine, and that Christ's human nature was only an appearance. This idea enjoyed a great success in the East. A council was convened in Chalcedon in 451 and condemned monophysitism. Juvenal, the bishop of Jerusalem, was himself suspected of heresy and made an *amende honorable*. In recognition of her leader's obedience Jerusalem was made a patriarchate and set over the three Palestines: Caesarea, Scythopolis and Petra, which involved seventy bishops.

But in spite of the council's condemnation and the position adopted by Juvenal, Eudocia took the side of the monophysites, followed by most of the convents. The administrative victory which the bishop had just won had lost him a large part of his spiritual influence. He was obliged to flee when the struggle led by Eudocia began to gain in violence. Juvenal's followers were massacred, a monk was proclaimed bishop in the Holy Sepulchre, and the worsening of the situation finally necessitated military intervention. A battle took place near Nablus. Concerned by these events, Eudocia went to ask the advice of a hermit in the north of Syria, St. Simeon Stylites, who sent her to Euthymes, the only abbot who had not followed her. She obeyed him and submitted to the Church.

Jerusalem was indebted to Eudocia for an episcopal palace, a large hostelry near the Anastasis for the pilgrims who until then had slept in the holy places, and a great many convents and churches: St. Sophia of the Judgment-Hall, St. Peter at the palace of Caiaphas and

Eudocia, Empress of the East (fifth century).

the church of Siloam at the pool of Hezekiah's conduit. Her favourite foundation was at the gates of the city, the Martyrium of St. Stephen, where she asked to be buried. 'The blessed Eudocia', wrote a contemporary, 'built so many monasteries and alms-houses for the poor and the aged that I am unable to enumerate them all.' They were to vanish as did almost all the Byzantine monuments in the Holy Land.

The Golden Gate, built in the fifth century, held to be the 'shut' gate of the prophet Ezekiel which is to be open for the passage of the 'Prince'.

207

Capital of Mary of Egypt driven out by the angel.

that of the empire, but the brilliance of her monuments and the unity of the Church concealed material poverty and profound moral disorder. Since the triumph of Christianity the position of the Jews in Palestine had become extremely precarious. They were so reduced in numbers as to have become insignificant. Their sufferings increased still further under Justinian. The impassioned zeal of the Christian clergy was responsible for terrible persecutions not only against heretics but also against the Jews and Samaritans. The emperor disqualified Jews from giving evidence against Christians, forbad them to celebrate the Passover and insisted that they used Greek and Latin translations of the Scriptures in their synagogues.

It was not surprising that the Jews came to hate Byzantine rule and did not hesitate to take advantage of the enfeeblement of the empire which perse-

cuted them. However, they do not appear to have taken any part in any attempt at revolt under Justinian. The Samaritans were the only ones to exhibit violent opposition. In 529 they took up arms, looted and set fire to churches and convents and laid waste the province of Jerusalem where the situation in the countryside was already bad enough. Tied to the soil and weighed down by taxes, the peasants were at the mercy of the great landowners who formed a landed aristocracy from which were recruited civil servants with every interest in preserving a situation to their advantage. The ravages of the revolt only added to the peasants' misery. But Justinian, a fanatical builder, gave Jerusalem a hospital and a church— St. Mary the New—which took twelve years to construct. Built on an elevated point of the western hill and supported on enormous sub-foundations, it has

It was in the Church of St. John the Baptist, built by the Empress Eudocia, that Mary of Egypt was converted after being thrust back into the porch by a mysterious force, and decided to dedicate to God a life which until then had been given up to the most complete depravity. But if the frequentation of the holy placed could produce such sudden conversions the malaise of the Church, however, only grew worse. The conflict over monophysitism went from bad to worse and weakened the Eastern Empire. The emperors who succeeded Theodosius II, who had died in 450, tried in vain to re-establish religious peace, which was becoming more and more urgent by virtue of the threat of the Huns at their frontiers. The edict of union promulgated in 484 by the Emperor Zeno, who was on the side of the monophysites, consequently gave rise to the first schism between the Eastern and Western churches which was to last until 518.

In the midst of these troubles Jerusalem continued to grow and adorn herself. Deprived of a role in the forefront of the intellectual, administrative or even religious life of the empire (having been supplanted by Athens, Constantinople, Alexandria and Antioch), she grew in prosperity which she owed to her preeminence as a reliquary city recognised by emperors, bishops and pilgrims.

Under the long reign of Justinian the history of the city became merged with

Remains of a Byzantine basilica of the fifth century brought to light below the Mosque of el-Aksa.

mosaics ever brighten the greyness of Byzantine quarrels?

been brought to light close to the Mosque of el-Aksa. It had sumptuous colonnades and was framed by porticos. St. Mary the New appears on a mosaic *(see right)* which gives a fairly precise cartographical picture of Palestine. The sizes of the towns correspond in this to their actual importance, establishing a 'scale' of cities; Jerusalem was particularly large.

It has proved possible to identify some thirty monuments: the Damascus Gate to the north of the city which, under its Arab name of Bab el-Amud, perpetuates the 'Amud' column which stood along on the square before the gate. The principal Roman street: the *cardo maximus*, with its double row of columns. The South Gate, the Gate of Zion, close to the Mosque of el-Aksa. The Holy Sepulchre. The palace of the patriarch. The hospice of the servants of the Holy Sepulchre. The house of the jewel-casters. The church of St Theodore. St Seraphion, known at the time of the Persian conquest, in 614, by its Arab name of Mar Srapion. St Sergius. The Jaffa Gate. A public square. Fountains. A fortress. The house of Caiaphas. The church of Our Lady of Zion, on the hill upon which the Cenaculum stands today, the tomb of David and the church of the Dormition. The tower of David. The church of the Repentance of Peter, on the left. That of St Mary the New, near the pool of Siloam. The church of Justinian. A gate. A court. St Sophia. A church. The street of the Tyropoeon bordered by a single colonnade. A building which is possibly the Wailing Wall where the Jews who did not have the right to enter the city were already coming to weep. A building at the limit of the Temple court. The Golden Gate. The Lion Gate through which the Via Dolorosa passes today. St Anne, the church of the pool of Bethesda. A church. The Empress Eudocia's place.

The Samaritan revolt revealed the acuteness of the domestic difficulties of Justinian's reign. An authoritarian and intransigent sovereign, he was inclined to govern without sufficiently taking into account the reality which surrounded him. Ruled by the dream of a world-wide Roman Empire, he subordinated the interests of the East to his desire to conquer the West. He succeeded in re-establishing imperial influence over the Mediterranean basin, but failed in his attempt at religious unification. Though orthodox, he disappointed the West by

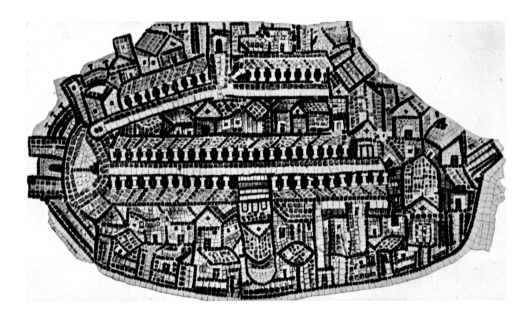

Jerusalem on the mosaic discovered at Madaba depicting Palestine in the sixth century.

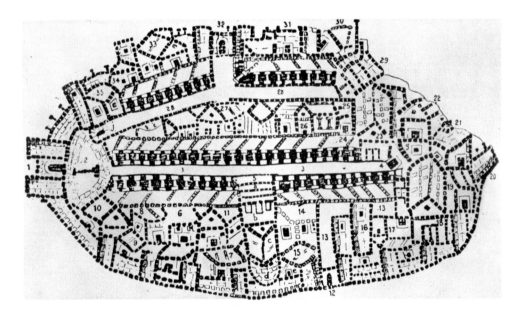

his attitude towards the popes whom he appointed and deposed without scruple. Although under the influence of the Empress Theodora he adopted a more moderate policy towards the 'heretics', he created a separatist climate in the Eastern provinces which rendered the cohesion of the empire extremely fragile. His reduction of military expenses discredited him in the eyes of the army at a period when serious revolts were breaking out in Syria and Egypt, while the landed aristocracy was rebelling in its turn in order to defend and maintain its

privileges. At his death the empire was weakened by religious struggles, disorganised by revolts and impoverished by building and military expenses, although deprived of troops capable of defending it. Persia, concerned at the penetration of her states by Christianity which was confused, in her eyes, with the Roman Empire, took advantage of this precarious situation to launch an attack. Her sovereigns claimed dominion over the entire Orient. In 572, Chosroes I Anushirvan crossed the Euphrates and seized Syria.

from Omar to Suleiman the Magnificent

Of all cities,
Allah chose four in preference;
Mecca, which is the city par excellence,
Medina, the city of the date-tree,
Damascus, the city of the fig-tree,
And finally Jerusalem, which is the city of the olive-tree.

Abu Horayrah

Godefroy de Bouillon (wood-cut, Swiss National Museum).

In the seventeenth year of the hegira the city linked with the fate of the Byzantine Empire is caught up in the prevailing currents of the East and opens its gates to the Arab conquerors.

Coin depicting Chosroes II (seventh century).

At the beginning of the seventh century the fate of Jerusalem, which had been linked for three hundred years with that of the Byzantine Empire, was thrice thrown into the balance. In 614 the city was besieged by the Persians who, ever since Byzantium had begun to be involved in a military revolution, had been trying to assert their supremacy. Their king, Chosroes II, had already conquered Syria and Palestine where the populations who had been persecuted by the Byzantines welcomed him as a liberator. In Galilee 26,000 Jews joined his army. Antioch and Damascus surrendered to avoid certain ruin and Chosroes expected the capitulation of Jerusalem, which was isolated and defenceless. In spite of its desperate situation the city decided to resist. The Persians organised a siege and on 20th May they opened up a breach and entered the town, which was abandoned by its garrison. Assisted by the Israelites who were bent on revenge for the humiliation of Byzantine domination, the soldiers massacred, looted and set fire to churches and convents. The Anastasis, the churches on the Mount of Olives and the basilica built by Justinian were largely destroyed. The victors carried off the relic of the cross. A long column of prisoners, the patriarch at its head, left Jerusalem and the Jews regained the freedom of the city for a time.

Heraclius, the new Emperor of Byzantium, organised a counter-attack, however, and carried the war onto Persian soil, where he defeated Chosroes on several occasions, obtained the restitution of his territories and regained possession of the relic of the cross which he personally brought back to Jerusalem in 629. When he arrived at

In 629 A.D. Heraclius, Emperor of Byzantium, brings back the relic of the cross to Calvary, humbly passing through the Golden Gate on foot (Louvre, Paris).

In a single night Mohammed is borne by his winged mare Borak to the Dome of the Rock before ascending to heaven (thirteenth-century miniature).

the Golden Gate he laid aside his ornaments and went on foot to deposit the relic at Calvary where the patriarch, who had returned from captivity, awaited him.

The Christians rebuilt the ruins and the Israelites abandoned Jerusalem, which they were forbidden to enter on pain of death. Persian power was annihilated, but Byzantium itself was left exhausted by this protracted struggle. When conquerors with fresh forces appeared in 632—the Arabs—Byzantium was in no position to undertake the defence of the East alone.

In a cave in the Arabian mountains, at the dawn of the seventh century, the book descended into the heart of a man who was praying. A new prophet, Mohammed, had just been born who claimed kinship with Moses and Jesus. Up till 624 (the date of the rupture between Islam and the Jews) all the adherents of the new religion prayed in the direction of Jerusalem. After the death of the Prophet, when Arabia had been completely won over to Islam, a general who had been appointed caliph in 635, Omar I, realised Mohammed's schemes of conquest over Palestine. The patriarch Sophronius decided on capitulation, which was guaranteed by the presence of the caliph in person. Without an escort, simply dressed and seated on a camel which bore his supply of dates for the day, Omar I entered the city beneath the surprised gaze of the population who were accustomed to the pomp of the emperor and his representatives.

Water-carriers talking in front of the so-called Mosque of Omar on the former Temple esplanade.

The Temple esplanade becomes the Haram Ash-Sharif and the Rock of Abraham is enshrined in the Mosque of Omar. Jerusalem is merely the rival of Mecca.

'Omar rebuilds the Temple' (fifteenth-century miniature).

Caliph Omar had given Jerusalem peace terms that surpassed all Sophronius' hopes. 'In the name of Allah . . . you have complete security for your lives, your possessions, and for your churches which shall not be occupied by the Moslems or destroyed.' From henceforth Jerusalem was to form part of the *jund Filastin* which combined Judaea and Samaria, with Caesarea as capital. Few changes were effected in civilian life under these new overlords who slipped into the Byzantine administrative structures. Once again a few Israelites were seen in the streets. Despite pressure from Sophronius, Omar had given them back their rights. The Christians were authorised to make pilgrimages on payment of a tax and pilgrims' accounts tell us that an annual fair was held in September on the Hill of Calvary which attracted large crowds. Men and beasts invaded the city which was regularly cleansed by a miraculous fall of rain at the end of the fair. Henceforth dedicated to the Moslem religion, the Temple esplanade became the Haram Ash-Sharif. Reverting to its Semitic role of a sacred precinct it is traditionally, for the Arabs, the scene of the Last Judgment. Caliph Omar had a house of prayer set up there, but the luxury of later Arab momuments has made people forget that this first mosque was a fragile construction in wood modelled on that in which Mohammed and his followers used to meet. It was doubtless no longer in existence when the Dome of the Rock (which is mistakenly called the Mosque of Omar and in Arabic *Kubbet es-Sakhrah*) was built.

In 685, the year 66 of the hegira, caliph Abdul Malik decided to make Jerusalem his religious capital and a rival centre of pilgrimage to Mecca. Setting up the sacred Rock in competition with the Black Stone of the Kaaba, he undertook the construction of the dome. The work was entrusted to Rajah Ibn-Hayat Jud al-Kindi, a scholar of Islam, and to Yazid Ibn Sallam, of Jerusalem. Seven years of revenues from Egypt were assigned to it, and in order to use up the whole of this sum the dome was covered with gold. The architects borrowed a plan from Hellenistic buildings which was adapted to the ritual requirements of the pilgrimages; the processional rounds performed round the Rock suggested a circular architecture. The proportions were borrowed from the basilica of the Ascension on the Mount of Olives, which provided the model for an octagonal plan. A door was set at each of the cardinal points, two concentric rows of columns and pillars divided the interior of the building into three parts: two ambulatories and a central area reserved for the Rock.

The dome stands on a platform at the highest point of the sacred esplanade, which is reached on all sides by broad staircases at the top of which are arcades, in Arabic *mawazin* or scales, as the legend has it that the scales of the Last Judgment will be suspended from them. The walls, which are some thirty-three feet high, are covered at the base by grey marble with coloured veins. Persian faiences and porcelain decorated with white arabesques on a blue background cover the upper part. The voice of the muezzin sounding high over the esplanade calls the faithful to prayer three times a day.

The Dome of the Rock (mistakenly called the Mosque of Omar) from the north, as photographed in 1856.

The call to prayer above the city.

'For him who dies at Jerusalem it is as if he had died in heaven and for him who dies close by, it is as if he had died in the city.'

The sacrifice of Abraham and the Temple of Solomon make the Rock at Jerusalem one of the privileged sites of the earth. Islamic tradition asserts that it served as a springboard for Mohammed's ascent to heaven. with one beat of her wings, his mare Borak deposited him upon the sacred place where he had come to pray. The stone rose up under his feet just as his ascension began, and it was the archangel Gabriel who stopped its movement. Beneath the Rock well up the four rivers of Paradise.

Another legend makes the Rock the precise spot from which the trumpets of the Last Judgment will sound and which will bear the throne of God. Rough, bare and dark, and rising over six feet above the ground, it offers a curious contrast with the decorative profusion of the inside of the dome which displays the ostentatious taste of the Ommayad dynasty. A double row of columns in coloured marble, with capitals in various styles, borders the ambulatory. Mosaics cover every inch of the wall in tones of cobalt, turquoise, brown and black. One of the most famous is composed of minute pieces of glass encrusted with a kind of marble. The same motifs are repeated everywhere: a vase from which branches emerge and coil round one another, medallions of flowers and arabesques; Koranic inscriptions in the Cufic script (the Arabic cursive script whose architectural shapes lend themselves to infinite variations) and flowers mingled with crosses and stars.

Over the Rock the dome is more than sixty-five feet in diameter and the same in height. All round are windows, added in the eighteenth and nineteenth centuries, and filled with stained-glass. Beneath the Rock a cave bristling with projections and pitted with holes is the site of numerous legends. With one of its spurs the Rock replied to Omar who was praying before it: '*Aleik essalam*, it is thou whom I salute.' While he was praying Mohammed knocked his head against the ceiling of the cave which immediately took on the form of his turban. Beneath the crypt is the hole of the dead where, three times a week, the souls meet to pray. Outside, to the east of the mosque, a small octagonal edifice constructed prior to the dome to house the treasury served as a model, and is said to reproduce the plan and proportions of the *Kubbet es-Sakhrah*: this is the *Kubbet es-Silseleh*, where the merits and faults of men will be weighed, as an old Hebrew tradition had already foretold. According to this David had received a chain *(silseleh)* from the archangel Gabriel which he stretched between the columns. When litigants touched the chain, a bell rang to indicate the innocent party.

The sacred rock of Mount Moriah enshrined in its sumptuous edifice.

The dome above the sacred rock, decorated with carved and painted wood.

From the sacred rock of Abraham's sacrifice Mohammed ascends to the throne of God (sixteenth-century Persian miniature)

Upon the Haram the Mosque of el-Aksa, the distant, looks towards Mecca.

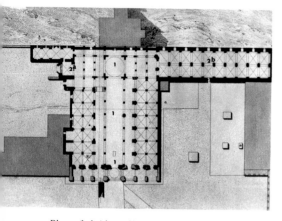

Plan of el-Aksa: (1) Arab constructions.
(2) Templar constructions: (a) Oratory of Zacharias. (b) Hall with two naves.

At first sight el-Aksa presents a large porch with seven groined arches, in front of a facade with seven doors and a dome on pendentives. Nothing now remains of the original mosque, built c. 780 by Adb-al-Malik or his son al-Walid, and of which archaeological researches have revealed the approximate plan. It comprised 280 columns in fourteen rows or, to give a scale of comparison, a third of the mosque at Cordoba, begun in 786. A high-pitched roof and a dome covered the central nave, and fifteen bays opened on the north and eleven to the south. A porch roof decorated with mosaics had been added to it betweeen 826 and 844. Damaged by several earthquakes, at diff-

erent times el-Aksa has been remodelled on a number of occasions until it has taken on the appearance of a Christian basilica.

Intended to serve as a house of prayer far more than the dome which remained a place of pilgrimage, el-Aksa replaced the wooden shelter built by Omar on the south of the Haram. It faced Mecca, and the *mihrab* pierced in the southern wall which precisely indicated its direction was supported by five marble pillars. Its *mimbar* (pulpit), one of the most delicately worked in the Middle East, was executed at Aleppo by order of Nur-al-Din Mahmud (Nureddin) of Syria, who made a vow to bring it to Jerusalem. But this wish was

Facade of the Mosque of el-Aksa orientated towards the Dome of the Rock. The decoration of the portals reveals the Frankish influence (photographed in 1877).

Interior of el-Aksa; the columns, of Carrara marble, are quite recent.

only accomplished in 1187 by his successor, Salah-al-Din (Saladin), after his reconquest of the city.

The *mimbar* and the *mihrab* are the only furnishings of the mosque whose seven empty naves give an impression of spaciousness. Ninety-one columns and thirty-three pillars support the edifice, some in marble and others in the pink stone of the region. Light pours in through the windows in the upper part of the central nave, which is higher and broader than the others. It falls on the mosaic which divides the main nave from the square of the transept and makes the gilded coffering of the ceiling sparkle. The dome, built by the Fatimites, is also covered inside with mosaics with Koranic inscriptions. El-Aksa can hold 5,000 faithful.

At the south-eastern corner of the apse is a second building, the chapel of Omar, almost one hundred feet long and twenty-six feet wide, with a *mihrab* remarkable for its Byzantine columns. This leads into a large, more or less square hall, 'the place of the forty martyrs', which is lined with marble below and with stained-glass. Koranic inscriptions commemorate the journey of Mohammed. It is to the Prophet, in fact, that the name of el-Aksa goes back. He used to give this title, 'the distant', to Jerusalem in contradistinction to Mecca. In this large hall is found the *mihrab* of Zacharias, whose rose window dates from the time of the Crusades. A vast vaulted underground chamber supports a large part of the mosque. Known as 'the stables of Solomon', it was here that the Templars lodged their horses. By the end of the eighth century the neighbourhood of the Haram had taken on the appearance of a Moslem holy city. The dome was its culminating point; all round it, inside the precinct, buildings continued to be constructed up to the time of the Crusades and, later still, under the reign of Saladin. Galleries, gates and fountains (generally covered with Koranic inscriptions), and minarets created an Islamic landscape at once both refined and rich-looking.

The first Arab dynasty, which lasted from 661 to 750, practised the same policy of toleration as Omar. But with the assumption of power by the Abbasid caliphs in 750, an uncertain period opened for both Christians and Jews in Jerusalem. They were compelled to wear a distinguishing costume, and the Jewish families who had been etrusted with the upkeep of the Haram Ash-Sharif lost the privileges that enabled them to pray on the site of the Temple.

The *mihrab* of the so-called chapel of Omar, in el-Aksa, decorated with wreathed columns of the thirteenth century.

The policy of toleration is short-lived. Protected for a time by Carolingian rebuilt, the Holy Sepulchre comes into the power of the Seljuk Turks. For

In spite of the state of insecurity in which the non-Moslems were living, it was at this period that a Jewish sect, the Karaites, installed themselves at Jerusalem, and that the Sanhedrin resumed the habit of assembling. In the bloody quarrel of the iconoclasts, the Church in Jerusalem took up a position in favour of the icons, which leads us to suppose that the Moslems, who were profoundly hostile to images, had remained neutral. In the ninth century a new event was to affect the religious history of the city. The caliph Harun-al-Rashid, who was fighting against the Eastern Empire, sought an alliance with Charlemagne, the rival of the Byzantines. Ambassadors were exchanged

and the caliph, who knew what value the Christians attached to relics, sent Charlemagne the relics of the patriarch of Jerusalem, among which were one of the nails of the cross, together with the keys of the Holy Sepulchre, conferring upon him a right of protection over the holy places. The emperor already possessed the famous 'iron crown', the precious diadem whose inner ring had traditionally been forged from one of the nails of the cross. Charlemagne replied with gifts to the Holy City, which made possible the construction of an abbey on the Mount of Olives, a church, a market and a library, together with the restoration of the church of St Mary, and improved the condition of the

Christians and pilgrims.

But towards the end of the ninth century, when Carolingian unity dissolved, the Christians again found themselves isolated. Moslem pilgrims poured into Jerusalem when the Karmathian invasions interrupted pilgrimages to Mecca and a mosque was built in the atrium of the Holy Sepulchre. But soon Islam divided into rival caliphates. The Byzantine emperor Nicephorus Phocas took advantage of this situation to invade and lay waste Syria and Palestine; the Byzantine army was in sight of Jerusalem when the emperor died suddenly (10th January 976).

The city then passed into the hands of the Fatimid caliphs of Egypt. In 996,

In exchange for his alliance with Harun al-Rashid, the Emperor Charlemagne receives the relics of the Patriarch of Jerusalem (fourteenth-century miniature).

power, almost recaptured by Nicephorus Phocas, successively destroyed and several centuries the Christian West attempts to snatch it from the infidel.

al-Hakim bi'amrillahi succeeded to the caliphate, and adopted a violently anti-Christian policy. In 1008 the Palm Sunday procession was forbidden and in 1009 the Holy Sepulchre was completely demolished following a report to the caliph, according to which 'the Christian priests were making the sacred fire (of Holy Saturday) descend upon the lamps of the Holy Sepulchre with the aid of a whole apparatus of greased cords covered with sulphur and other inflammable substances while making out that the fire was coming from heaven.' The church was rebuilt in 1048, under the caliphate of El Mostansir Billah, with the help of the Emperor Constantine IX (Monomachus) who, in exchange, re-

leased some Moslem prisoners and sent money for the work. This period of appeasement did not last for long. In 1701 the Seljuk Turks who had conquered the caliphate of Baghdad and a large part of Asia, attacked the Fatimites. Jerusalem fell into the hands of the Turks in 1077. Churches and mosques were looted and desolation and poverty invaded the city, which lost its principal source of income. The cruelty of the occupiers made pilgrimages impossible. The Jewish communities lived off gifts sent by Israelites abroad and the rabbinical colleges fled to Tyre. Once they were established in Palestine the Seljuks turned to Byzantium, which then sought aid from Pope Urban II.

The crown forged from a holy nail.

Combat of Seljuk Turkish horsemen, who seized the Holy City in 1077 (eleventh-century miniature from the album of Mohammed VII).

Exultation of the Crusaders at the sight of the Holy City, occupied by the Egyptian Fatimites, on 7th June 1099 (nineteenth-century illustration by Gustave Doré).

On Friday 15th July 1099, the Knights of Christ recaptured the Holy City from the Saracens.

Faced with the new outburst of Islamic hostility, as seen by the martial fervour of the Seljuk Turks, the Western powers, alerted by the voice of Pope Urban II, joined forces and opposed the Crusade, the holy war of Christianity, to the *jihad*, the holy war of Islam. The liberation of Jerusalem became the concern of a Europe in which was mingled the mystical thought of the

Middle Ages and the need for territorial and commercial expansion of a turbulent society. The First Crusade, under the leadership of Peter the Hermit, failed.

The Crusade of the Barons gathered together international contingents, led by the Papal legate, Adhémar de Monteil. After numerous defections and losses the Crusaders came within sight of Jerusalem on the 7th June 1099, 'exulting with

The Crusaders second assault, on 14th July: the moveable siege towers collapse beneath the Greek fire thrown from the top of the walls (illustration by Gustave Doré).

gladness, singing hymns and weeping with joy'. The town was no longer in the hands of the Turks. The Egyptian Fatimites had just recaptured it, and it was against them that the Crusaders organised the siege. A first attempt, on 13th July, showed the city's powers of resistance and the necessity for siege engines for a second assault.

The Crusaders constructed two wooden forts furnished with mortars and placed them on the city's weak point on the east. While this was going on, reinforcements and fresh supplies reached them, thanks to a Genoan fleet which had disembarked at Jaffa.

On Friday 15th July, after a procession round the city, the final assault was delivered. Towards noon Godefroy de Bouillon managed to throw a foot-bridge onto the wall. At the same time ladders were set up on every side, enabling groups of soldiers to enter the city. The defenders entrenched themselves in the Mosque of el-Aksa which was only taken after a fresh engagement. Tancred and Gaston de Béarn seized the Dome of the Rock. The Count of Toulouse seized the most difficult sector, the tower of David.

The conqueror refuses to accept a crown of gold where Christ had worn only a crown of thorns.

On the evening of 15th July 1099 Jerusalem was in the hands of the Crusaders who unleashed an appalling massacre. The Moslems perished in tens of thousands while the Jews were shut up in the synagogues and burned. 'One could not see this multitude of dead without horror', wrote William of Tyre; 'even the sight of the victors covered with blood was an object of terror.' After this, the Christians 'washed their hands and feet, laid aside their blood-stained clothes for fresh robes and made their way barefoot to the holy places'. On 17th, they met in order to give Jerusalem a leader and a constitution. Two names were put forward: Raymond de Saint-Gilles (the Count of Toulouse) and Godefroy de Bouillon. The Count of Toulouse, the more brilliant of the two, advocated a policy of alliance with Byzantium and the creation of a state which would be its vassal—a policy which would have had the advantage of ending Jerusalem's isolation. For reasons which are not clearly known, however, he was not awarded the throne and the barons elected Godefroy de Bouillon who was famous for his courage, strength and piety, rather than political ability.

Refusing the title of King, Godefroy de Bouillon took the extraordinarily modest one of 'Defender *(advocatus)* of the Holy Sepulchre'. The foundations of an independent Frankish state—virtually a colony with a feudal administration— were laid in the midst of an eastern country. The Supreme authority was vested in the body of the nobility assembled in a high court of justice, which alone had the right to legislate and grant fiefs, and to which the king had to swear to respect the feudal franchises and prerogatives. The great vassals, the princes of Antioch, Edessa, Tripoli, who recognised him as sovereign, were in fact free and themselves had vassals. The monarchy was hereditary and free of the Salic law; the right of succession belonged to the closest relation of the king present on Eastern soil.

The isolation of these Latin states and the dangers which they ran in common gave the kings of Jerusalem an *ipso facto* authority, each time that their personalities were able to assert themselves over the real independence of the nobility. The king's army was composed of feudal levies and included knights, mercenaries recruited from amongst the Syrians and Turcopuli, a light native cavalry. Beside the nobility and the king, the Latin Church constituted a third power. It owned estates, convents, abbeys, considerable wealth and an undeniable influence. The Greek patriarch had not been replaced and the other Christian Churches, the Syrian Monophysite, and the Nestorian, only had the importance of local confessions. The Latin Church consequently had no difficulty in taking the lead. The Latin patriarch crowned the king and the ceremony expressed the interdependence of sovereign and Church.

To those who had a share in power were added the middle classes and merchants who had their own institutions: the court of the burgesses, composed of twelve notables, judged freemen of common birth; a commercial court and a maritime tribunal were reserved for the merchants. The native population had their own tribunal: the court of the Raïs, which settled their disputes, but a special statute law, a fusion of western and eastern laws, adjudicated in the relations between Westerners and the native population. The domestic organisation of the kingdom is known from a number of manuscripts; 'The Assizes of Jerusalem', the lost original text of which was reconstituted in the thirteenth century, and several chronicles, one of the most famous being that of Godefroy de Bouillon.

'How Godefroy was made King of Jerusalem and refused to wear a crown' (National Library, Vienna)

Godefroy de Bouillon (Nuremberg Museum).

Illustrations of the conquest from Heraclius to Peter the Hermit (the thirteenth-century *Roman de Godefroy de Bouillon*).

Et auci   ouuertior   v drable
enmes lit   tempure de   Dsist ent
tores di   rommne ax   dint que
ent que   en sou tep   estoit pr
eracles   analhome   pheres

Bauduïn conte de rohez

les barons   les barons

Baudouin of Boulogne, the first king of the delivered Jerusalem, becomes the 'Frankish sultan'.

Crusader knight (fourteenth-century, Florence).

On 25th December 1100, Baudouin de Boulogne, the first Count of Edessa and the brother of Godefroy de Bouillon, had himself crowned king in the church of the Nativity at Bethlehem. He was the real founder of the kingdom of Jerusalem to which he dedicated his energetic personality, a realistic intelligence (which did not burden itself with scruples when the interest of the kingdom was at stake), and an unfailing military gallantry.

He swept his knights and soldiers into the conquest of the littoral which had remained in the hands of the Egyptians. He then fought the Turks, occupied Transjordania and pushed on as far as the Red Sea, cutting the Islamic world in half. The Franks thus occupied a defensible position in the East. At home Baudouin had to resolve a number of difficulties: in order to repeople the towns and countryside he called upon Christians of all rites (whether Greek or Syrian) scattered throughout Syria and Transjordania, gave them the freehold of the houses and estates which had been abandoned and encouraged the mixing of this population with the knights and pilgrims who had remained in Palestine. This policy of assimilation was so successful that a few years later the new Crusaders arriving from the West no longer recognised their predecessors who were completely adapted to the oriental environment. Baudouin himself reigned at Jerusalem like an eastern prince and was known as the 'Frankish sultan'. Dressed in a burnous woven with gold, his long beard accentuating his majestic appearance, and surrounded by oriental pomp, he accepted the adulation of foreign embassies and took his meals before them seated cross-legged on a carpet.

He was first and foremost a statesman who sought, sometimes by force and sometimes by guile, but always without scruple, to make his fragile kingdom into a strong military monarchy. Very different from the strict Godefroy de Bouillon, he did not hesitate, in order to marry the wealthy Adelaide of Sicily, to put his first wife as a 'nun in the church of Our Lady Saint Anne', which he enriched for the circumstance with considerable subsidies. Once the dowry was exhausted he repudiated Adelaide just in time to escape the scandal of a king excommunicated at Jerusalem for bigamy.

The Church of St Anne, rebuilt to a large extent thanks to the gifts brought by the first wife of Baudouin de Boulogne (photograph by Leclercq, 1859).

The coronation of Baudouin de Boulogne, on 25th December 1100 (early fourteenth-century miniature).

'The knight is without fear and without reproach who protects his soul with the armour of faith, as he covers his body with a coat of mail.'

In a few years Baudouin I succeeded in creating the kingdom of Jerusalem, having imposed the necessary discipline everywhere. He managed to unite the barons round the throne, thanks to his skilful diplomacy and indomitable energy, never hesitating to offer his assistance to his vassals in time of war or to act as arbitrator between them. Where the Church was concerned he maintained an equally firm position. He deposed Daimbert, the patriarch of Jerusalem, on the charge of simony and misappropriation of funds, and then replaced him by Arnulf, who was more amenable to his wishes. The successor of Baudouin I, Baudouin de Bourg, Count of Edessa, continued his work. He was a conscientious, active, shrewd prince well adapted to the oriental environment. He set about consolidating the position of the Frankish kingdom in the face of the Turks and was considerably assisted in this military task by the great orders of chivalry—the Templars, the Hospitallers and the Teutonic Knights—based on Jerusalem.

Although their modalities were different they sprang from a common necessity: the protection of travellers on the roads of the Holy Land and the maintenance of order in the country regions with Moslem populations, who were fre-

quently hostile. They had a common ideal, for which the Holy Land was in a favoured situation: to combine the lives of warrior and monk.

In 1118 a French knight, Hugues de Payns, joined with eight companions in order to accompany and protect parties of pilgrims. The king installed them in the Haram Ash-Sharif. They took the name of 'Templars' because the Dome of the Rock was built on the very site of the Temple of Solomon. As early as 1124 they turned el-Aksa into a church, constructed an adjoining hall and kept their horses beneath the mosque in the 'stables of Solomon', 'a stable of so marvellous a capacity', noted a German crusader, 'that it could hold over two thousand horses or one thousand five hundred camels'. Hugues de Payns returned to Europe and asked St Bernard to dictate the rule of 'the Knights of Christ' which was modelled on the Cistercian rule with the three vows of poverty, chastity and obedience, and was to comprise four classes: knights issued from the nobility, chaplains, sergeants belonging to the middle classes, and craftsmen. At their head was the grand master of the order whose powers were enormous although limited by the 'chapter'; below him came the seneschal and then the commanders who controlled

the provinces.

The life of these monk-knights was regulated down to the smallest detail where both physical and religious life was concerned. They wore a uniform with a red cross, their monk's tunic covering their armour. Services and Lenten fasts were obligatory. At the outset they were highly regarded for the help they gave the king, but they fell into a decadence bound up with their material prosperity. Having become bankers—since pilgrims deposited money with them at the start of their journey and reclaimed it on their arrival at Jerusalem—and organisers of voyages and tours for pilgrims, they acquired numerous estates, built castles and establishments in both the West and the East, opened a bank in Paris and lent money to the king until, in the reign of Philippe le Bel, the mysterious 'affair', the scandal which was to ruin them, exploded. The order was dissolved and its possessions were given to the rival order of the Hospitallers, which had been founded in 1070 as a charitable institution for the care of pilgrims. As early as 1120, Raymond du Puy had made the monk-knights of the Hospital of St John of Jerusalem into an army dedicated to the defence of the Holy Sepulchre. Its recruitment was, however, less aristocratic than that of the Templars

Seal of the Templars depicting two knights on the same mount.   Seal of the Hospitallers depicting seven knights kneeling before a relic of the true cross.

The Knights Templar, evoked on a fresco of the Templar chapel at Cressac (twelfth century), leave for battle beneath the gaze of the inhabitants of Jerusalem.

and the order was more religious and less centralised. The knights of the Hospital wore a uniform with a white cross.

Quickly realising of what assistance these knights could be to them, the kings of Jerusalem entertained close relations with them in spite of their frequent insurbordination. They gave them the most dangerous posts in the defence of the territory and in exchange granted them castles and privileges.

A letter of Louis VII testifies to the importance and confidence which the orders of chivalry, and in particular the Templars, enjoyed in the middle of the twelfth century. 'We cannot see, we cannot imagine how we could have existed one moment in these lands without their help and assistance. This help has never failed us from the first day of our arrival up to the moment when these letters leave us, and they render themselves ever more obliging. We therefore pray that you will redouble your sympathy towards them in order that they may be sensible that we have interceded on their behalf. In addition we are notifying you that they lent us and borrowed in their own name for us a considerable sum. This sum must be returned to them lest their house be defamed or destroyed. We must not cause them to break their word nor bring dishonour upon all of us at once. We therefore beseech you to repay them without delay the sum of two thousand silver marks.' The role of these orders of chivalry thus extended far beyond the mere surveillance of the kingdom. Their particularism, their independence, their pride and also their thirst for power eventually gave rise to serious conflicts with the clergy, to the point where the order of the Hospitallers came to make an armed attack on the chapter of the Holy Sepulchre. However, they were exempt from the jurisdiction of the patriarch of Jerusalem and the Vatican (to whom they were answerable), although condemning their excesses, preferred to tolerate a certain amount of disorder rather than increase the power of the local clergy who were more closely linked with the kings of Jerusalem than with the Holy See.

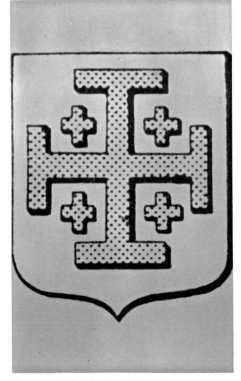

The arms of the kingdom of Jerusalem.

Beth phage.
Mons Oliveti, Ascensio Domini.
Villa Gethsemani.
Mons excelsus.
Jhericho.
Bethania.

Ecclesia Sancte Marie, sepulcrum.
Recessus Jhesu trans torrentem Cedron.

Vallis Josaphat.

Aurea porta, qua ingressus est Jhesus sedens super asinam.

Templum S. Marie.
Templum Domini.
Templum Salomonis.

Fons Syloe.

Porta speciosa.
Claustrum Salomonis.

Aceldemach.

Cambium monete.
Forum rerum venalium.

Vicus porte Sancti Stephani.
Vicus porte montis Syon.

Lapis scissus in morte Domini.
Calvarie locus.
Golgota.

Turris David.
Ecclesia latina.
Cenaculum.

Sepulchrum Domini.

Vicus ad Templum Domini.

Mons gaudii.

Processio Sepulcri Sancti.
Sepulchrum Rahel.

Ecclesia beati Stephani.

Vicus ad civitatem.
Porta David.
Vicus ad Beth. Effrata.

Mons Syon.
Beth leem.

Sanctus Georgius.

One cannot deny the whole of the Orient. The Latin kingdom frequently combines Moslem and Christian traditions.

When the Frankish architects rebuilt the fortifications of Jerusalem they followed the lay-out of the Roman surrounding wall, replacing the Damascus Gate by the Gate of St Stephen and keeping the Gate of Zion open on the south and that of Josaphat on the east. The town thus delimited corresponded more or less to the present old city. It was intersected by two perpendicular streets which were orientated north-south and east-west. Two towers constituted the principal points of defence: the tower of Tancred and the tower of David. The one we see today is a fourteenth-century construction, erected on the site of Herod's towers of Phasael, Hippicus and Mariamne which had been destroyed during the Byzantine period.

The citadel built by the Crusaders, and which was to disappear in 1239, became the residence of the king and the place of refuge of the townpeople in case of alarm when, in 1128 the king left to the Templars the residence he had arranged for himself in the Mosque of el-Aksa. The neighbourhood which surrounded it was then given the name of Mount Royal. To the east were the bakers' shops; descriptions of the city permit the location of a grain market between the towers of David and Tancred. Inhabited by the Georgian and then the Armenian populations, the neighbourhood saw the erection in the twelfth century of the church of St James which was surmounted by a dome with intersecting ribs, characteristic of Armenian buildings.

Great animation reigned in the centre of the city around the building yard of the Holy Sepulchre. This was the market quarter and one still comes across the inscriptions indicating streets or markets. A cattle market, tanneries and a poultry market were held there together with a herb bazaar. Apart from the Templar constructions around the Mosque of el-Aksa the crusaders did not touch the Haram Ash-Sharif and, in particular, they did not harm the Dome of the Rock which was given to the Augustinian canons and was simply turned into a church, under the name of *Templum Domini*, by the addition of an altar on the Rock and a cross on the Dome. The Rock was protected from the pilgrims by a wrought-iron grille.

Surprisingly, the building was to have a powerful appeal for the Christians and, in Europe, several Templar churches adopted a circular construction in imitation of it.

The influx of Christians of various rites, Nestorians, Syrian Monophysite, Armenian, Latin and Syrian, necessitated the transformation into churches of most of the mosques, which had been abandoned by the Arabs, and the restoration of numerous Byzantine edifices which took on a western appearance. In the Valley of the Kidron the church of St Saviour replaced the basilica of Gethsemane; the abbey of Our Lady of Josaphat was built over the tomb of the Virgin and the dome of the Ascension; St Stephen and the church of the Cenaculum were repaired. The most characteristic buildings, however, remain St Anne's and, above all, the Holy Sepulchre.

Remains of the medieval fortifications built on the site of Herod's fortress and generally called the tower of David (photograph by Bonfils, 1877).

Plan of the city in the thirteenth century orientated east-west according to an ideal geometry (Royal Library, The Hague).

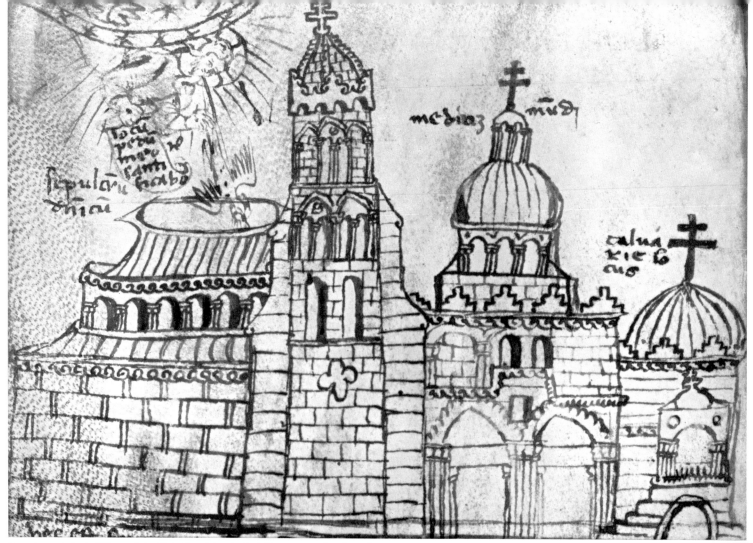

Drawings of the buildings of the Holy Sepulchre in their first state at the time of the Crusades. Above left: an evocation of the sacred fire (Vatican Library).

The Holy Sepulchre: the two-storied Romanesque belfry, dome of the rotunda and smaller one dating from the Crusades. Behind, the convent of Notre Dame de France.

Christ's tomb, 'the ideal centre of the world', is covered with new architecture to accommodate the crowds who come in pilgrimage.

The Latin kings were anxious to put their mark on the holy places that had been the pretext for the Crusades and which continued to be the goal of pilgrims. Between 1131 and 1187 their architects erected the Romanesque building which, except for a few modifications, constitutes the present Holy Sepulchre and was consecrated before its completion, in 1149. A traveller's drawing *(see opposite)* recaptures it at the moment when, completely finished, it had not suffered the attacks of time and successive restorers that have given it its present appearance *(see below opposite)*. In the foreground stands a Romanesque belfry with three tiers of windows supported by fine columns and terminated by a faceted dome standing on battlements. Behind this belfry, which hides part of the facade, is outlined the body of the building, a composite mass whose left-hand side is crowned by a truncated dome with a wide opening to the sky while to the right of the belfry the facade is crowned by a rounded dome surmounted by a cross. Another similarly shaped but smaller (which is no longer in existence), doubtless corresponds to a baptistry attached to the building.

The same elements appear in an engraving of the beginning of the nineteenth century *(see below)* in which the belfry is more or less reduced to two storeys and appears to be in ruins. In the present building alterations have affected the domes. The roof in the shape of a truncated dome has disappeared and has been replaced by a modern dome which has recently been restored. The body of the building still exists, however, in its original complexity and only history makes possible an explanation of its arrangement. When the Crusaders entered Jerusalem they found a Byzantine church, the Anastasis, on the site of the holy places, as restored by Constantine Monomachus, who had respected the essentials of the building. A rotunda, it covered the tomb of Christ with a roof in the shape of a truncated cone. The interior was richly decorated with paintings, mosaics and brocades woven with gold. Next to it, the former martyrium was in ruins, and all the way round small chapels marked Calvary and the chapel of the Invention (discovery) of the Cross and of St Helena.

The western plan consisted in joining up these scattered buildings and the Anastasis into an enclosed space as already done in the great pilgrimage churches of the South of France, Limoges, Toulouse and Santiago de Compostela in Spain. The rotunda thus lost its architectural autonomy. Open on the east it became the apse of a very large church which had as its choir the spot where tradition located the centre of the world, 'the omphalos', whose arms enclosed Calvary and a considerable number of chapels and galleries constructed previously. Erected later, the belfry added still further to the Romanesque and western appearance of this new Holy Sepulchre.

The Holy Sepulchre before the Greek restoration of 1809: the dome in the shape of a truncated cone and the three-storied belfry can be seen (National Library, Paris).

233

The prudent Foulque d'Anjou gives the kingdom of Jerusalem a period of peace. Franks and Moslems learn co-existence.

On 14th September 1131, Foulque d'Anjou was crowned King of Jerusalem with Melisende his wife. Ever since the Holy Sepulchre contained the royal tombs, the ceremony no longer took place in Bethlehem but in the Holy City. The King was received by the clergy at the door of the church and took the oath to defend the patriarch and his church, together with the laws and customs of the kingdom. In return the patriarch swore to uphold the king's crown. When these oaths had been exchanged the king received the kiss of peace from the priest and the people acclaimed him the true heir of the kingdom. To the singing of the *Te Deum* the new king proceeded to the choir, followed by his barons who bore the crown and the golden orb or 'apple', the high constable who bore the banner and the seneschal with the sceptre. During this ceremony, which made him into a semi-sacred personage, the king was dressed like a deacon and received the unction of the holy chrism.

When he took charge of the kingdom of Jerusalem Foulque was in his forties and had a particularly useful political experience in the face of the new situation created by the accession of the 'atabeg' (in Turkish: father prince) Zangi in the principality of Aleppo. Zangi had an objective: the unification of the Moslem world. He wished to seize the independent Moslem kingdom of Damascus.

A Franco-Byzantine coalition would have seemed natural, but the instinctive mutual distrust between Latins and Greeks prevented any such realisation, even though the principle was accepted. Foulque preferred alliance with the kingdom of Damascus which was being threatened by Zangi. This alliance deterred the atabeg who, in 1140, withdrew his troops.

The rapprochement was a lasting one; close relations were established between the Frankish barons and the emirs of Damascus with a spirit of religious toleration on both sides far in advance of their time. At Jerusalem, the emir Ousama became friendly with the Templars and himself recounts his visit. One day when a freshly disembarked Crusader wished to prevent the emir from making his Koranic invocations, the Templars rushed forward, ejected the new arrival and apologised to Ousama: 'He is a stranger and does not know the country' and Ousama went on to emphasise how much their cohabitation with the Moslems had modified the attitude of the Syrian Franks. For his part, while visiting a church one day, the emir was suddenly overwhelmed by the fervour of the Latin monks he had

The coronation of Foulque I and his wife Melisende in the Holy Sepulchre on 14th September 1131 (fifteenth-century miniature, National Library, Paris).

Facade of the Holy Sepulchre. Left, the baptistry; right, chapel of the Franks (photograph by Bonfils, 1877).

seen saying divine service. Foulque's wise administration had therefore resulted in solid ties; the friendship of the vizier of Damascus secured him against any attack from Aleppo.

Meanwhile the Holy Sepulchre was being completed, the decoration of the facade uniting the style devoid of human representation inherited from the Semitic East with figurative scenes inherited from the West. The squat capitals had only two rows of curled leaves surmounted by scrolls but the lintels of the portal show episodes from Christ's life at Jerusalem (the raising of Lazarus and Palm Sunday) or else a chain of naked men in a forest of tracery. This motif, said to go back to antique funerary art, is met with again in Christian art of the East (in Coptic art in particular) and also in the Romanesque art of the South of France.

The Holy Sepulchre in the fifteenth century (wood-cut from Breydenbach's *Sanctae Peregrinationes*).

Romanesque capitals of the portal (twelfth century).

Christ's tomb in the Middle Ages (manuscript, Vatican Library).

Interior of the Holy Sepulchre (reverse of the Bull of the Hospitallers).

Seventeenth-century engraving showing a section through the Holy Sepulchre with the dome not yet transformed by the Greek restoration of 1809.

The Turkish threat grows: Christendom sharpens its sword for a second crusade.

The original appearance of the Holy Sepulchre itself is now known only from documents anterior to the fire which completely devastated the building in 1808 (for the present state of Christ's tomb, *see* pp. 254–255); but the engravings of the seventeenth century still show the Romanesque choir and the earlier dome in the shape of a truncated cone with its broad aperture open to the sky, at the foot of which the kings of Jerusalem had themselves buried.

At the accidental death of Foulque, in 1143, his son Baudouin III was proclaimed king under the regency of Melisende. The Turks continued their offensive. In 1144 Zangi seized the county of Edessa, which formed the northern bulwark of Palestine. The threat became so serious that a second Crusade was preached in the West. The King of France, Louis VII, and the Emperor of Germany, Conrad III, embarked for the holy places. While the German army, deserted by its Byzantine guides and beset by the Turks, beat a retreat, Louis VII reached Antioch, accompanied by his wife Eleanor of Aquitaine. An astonishing incomprehension of events diverted the king from the reconquest of Edessa which was the only means, however, of arresting the Turkish advances. Louis VII suddenly left Antioch for Jerusalem. Melisende then involved him in a useless and even fatal operation against Damascus, which could have constituted a precious ally against Zangi. In this way the Palestinian barons brought about the failure of the Frankish operation. The result was the collapse of Louis VII's attempt and he left Jerusalem in 1149.

The young Baudouin's majority was approaching and he was crowned at Easter in 1152. The queen, however, seemed unwilling to hand over power and Baudouin had to take up arms against his mother. Seeing that success was impossible, the dowager accepted defeat.

Baudouin consolidated the southern frontier of the kingdom by the capture of Ascalon and resumed against Nureddin, the son of Zangi, the policy of alliance with Damascus inaugurated by Foulque; but he was unable to prevent Moslem unity and, in 1154, Nureddin made himself master of Damascus.

Crusade and counter-crusade were now face to face. Victor in the first part of the struggle, Baudouin realised the necessity of forming a Christian coalition and asked for the hand of a Byzantine princess, Theodora, the niece of Manuel Comnenus. Despite the sympathy which sprang up between emperor and king, the mistrust of the Byzantines prevented the allies from achieving definite success in the face of the Moslem peril. Baudouin died in 1162 and Amaury I, his brother, succeeded him.

Rotunda of the Holy Sepulchre at end of seventeeth century and tomb of Christ beneath the dome with its broad aperture open to the sky (National Library, Paris).

Hezekiah's reservoir, near the Holy Sepulchre, the dome of which can be seen in the background at left (photograph by Bonfils, 1877).

The anointing of Baudouin IV, the future leper king, in 1174 (fifteenth-century miniature from Sebastien Mamerot's *Passages faits Outre-Mer par les Français*).

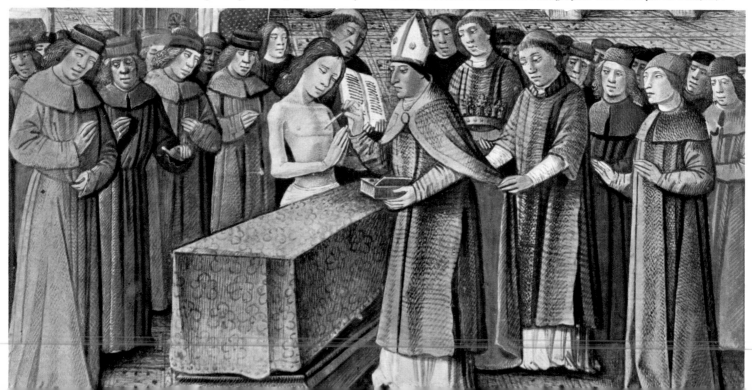

'Come, Sire, and receive this crown, I could not employ it better.' At the death of the leper king, Sybille crowns the handsome Guy de Lusignan.

At Jerusalem the Frankish architects restricted themselves to military and religious constructions. They do not appear to have attended to modernising the water supply. The Jewish and Roman conduits continued to supply the town, and the Crusaders merely used the reservoirs and pools which had doubtless already been repaired by the Moslems, such as that of Bethesda, or the probatic pool, and the pool or reservoir of Hezekiah.

The year 1174 marked a serious turning-point in the history of the kingdom. Two simultaneous events suddenly changed the relations of the forces in the East. King Amaury died before he had brought the urgent policy of alliance with Byzantium to a satisfactory conclusion. A youth, Baudouin IV, succeeded him, whose lively qualities were described by his tutor William of Tyre, but who was stricken with leprosy. Nureddin also died, leaving a minor to succeed him. Immediately Saladin, who had been vizier of Egypt since 1169, set about realising Moslem unity and King Baudouin, assisted by the regent Raymond III of Tripoli, did his utmost, by pursuing the traditional policy of support to Damascus and the small states against Moslem hegemony, to prevent him from doing so. They only succeeded in delaying him for a few years. By 1183 Saladin was master of Aleppo and Damascus and had both Egypt and Syria under his dominion. The kingdom of Jerusalem was encircled. At the moment when the Moslems were united beneath the command of one of the greatest figures in the history of the Near East, the Franks were disputing Baudouin's succession and bringing the country to the verge of civil war.

Princess Sybille, the king's eldest sister, was his rightful heir, but her husband Guillaume de Montferrat had died a few months after her marriage leaving her pregnant with the future Baudouin V, and Sybille turned down the suitors contemplated by Baudouin. In the midst of all this there landed in Palestine an elegant young Poitevin called Guy de Lusignan, penniless and unknown but said to be the most handsome man of his time. The passionate young widow was instantly captivated and declared that she had chosen her new husband.

Increasingly ill, Baudouin IV did not oppose his sister's entreaties and authorised the marriage, but in view of

The Countess of Jaffa crowns her husband, the handsome Count of Lusignan (miniature, about 1300).

Saladin, victor in 1187 (Gustave Doré).

Lusignan's unfitness to govern the king ordered the barons, on his death bed, to crown the child Baudouin V king and confer the regency of the kingdom upon Raymond of Tripoli. On 16th March 1185 Baudouin IV died at the age of twenty-four. Two years later Baudouin V also died, leaving the way open to Guy de Lusignan who was supported by the patriarch, the Grand Master of the Templars and the prince of Antioch, all of whom were enemies of the regent, Raymond of Tripoli. While the barons met at Nablus in an attempt to oppose the coronation of Lusignan, the patriarch Heraclius crowned Sybille at Jerusalem and she in turn crowned her husband. Immediately Saladin, provoked beyond measure by the brigandage of the prince of Antioch attacking caravans of pilgrims leaving for Mecca, unleashed a general war.

'The cross fell and a general cry was raised in the city and its environs. They part of the Moslems and cries of sorrow and rage on the part of the Christians.'

At the beginning of July 1187, Saladin, who was determined to seize Jerusalem, invaded Galilee. The meeting between his army and the Franks took place at Hattin, in the burning heat of the Palestinian summer. In a single day the entire Frankish cavalry was annihilated. Guy de Lusignan was taken prisoner, together with the prince of Antioch and the Grand Master of the Temple; only Raymond of Tripoli succeeded in making a break-through and escaped. The disaster was total, the kingdom no longer had an army. In order to prevent all help from outside Saladin made for the coast and seized all the ports. Then he turned towards Jerusalem.

The situation of the city was desperate and the population panic-stricken. A baron, Balian d'Ibelin, whom Saladin had set free to go and look after his wife, the former Queen Maria Comnena, organised a precarious defence with the elements left in the city—the sons of killed or captured knights, mere children of fifteen, upon whom he conferred knighthoods as he did upon the townspeople. Despite Saladin's solicitations they refused to surrender. On 20th October the sultan ordered the attack to which the beseiged attempted to reply. However, on the intervention of the patriarch Heraclius who saw the city going to its ruin, Balian d'Ibelin solicited

an interview with Saladin: 'We shall kill our sons and wives, we shall set fire to the city, we shall slaughter five thousand Moslem prisoners, then we shall come out in a body and not one of us shall die before having struck down one of your men.' Saladin allowed himself to be swayed by the fierce courage of the baron and consented that the population should ransom itself. 'It was agreed with the Christians that each man in the city, whether rich or poor should pay ten pieces of gold for his ransom; the women five, and the children of both sexes, two. A delay of forty days was accorded for the payment of this tribute', reports a Saracen witness.

The avarice of the Templars limited the number of freed prisoners to 7,000; in addition Saladin granted freedom to 500 paupers while his brother purchased that of a thousand more. The sultan scrupulously observed his promises, and forbad that the Holy Sepulchre should be touched. Moslem horsemen escorted the crowd of emigrants as far as the ports where Saladin compelled the Genoan and Venetian ships to embark them. When the city had been set in order the sultan made a triumphal entry, his first concern being to restore its sanctuaries to Islam. The golden cross erected on the Dome of the Rock was pulled down and the walls and court washed in rose-water brought from Damascus. The Mosque of el-Aksa was restored to its original purpose and covered with the mosaics which still decorate the dome and *mihrab*. In it was installed the cedar-wood pulpit inlaid with ivory which had been carved at Aleppo on the orders of Nureddin who had destined it for Jerusalem.

The Latin kingdom was lost with the exception of Tyre, and not a single military operation destined to recapture Jerusalem was successful. In the course of the Crusade of 1192 Richard Coeur de Lion achieved considerable success over Saladin who put him in a favourable position to negotiate a compromise peace. The Franks retained the coast of Palestine which they had reconquered and the Christians were to have the right to come freely to Jerusalem on pilgrimage. In 1217 a fifth Crusade attempted to reach Cairo to recover the keys of Jerusalem, and ended in total failure. St Francis of Assisi accompanied it; he landed in Egypt in 1219 and obtained an interview with the sultan. In order to convert him to the Christian faith, he challenged the imam of

The Dome of el-Aksa sumptuously decorated with carved wood and restored in twelfth century by Saladin.

were cries of joy on the (Arab chronicler)

Damietta to pass with him through the flames of a pyre but the Moslem preferred not to undergo the trial. It was in the course of this journey that St Francis, the founder of the Franciscans, the future guardians of the Holy Sepulchre, visited Jerusalem.

Nevertheless the West had not renounced the recapture of the Holy City. The title of King of Jerusalem, which had been preserved despite the disappearance of the kingdom, fell in 1225 to the Emperor of Germany, Frederick II, following his marriage to Isabelle, daughter of Jean de Brienne, and heiress to the kingdom. This match was the work of Pope Honorius III who attempted in this way to give the most powerful sovereign of Europe some personal reason for putting into effect his oath to take the cross, and reconquering Frankish Syria. But Frederick was in no hurry to enter into a war against Islam, a religion in which he showed keen interest. He was a free thinker in advance of his time, a cultured sovereign, and he had a passion for the mathematical sciences to which the Arabs had at that time given their greatest development. It was to al-Kamil, the sultan of Egypt, who was master of Jerusalem and the nephew of Saladin, that he put questions concerning the theory of numbers.

Moreover Frederick made a point of admiring Islam because of his aversion for the Roman Church. Even beneath the pens of Arab Chroniclers, his praises of Moslem society take on the appearance of a malicious satire of the papacy: 'The caliph,' replied an ambassador to Frederick who was questioning him, 'is the descendant of the uncle of our Prophet Mohammed. He received the caliphate from his father and his father from his father before him so that the caliphate has always remained in the family of the Prophet without a break.' 'That's capital,' exclaimed the emperor, 'and far superior to what exists among those idiotic Franks who take an ordinary man completely unrelated to the Messiah as their leader, and turn him into a sort of caliph. This man has no right to such a rank while your caliph, who is related to the Prophet, has every right to it.' At the time when the papacy was enjoining Frederick II to become the leader of the holy war, the sultan al-Kamil was himself sending him an invitation, but as an ally, to defend him against the sultan of Syria, who was threatening him with his bands of Turks.

The second seal of Richard Coeur de Lion, the vanquisher of Saladin's forces in September 1192.

St Francis of Assisi proves the Christian faith by the trial of fire (Sassetta, National Gallery, London).

The strange crusade of Frederick II of Germany, the excommunicated emperor, charms the sultan but rouses Christianity to indignation.

In this delicate situation Frederick temporised and it was not until 1227, after he had been excommunicated, that he decided to embark for the East without people knowing exactly what manner of visit the emperor was going to make to the sultan. Everything went off perfectly and, without having recourse to war, al-Kamil and Frederick signed the treaty of Jaffa in which, each taking care of the interests of the other's subjects, they attempted to lay down a policy of religious toleration. Jerusalem, Bethlehem and Nazareth were restored to the Franks together with a large territorial zone.

At Jerusalem herself a kind of ecclesiastical *condominium* was worked out. The town was declared a holy city for both Christians and Moslems; the Christians regained the Holy Sepulchre while the Moslems kept the Haram Ash-Sharif together with the right to keep an unarmed guard there. Where all disputes were concerned, the Moslem community was placed under the jurisdiction of a resident cadi who acted as an intermediary with the Franks.

Concluded without bloodshed, this settlement appeared unhoped-for, and on 17th March 1229 Frederick made his entry into Jerusalem, which he received from the cadi Chems ed Din, who was representing al-Kamil. The emperor's policy was far from having the support of the Frankish barons, however, for as far as they were concerned he had

Frederick II makes peace with the sultan (fourteenth-century miniature, Vatican Library).

accumulated blunders; nor did it have that of the Templars, who refused to recognise the treaty of Jaffa on the pretext that Frederick was excommunicated. Going even further, the Pope placed an interdict on the city. The coronation ceremony was consequently completely secular and 'it was to the

sound of arms alone' that Frederick himself took the royal crown from the altar of the Holy Sepulchre and placed it on his head. The Teutonic grand master then read a proclamation justifying the emperor's policy. On leaving the the Holy Sepulchre Frederick paid his court at the headquarters of the Hospitallers, then attended to the fortification of the Holy City and gave instructions for the repair of the tower of David and the Gate of St Stephen.

He manifested his desire for religious appeasement by numerous gestures of tolerance, and an Arab historian records one of his remarks which greatly offended: 'My principal purpose in coming to Jerusalem was to hear the Moslems, at the hour of prayer, invoking Allah during the night.' He even reproached the sultan for having forbidden the prayer of the muezzins: 'You are changing your religious rites on my account? What a mistake!'

This way of thinking was too far in advance of its time, and only provoked suspicion among the Franks and even among the Moslems. On 21st March, on the arrival of the patriarch who had been entrusted with the enforcement of the interdict placed upon the town, Frederick left Jerusalem.

Pilgrims before the Holy Sepulchre guarded by the Saracens (fifteenth-century miniature, detail).

A Saracen before the tomb of Christ (fifteenth-century miniature, detail).

The end of the Latin kings. Persecutions commence for both Jews and Christians.

Once Frederick II had departed the Frankish princes expelled his representatives and, assisted by the reinforcements furnished them by a new French Crusade, attacked the Egyptians. The truce was broken: the Crusaders were defeated at Ascalon in 1239. Jerusalem remained open to Christians, however, thanks to the skilful diplomacy of Richard of Cornwall, Frederick's brother-in-law, who in 1240 obtained from the sultan the renewal of the treaty of Jaffa. But prepared to join in any coalition against Egypt, the Franks allied themselves with the sultan of Damascus. Egypt then sent savage bands of Khwarizmian mercenaries against them who sacked Syria and Palestine. On 23rd August 1244, they fell upon Jerusalem, butchered 7,000 Christians including the grand masters of the Templars and Hospitallers, carried the women away into captivity and sacked the city. Three years later the Egyptians got rid of these mercenaries and themselves took control of the city.

The Arabs remained in possession of Jerusalem and Palestine until 1517, and the latter was divided into three *mamlakas* or principalities. The first sultan attempted to restore order. The Christians were given permission to enter the Holy Sepulchre on payment of a tribute. But in 1305, during the reign of al-Nasir, the first discriminatory measures against Jews and Christians made their appearance. They were compelled to wear the turban, yellow for the Jews and blue for the Christians, and were excluded from civil office and employment. This climate of intolerance continued to worsen: all Latin churches posterior to Islam and synagogues were to be pulled down while the economic pressure made itself increasingly felt, and both Jews and Christians began to flee the city. It is said that the Christian merchants used to be shut up in their shops each night while the Moslems used to open in the morning at whatever hour they pleased. A pilgrim declared that he found only two Christian monks in the whole city. For the first time Jerusalem became a predominantly Moslem city endowed with a fairly considerable administrative role. The Mamelukes built centres of Islamic studies, *zawiyets* (monasteries) and *tekiyets* (houses of prayer) or had them repaired. Part of the walls were restored and, within the precinct of the Haram, minarets, marble pulpits and fountains were erected. The arcades which lead up to the Rock and the arches which give access to the Haram date from this period.

In 1452, during the reign of Malik Dhaher Djamak, a violent persecution overtook the remaining Christians. On the order of the sultan, his soldiers laid waste the convents, the buildings on Mount Zion, the Holy Sepulchre and Bethlehem. The Jews, on the other hand, were not treated so badly, and a celebrated court case which lasted for two years between Jews and Moslems shows that justice was done to them.

In 1492, the sultan Bayezid even opened his gates to the Jews expelled from Spain, who came in this way to augment the community at Jerusalem.

All Western attempts to reconquer the holy places during the fourteenth and fifteenth centuries failed. They were motivated essentially by the fear inspired in Christendom by the new infidels, the Ottomans, and their army of janizaries.

Behind the Haram, arches and minarets built by the Mamelukes in the fourteenth century.

Janizaries (wood-cut from Breydenbach's *Sanctae Peregrinationes*, 1488, Condé Museum. Chantilly, France).

The Holy Sepulchre and Arab buildings (fifteenth-century miniature, British Museum, London).

In 1517 Selim the Inflexible seizes the city. For four hundred years the Sublime Porte will administer Palestine.

In the sixteenth century the expansion of the Ottoman Empire extended to Syria and Egypt. In 1517 Selim I, the Inflexible, seized Jerusalem and Cairo. The Holy City became Turkish for four hundred years, up to World War I. The Sublime Porte, as the Ottoman government was called, carried out for half a century a beneficial administrative task, after the ruinous Egyptian domination. A province of the Ottoman Empire, the 'Pashalic' of Palestine had as its administrative capital sometimes Jerusalem and sometimes Gaza. With peace restored a revival of the traditional agriculture was made possible and olive-oil manufacturers were set up at Jerusalem.

It was at this period that a Spanish officer, Ignatius Loyola, made a pilgrimage to the Holy Land which determined his vocation. Abandoning henceforth the military life for the convent, he devoted himself to the study of philosophy and theology. With six of his disciples he made a vow to dedicate himself to the conversion of the infidels and founded the order of the Jesuits.

Suleiman II, the Magnificent, who reigned from 1520 to 1566, paid particular attention to the improvement of the city. He increased its supply of drinking water by repairing the aqueducts and erecting fountains, and overhauled the fortifications. The present walls, together with the Damascus Gate and the tower of David, date from this period. Important restorations and improvements were carried out to the Haram Ash-Sharif. Suleiman had the exterior walls of the Dome of the Rock covered with marble and mosaics and pierced sixteen windows in the drum of the dome which were set with gilded glass. Persian faiences covered the north door of the Kubbet es-Sakhrah and the *mihrab* of the Dome of the Chain. A plaque commemorated these works: 'In the reign of the great sultan and highly honoured . . . Suleiman khan, . . . was restored the dome of the mosque of the Rock, at Jerusalem the majestic.'

As a reult of the agreements made in 1535 between France and the Sublime Porte, which gave the French fleet a monopoly of maritime trade, the situation of the Latin Church in Palestine was considerably improved. The Franciscans, who had been expelled from the Cenaculum and transferred to the monastery of St Saviour, managed to secure rights to the church of the Holy Sepulchre, in preference to all the Eastern churches. In 1555 Charles V and his son Philip II obtained permission to rebuild the chapel of the Holy

Ottoman characters, veiled woman and men-at-arms (wood-engraving from Breydenbach's *Sanctae Peregrinationes*, 1488).

246

St Ignatius Loyola (Zurbaran, château de Saint-Landry, France).

Suleiman II, the Magnificent (1520–1566) (Topkapi Museum, Constantinople).

Sepulchre which became a Latin possession from then on. A bitter struggle broke out with the Eastern churches. For their part the Turkish authorities desired the continuation of pilgrimages, which were a source of profit, and that of the conflicts between the churches which enabled them, by playing off one church against another, to secure considerable revenues from that source also. The bringing together of the patriarchates of Jerusalem and Constantinople under the same authority was to increase the rift between Greeks and Latins.

It was at this period that the first Protestant pilgrims made their appearance and were received, it should be added, by the Franciscans, as well as the others. At the beginning of the seventeenth century it was the turn of the Russian Orthodox Church, which provided the Georgians with the means to acquire rights. This race for the holy places was to continue throughout the following centuries while the indolence of the sultans of Constantinople and the corruption of the civil servants prevented any development of Palestine and created a permanent climate of insecurity.

Detail of the mosaics on the outside of the Dome of the Rock, decorated by Suleiman in the sixteenth century.

An unstable equilibrium is gradually established between the religious

The Kidron valley road, on the south-east of Jerusalem, at the time of the Turkish occupation (fifteenth-century engraving).

The results of the Turkish occupation in Palestine, with the exception of the few years of Suleiman's reign, were negative in many respects. All authorities are in agreement over the rapid decline of the administration, and without going so far as to declare that 'the Turks were completely ignorant of architecture', it is not possible to find a single building at Jerusalem which gives evidence of any particular originality. On the whole the Turks confined themselves to the restoration of ancient monuments and it was among Hellenistic, Roman, Byzantine and, above all, Arab buildings that the turbaned throng of the sultan's subjects strolled. Only the walls provide a lasting, but not very original, example of military architecture. The Damascus Gate is certainly one of the most interesting parts of it and has remained intact throughout the centuries, preserving an appearance close to the period of its construction.

In a very different field, however, the Turks brought with them a spirit that the Europe of the same period could envy. With few exceptions they were relatively tolerant to the Jews, and in this way attracted a large number of those who had been expelled from Christian countries. The influence wielded by the Duke of Naxos at the court of Suleiman the Magnificent was one of the reasons for this. Having openly reverted to his original religion, the duke dreamed of establishing a Jewish state in a small territory that the sultan had given him along Lake Tiberias. He did not carry out this project, but his co-religionists enjoyed a freedom which enabled them to establish flourishing communities in a number of towns in Palestine. They settled at Jerusalem just when the decline of the central authority was giving rise to certain fears. A synagogue was built, attributed to Johanan Ben Zakkai. It became one of the most famous, together with that of the Hourva, erected in 1743 by Rabbi Juda Ha Hassid, which was destroyed twenty years later and restored

communities: Christians and Jews, pilgrims and immigrants mingle with the sultan's subjects.

in 1820, only to disappear in 1948 during the fierce fighting which took place in the old city. A whole climate of Messianic expectations developed which encouraged the immigration of Jews who were being maltreated in Europe. A broad current of mysticism made its appearance with the Cabbala, of which Safed, in Galilee, was one of the most important centres. Isaac Luria Levi, one of the most celebrated of the cabbalists, was born at Jerusalem in 1534.

The middle of the seventeenth century saw the irruption of the most celebrated of the false messiahs, Sabbatai Zebi. Accumulating proofs of his mission and charming crowds and heads of communities alike, he set in motion a wave of migration. The Jews of Europe, convinced that the Messiah had come, sold their possessions in order to set out for the Holy Land in their thousands.

The epic of the pseudo-Messiah ended ignominiously however . . . with the conversion of Sabbatia to Islam. Many of his disciples also became converted at the same time, convinced that this conversion was a necessary stage before the proclamation of his glory; the 'Donmehs' are their descendants.

Although they were supported by the central administration, the Jews were nevertheless subjected to the arbitrariness of the governors of the city. Having few possibilities for earning a living, those who lived at Jerusalem and had come there, for the most part, in order to pray, study and die, had to count on the assistance of the Jewish communities. Emissaries regularly set out for abroad to collect funds which were then divided amongst the various synagogues of the Holy City and the Talmudic schools. This was called the 'Halukah' or distribution. This rather moving fidelity to Jerusalem created a foundation upon which Zionism was to rely later.

The end of the eighteenth century ushered in a new phase of European interest in Palestine, this time of a purely political nature. The conflicts between the great powers came to a head in this area of the globe. One of which was to be Napoleon's abortive expedition. Having arrived at Jaffa he appealed to the Jews to fight at his side. But compelled to evacuate his positions by the fleet of the pasha Ahmed el-Djezzar, who was supported by the English, he was unable to reach Jerusalem.

The Damascus Gate, on the north of the city, built in 1537 (photograph by Bonfils, 1877)

The Damascus Gate in its present state with the bustle of the inhabitants and tourists.

6 DIVISIONS AND REUNIONS

Jerusalem of the Israelis and the Jordanians

For Jerusalem's sake I will not rest, until her vindication goes forth as brightness, and her salvation as a burning torch.

_____

You shall be a crown of beauty in the hand of the Lord, and a royal diadem in the hand of your God.
You shall no more be termed Forsaken, and your land shall no more be termed Desolate; but you shall be called Hephzibah (my delight is in her), and your land Beulah (married) . . .

Isaiah LXII. 1, 3-4

Prospect of the city in the nineteenth century.

The romantic century, but Jerusalem, a 'city of desolations in the midst of desolate solitude', disappoints her pilgrims.

François René de Chateaubriand (1768–1848).

Alphonse de Lamartine (1790–1869).

The anarchy which had progressively invaded the Ottoman Empire reached its peak at the beginning of the nineteenth century and brought about the ruin of the small towns subjected to the arbitrariness of governors who were practically independent. Jerusalem, which theoretically belonged to the pasha of Damascus, was in fact cut off from her administrative capital. The road from one city to the other was dangerous and infested with brigands. It was impossible for an inhabitant of Jerusalem to go to Damascus to seek help against the injustices and exactions of the administration or the cruelty of the janizaries without risking his life. Even if he succeeded there, he only came up against the complicity of officials who, at all levels, were exploiting their privileged position as occupiers and enriching themselves to the detriment of the population. The pasha, also corrupt, generally became the man most to be feared in the country he administered. In these conditions Jerusalem suffered an eclipse. The population declined, became impoverished and retired within itself, living in fear and discouraging visitors.

Chateaubriand ventured there in 1806, his 'pistol at the ready', in order to defend himself against the bandits. What drew him to these dangerous parts? He came to 'seek impressions' for the Christian epic which he was to call *Les Martyrs*, and for a 'Journey from Paris to Jerusalem' which was singularly lacking in enthusiasm.

'The houses of Jerusalem are heavy square blocks, very low, without chimneys or windows . . . which resemble prisons or sepulchres. On seeing these stone houses set in a stone landscape, one might wonder whether they are not the disordered monuments of a cemetery in the midst of a desert! Go into the city, nothing will console you for the bleakness outside. You lose your way in little unpaved streets which rise and fall over the uneven ground, and walk along in clouds of dust, or over loose pebbles. Awnings slung between the houses increase the obscurity of this labyrinth while noisome vaulted bazaars succeed in taking away the last light from the desolate city. A few wretched shops display only poverty to one's gaze, and frequently these shops are closed in the fear that a cadi will pass by. There is no one in the streets, no one at the gates of the city, except that from time to time a peasant glides along in the shadows, hiding beneath his clothes the fruits of his toil in the fear of being robbed by the soldiery. In a distant corner an Arab butcher cuts the throat of some beast or other suspended by its feet from a tumble-down wall . . . the only sound heard in the city is the occasional galloping of a desert mare; it is a janizary bringing back the head of a bedouin or going to plunder a fellah . . .

'. . . Let us turn now to the particulars of the streets: haret bab el-Amud, the street of the gate of the column, traverses the city from north to south; suk el-Kebiz, the street of the great bazaar, runs from west to east; haret el-Alam, the via dolorosa . . . One then comes across seven other little streets: haret el-Musmin, the street of the Turks, haret en-Nasara, the street of the Christians . . . haret el Asman, the street of the Armenians, to the east of the castle; haret el Yud, the streets of the Jews; the city's butchers' shops are in this street; haret bab Hotta, the street near the Temple and haret el-Zahara. My dragoman . . . used to assure me that the rebels and wrong-doers lived in this street . . . haret el-Mugharibeh, the street of the Mohgrebins . . .' Twenty years after the author of the *Martyrs*, Lamartine came to Jerusalem to draw his inspiration for *Jocelyn*, but contented himself with a very brief visit. In 1831, knowing that Turkey, already weakened by the Serbian crisis and the Greek war of independence, was incapable of resisting him, Mehemet Ali, the pasha of Egypt, invaded Syria and turned Jerusalem into the capital of the province. Ibrahim Pasha, his son, then provoked a peasants' revolt by attempting to impose compulsory military service. The peasants managed to enter the city through the conduits that carried the water inside the walls, and seized the citadel.

With the help of the great powers, and in spite of their military inferiority, the Turks recovered their territory in 1840. The sultan Abdul Mejid gave guarantees for the lives and possessions of the occupied populations, but these remained a dead letter, and the 'infidels' rapidly became the object of discriminatory measures. The Jews were forbidden to buy land or build synagogues. In the face of a new outburst of brigandage they no longer dared go outside the walls.

Under Turkish rule Jerusalem slumbers in her poverty. Vegetation has invaded the medieval buildings of Hezekiah's reservoir.

Several years have passed, the Turks are still in power and the reservoir is now merely a shapeless pit abandoned and filled with earth and rubble.

Quarrels for the custody of the holy places. The Christian communities wage

The situation improved towards the middle of the nineteenth century. The strengthening of the sultan's personal position enabled him to appoint better administrators. Abuses were suppressed and brigandage combatted by the army so that the caravans conveying goods and merchandise henceforth reached Jerusalem without let or hindrance.

The great European powers showed a growing interest in what was called the 'Eastern Question', and Jerusalem became one of the spots where the various foreign influences came face to face. The installation of consuls, who until then had lived at Saint John of Acre because of the disturbances in the country, showed the desire of the great powers to take part in Eastern affairs. The British installed themselves in 1839, France, Prussia and Sardinia in 1843, soon followed by the United States, in 1844, then by Russia, Austria and Spain. The presence of foreign consulates provided safeguards for the various religious, social and cultural groups which comprised European elements, but rapidly aggravated the conflicts over the custody of the holy places and the Holy Sepulchre. France, responsible for the protection of the Latins, came to the assistance of the Franciscans who saw their rights being threatened by the Greeks. Russia opposed the decisions of the Turkish government, about to give satisfaction France, and set herself up as the protector of the Orthodox Church.

A firman from the sultan, dated 1852 and addressed to the governor of Jerusalem, defined the division of the holy places as it still exists today, distinguishing, in the Holy Sepulchre, those parts common to all Christians and those that belonged more especially to one confession or another. The Sepulchre,

Beneath the rotunda, the nineteenth-century chapel of the Sepulchre.

Faithful from the various Christian confessions around the Sepulchre.

a minor war amongst themselves which is exploited by the European powers.

the Chapel of the Angel and the Stone of Unction constitute the parts held in common, and from hour to hour one sees pilgrims and delegations of all confessions following in each other's steps. Calvary is divided into two parts; the northern part belongs to the Greeks and the southeastern part, with the chapel of Golgotha and the altar of the Crucifixion, to the Latins. Each of them has a choir, the choir of the Greeks and the choir of the Latins, while the Armenians occupy the chapels of the Parting of the Raiment and the Invention (discovery) of the Cross. The Copts and

Syrians also obtained a chapel each. To cite only one example of the violence of the disputes between the various congregations, the number and disposition of the lamps in the various sanctuaries has to be strictly regulated. Out of a total of 360, 170 are allocated to the Orthodox Church, 94 to the Roman Catholics, 77 to the Armenians and 18 to the Copts. Each of the communities still keeps its position today.

The division of the basilica of the Holy Sepulchre between the confessions is so complicated that one never knows if one is amongst the Latins, the Greeks,

the Maronites or the Armenians. If the English had not erected a scaffolding during World War II the dome of the basilica would have collapsed already. At the time of his visit in 1964, Pope Paul VI had to make his way past heaps of rubble, since the religious authorities responsible had been unable to arrive at an agreement so as to proceed to the necessary repairs. But since that visit a new desire for co-operation has appeared among all the communities so that the Holy Sepulchre may be restored to its original appearance and saved from ruin at least.

The so-called chapel of the Angel in front of the Holy Sepulchre.

The altar of the chapel of Golgotha, of the Latin rite, on the south-east of Calvary.

Moslem prayers in the Mosque of Omar (nineteenth-century lithograph).

The Church of St Mary Magdalene, built by Tsar Alexander III.

Crowning the Mount of Olives, the tall square tower of the Russian convent is a focal point from the hill-tops of Judaea and Jordan.

Arabs, Jews and Christians live side by side without merging with one another. With the influx of pilgrims and religious communities the city returns to life.

Far from having a calming effect, the firman of 1852 set in motion intense diplomatic activity. French and Russian embassies to the sultan followed on one another's heels. Napoleon III tried in vain to dissociate the conflict over the holy places from that resulting from Russian ambitions to rule the Dardanelles. In 1854 the Crimean War broke out. Jerusalem, which was its pretext, suffered little from it. On the contrary, the conflicts over the Holy Sepulchre brought all kinds of advantages to the city and a new influx of pilgrims and travellers.

At the same time the Turkish government accorded to certain rabbis the right of representing their co-religionists of the same nationality. A great rabbi, Sepharadi, was given responsibility for the Jews of the Mediterranean basin, while another rabbi looked after the Russians and Austrians. With an increased sense of security the various communities built residential districts. The Jewish revival was marked by building of synagogues and the foundation of a Hebrew hospital and infirmary.

Round about 1850 the total population of Jerusalem did not exceed 15,000: 2,000 Christians, 6 to 7,000 Jews and almost as many Moslems.

The old city still retained its strict divisions: to the south, the Arab quarter with the Mosque of Omar which had been restored under the Ottomans on several occasions; to the south-west, the Jewish quarter with its synagogues, and the Armenian quarter round the convent of the church of St James. Finally, to the north-east, the Christian quarter, The whole of the old city was surrounded by the strong wall rebuilt by Suleiman the Magnificent. The Sublime Porte appointed each pasha or governor of the city for a period of one year only for fear that, having become too well ensconced in the city and in their functions, they would revolt. The pashas consequently turned this very short period to their advantage so as to make their fortune and exploit the subject population. All economic development consequently remained impossible just when Europe was undergoing the great industrial and financial explosion of the nineteenth century.

The Christians drew their resources from their religious institutions. The Moslems traded in spices, cereals and imported cotton goods, or manufactured oil and soap. The Jews were craftsmen or pedlars. The communities depended on one another: the Jews manufactured articles which they exchanged for agricultural produce sold them by the Arabs. Twice a year the merchants went to Beirut to make their purchases for the season.

The presence of foreign consuls encouraged the growth of the population. The city numbered 36,000 inhabitants in 1874: 11 per cent of them Christians, 36 per cent Jews and the rest Moslem.

Christian pilgrims also became more and more numerous and, from 1870 onwards, the Templars founded establishments to accommodate them. The Christian communities maintained and administered convents and monasteries, and in this way the American, Greek and Armenian colonies came into being. The Russians built what was known as the Russian Enclosure with the church of St Mary Magdalene and its convents on a former Turkish army parade-ground. On the Mount of Olives rose the tall tower of the convent from which pilgrims could gaze upon the Jordan which they sometimes no longer had the courage to reach. The aims of the Christian institutions were varied, and ranged from archaeology to the propagation of their faith. The Queen of England and the King of Prussia together founded an Anglo-Prussian mission, which ended by becoming entirely Anglican, and built St George's cathedral on the road from Jerusalem to Nablus. A Jewish convert to Catholicism, called Ratisbonne, founded the institution and convent of Notre Dame de Sion which was directed in particular towards the conversion of Jews. It was at this period also that were built the hospice and church of Notre Dame de France which were seriously damaged during the Arab-Jewish war, but are once again able to receive pilgrims today.

The hospice of Notre Dame de France, with a military guard, stands at the limit of the old city.

A longing for Zion brings back to the Wailing Wall the pious Jews from all

For centuries the Jews have come to weep before the sole vestige of the power of Jerusalem: the Wailing Wall (photograph of 1877).

over the world who, for thousands of years, have bewailed the destruction of the Temple.

Archaeological excavations multiplied. In 1838 Edward Robinson had already embarked on researches on the third surrounding wall, that known as Agrippa's wall. In 1850–51 and 1863, F. de Saulcey brought to light what have since been called the Tombs of the Kings. Founded in 1865, the Palestine Exploration fund enabled Charles Warren to start his excavations right in Jerusalem. He laid the foundations of all later archaeological work, despite the mistakes made at the outset. Warren dated, for example, the subfoundations of the Temple to the period of Solomon, while in reality they only date from that oe Herod. Captain Charles Wilson identified the arch which now bears his name. The French archaeologist Charles Clermont-Ganneau, who was in the consular service at Jerusalem, made discoveries which revolutionised Palestinian archaeology. In 1870 the Palestine Exploration Society was founded, and from then on digs took place every year, conducted by Guthe (1881), Maudsley (1884) and the Dominicans of St Stephen.

Jewish pilgrims also flocked there. At first they lived on the 'Halukkah', the distribution of the funds collected abroad, but as the Jewish population increased it came to exercise more and more different callings and began to play a much larger part in the economy of the city.

The first school which could be termed modern was founded in 1856; this was the Lämel school. Then the Anglo-Jewish Association founded the Evelyne de Rothschild school and the *Alliance israelite universelle* introduced the French element. Founded in 1860, the *Alliance* had as its object the raising of the moral and intellectual level of the Jews, particularly of the Jews of the Middle East and North Africa. In 1869 it founded the first school of agriculture in Palestine, Mikveh Israel, at which thousands of young immigrants have been trained. With the influx of arrivals the first agricultural communities were being founded, but in the midst of this activity the pious Jews assembled near the mosque, at the foot of the Wailing Wall which constituted a subfoundation to the Temple and was the last vestige of Herod's *enceinte*. They came to bewail the loss of their independence and the destruction of the first and second Temples.

Old Hebrew inscriptions cut in the massive stones of the Wailing Wall.

Old men weeping and praying before the remains of Herod's surrounding wall (photograph of 1912).

From twenty-four countries the Jews flock to Jerusalem, each one bringing his customs and his rites: new and traditional communities spring up.

The Montefiore district—one of the first to be built outside the walls—with its picturesque mill.

A new city began to rise outside the traditional walls that encircled the old city. Sir Moses Montefiore created entire suburbs and encouraged the establishment of productive activities. The most enterprising members of the Jewish community became farmers and began planting vineyards and olive-groves at Motza.

In 1939 Sir Moses Montefiore, the precursor of Zionism, noted in his diary: 'It is a country which could produce almost everything in abundance with very little technical knowledge or labour. If the plan which I contemplate is realised, I am certain that it will be the means of bringing happiness and prosperity to the Holy Land.'

The founding of the first suburb of 'peaceful residences' *(mishkenoth shaananim)*, with Montefiore's impulse, was a revolution. Houses were built along the Jaffa road and they now constitute the oldest quarter of modern Jerusalem: Nahlath shiva, the 'foundation of the seven'. A group of about a hundred families followed this example and created a new district with numerous houses linked by inner courtyards: this is Mea shearim (the hundredfold or the hundred gates), now the district of the ultra orthodox Jews and the *natore karta* (guardians of the city), a sect which does not recognise the secular State of Israel and is awaiting the coming of the Messiah to restore the splendour of David.

The quaint district of Mea shearim, where Isaac sowed and received an hundredfold *(mea shearim)*.

Street of Mea shearim, a stronghold of orthodoxy.

The feast of Purim in the Mea shearim district.

'If this novel does not become action, action can become a novel. Its title: The Promised Land.' Theodor Herzl.

The Emperor Wilhelm II's entry into Jerusalem in 1898 gave rise to anxiety among the inhabitants.

Theodor Herzl, founder of the Zionist movement.

The house where Herzl had a room.

Prominent European figures made pilgrimages to the holy places, stage-managed so as to impress the inhabitants of the city and create a climate favourable to the illustrious pilgrims' native land. A road was prepared for the first of them, the Emperor Franz Joseph (1864), who halted at Jerusalem before going on to attend the opening of the Suez canal.

A few years later Prince Friedrich Wilhelm, the heir apparent of Prussia, visited the city; in 1898 it was the turn of his son Wilhelm II. The German emperor wished to make his entry on a white stallion. According to an old legend, Jerusalem would be conquered by the emperor who passed through one of its gates on horseback. In order to calm the anxieties of the inhabitants, a breach was made in the wall. The emperor was satisfied; he was entering the city on horseback: the inhabitants were reassured; he was not doing so by one of its gates.

This visit made possible a meeting which had historic consequences. The previous year a Jewish journalist from Vienna, Theodor Herzl, had founded the Zionist movement for the creation of a Jewish state and had called together the first Zionist Congress at Basle: 'I have just created the Jewish State', he noted in his diary. 'In five years perhaps, certainly in fifty, everyone will understand this.' Herzl had undertaken to win the principal European heads of state over to the cause of Zionism. Although Palestine was a province of the Ottoman Empire, Herzl was thoroughly aware that the support of the Emperor of Germany would be important, and he left no stone unturned in order to meet him. In Palestine, at Mikveh Israel, on the road from Jaffa to Jerusalem, the Kaiser met a Zionist delegation; he met it a second time at Jerusalem where Theodor Herzl was waiting for him. Although he made no promises and his statements to Herzl were somewhat vague, the very fact that he had agreed to discuss the future of a Jewish state in Palestine gave great international prestige to the Zionist movement and its leader.

The Kaiser's visit was also the occasion of the construction of a large Lutheran church on Mount Muristan. Another church, the church of the Dormition, was built between 1900 and 1910 on a plot of land presented by Wilhelm II to the German Catholic Society of the

The Church of the Dormition, on the hill of Mount Zion, built between 1900 and 1910 by the German Catholic Society of the Holy Land.

Holy Land at the spot where Mary is said to have fallen asleep for the last time. The first banks also made their appearance. In 1892 the French Crédit Lyonnais opened a branch. In 1904 the Anglo-Palestine Bank was founded. The railway from Jaffa to Jerusalem, completed in 1892, was another revolutionary development. Its promoter, Joseph Navon, the leader of the Jewish community, gave the work to a French company.

At the census of 1912 there were 72,000 inhabitants, of whom 64·4 per cent were Jews, 22·2 per cent Christians, and 13·4 per cent Moslems. The growth of the Zionist movement and the immigration of the Zionist pioneers had already put their mark on the old city. Kindergartens, secondary schools, teachers' training colleges, a school of fine art and the Bezalel museum, founded by Boris Schatz, contributed to the development of cultural life. Having settled at Jerusalem, Eliezer Ben Yehuda did much to promote the revival of the Hebrew language.

The peaceful little station of Jerusalem today serves only Tel Aviv and Haifa.

'His Majesty's Government view with favour the establishment in Palestine of a national home for the Jewish people . . .' (November 1917)

In October 1914 Turkey entered the war on the side of the Axis. A difficult period commenced. Many of the city's inhabitants, who originated from countries hostile to Turkey, were expelled. Others were forcibly drafted into the Turkish army or the labour corps. All Zionist activities were forbidden because the movement had aligned itself with the Allies. The passage or presence of armies, requisitions, and the absence of links with the outside world weighed upon the economy. The supply lines were cut, and the Turkish currency lost ninety per cent of its value. As a crowning misfortune, plagues of locusts destroyed almost all the crops.

For three years the population of Jerusalem endured great sufferings. The German officers on the staff of the Turkish commanders of the garrison were powerless to calm them. Once more poverty and despair reappeared in the place they had occupied for so long.

But the Zionist movement had undergone considerable development during these same three years. In November 1917 the British Government, in the person of its foreign minister, Lord Balfour, accepted the principle of a Jewish national home in Palestine. This declaration, which was communicated to Lord Rothschild, was obtained through a Russian chemist employed by the British Navy who had just rendered an invaluable service to the Allies: the discovery of the formula of synthetic acetone indispensable in the manufacture of explosives. This chemist, Chaim Weizmann, became the leader of the Zionists of Zion movement which was opposed to the scheme — accepted by Herzl — to establish a Jewish state in Uganda. For Weizmann a Jewish state could only come into existence in the land of Israel, in Palestine. One day he was to be the first president of the State of Israel.

Supported by France and the Allies of Great Britain, the Balfour declaration stated that 'His Majesty's Government view with favour the establishment in Palestine of a national home for the Jewish people, and will use their best endeavours to facilitate the achievement of this object, it being clearly understood that nothing shall be done which may prejudice the civil and religious rights of existing non-Jewish communities in Palestine, or the rights and political status enjoyed by Jews in any other country.' One month later, in December 1917, General Allenby drove out the Turkish armies and reached Jerusalem. For the first time since the Crusades a non-Moslem army entered the Holy City. Nevertheless on that historic day the Vatican refused to have the bells of the churches of Christendom rung, for fear of offending the Sublime Porte.

Alongside the British soldiers were units of the Jewish Legion composed of volunteers who had enlisted on the Allied side and who were fighting for the liberation of Palestine. Among these volunteers was a corporal: David Ben-Gurion. 'An extraordinary period, filled with an exhilarating joy . . . We were free, free of the Turks, completely free. We believed that the Jewish state was already in existence because that was how we had interpreted the Balfour declaration' recounts a contemporary, Joseph Baratz. The city naturally became the centre of the new administration of Palestine. In 1922 the League of Nations gave Great Britain a mandate over Palestine, with a mission to carry out the promises contained in the Balfour declaration. Jerusalem regained her rank of capital, but a long and very arduous path had still to be travelled.

Djemal Pasha, the Turkish politician and general, surrounded by German officers in 1917.

Foreign Office,
November 2nd, 1917.

Dear Lord Rothschild,

I have much pleasure in conveying to you, on behalf of His Majesty's Government, the following declaration of sympathy with Jewish Zionist aspirations which has been submitted to, and approved by, the Cabinet.

"His Majesty's Government view with favour the establishment in Palestine of a national home for the Jewish people, and will use their best endeavours to facilitate the achievement of this object, it being clearly understood that nothing shall be done which may prejudice the civil and religious rights of existing non-Jewish communities in Palestine, or the rights and political status enjoyed by Jews in any other country".

I should be grateful if you would bring this declaration to the knowledge of the Zionist Federation.

Lord Balfour's declaration of 1917.

General Allenby, the Commander-in-Chief of the British forces in Palestine, is ceremonially received at the entrance to the city in December 1917.

The victorious English troops. For the first time since the Crusades a non-Moslem army entered the Holy City.

'Palestine was a different country from what it had been under Turkish rule, efforts. We were no longer isolated, dreaming of a Utopia in which nobody

Laying of the foundation stone of the Hebrew University, on Mount Scopus, opened in April 1925.

It is significant that one of the first acts decided upon by the Jewish authorities in Palestine, as early as 1925, should be the foundation of a Hebrew university on Mount Scopus. The first British High Commissioner for Palestine, Sir Herbert Samuel, attended its inauguration. Later Winston Churchill, secretary to the Colonial Office, himself planted a tree at the foot of the buildings. The empires which had brought about the destruction of Jerusalem no longer existed, and Hebrew became a living language again. At Jerusalem, as a preparation for its return to its ancestral land, the Jewish people opened a university in which was taught the language which had been its own in this same country, close on two thousand years before. A new era began for Jerusalem, which rose again from her ruins for the seventeenth time. On the administrative, cultural, social and economic planes, she soon became the most important city in the country once more. Outside the limits of the old city suburbs were built. For the first time in their history the inhabitants of Jerusalem had running water. Then came electricity and buses; the city was becoming modernised. In the approach corridor, through the mountains of Judaea, the Jewish pioneers created an agricultural

Winston Churchill planting a commemorative tree.

The return of the scrolls of the Law in 1918 gives back to the city its role as a religious capital.

when stagnation and corruption were like quicksands which stifled all our believed except ourselves— we were recognised at last.' (Joseph Baratz)

hinterland so that the city could be provisioned from near-by agricultural centres. The installation of the offices of the Chief Rabbinate, together with those of the Grand Mufti, confirmed the spiritual and religious supremacy of Jerusalem. The educational system and health services were developed and on Mount Scopus, the bold architecture of the Hadassah hospital became part of the city landscape.

Archaeological researches underwent a rapid extension. The British authorities created a department of antiquities, while the university opened a department of archaeology. Excavations undertaken in 1923 and 1928 on the site of the hill of Ophel made possible the exact location of the centre of the City of David. The American School of Oriental Research brought to light the site of the Biblical Mizpah, to the north of Jerusalem, and another group of scholars identified Bethel and Ai. The first major excavation conducted by Professor Sukenik—who became a specialist of the first rank in the identification of the Dead Sea scrolls —and Professor Mayer, for the Department of Archaeology of the Hebrew University, concerned the line of the third surrounding wall. The areas around the walls of the city were tidied up and building in the vicinity was controlled. Special measures were also taken to preserve the Valley of Kidron.

The residential quarters clung to their Jewish or Arab characters, almost as if preparing for the division of the city. In 1924 the village of Ramat Rachel was founded, a kibbutz close to the city, which was to play a role of the utmost importance in 1948 in the defence of Jerusalem. The modern quarters of Beit Hakerem, Talpiot and Rehaviya came into being one after another. In 1931 Jerusalem numbered 93,118 inhabitants, of whom 57·7 per cent were Jews, 21·4 per cent Moslems and the rest Christians. In 1946, out of a population of 164,440 inhabitants, more than 100,000 were Jews, originating in equal parts from the countries of central Europe and those of the Mediterranean basin, and known respectively as *ashkenazim* and *sephardim*. 'The camps are full of shortcomings', wrote Henrietta Szold, the founder of one of the most important Zionist associations, the Hadassah, 'the workers are full of them also, but taken all round the movement has something miraculous about it.'

The buildings of the Hadassah medical centre on Mount Scopus (now abandoned).

The faculty of letters of the university on Mount Scopus. In the background, the Weizmann school of chemistry.

Sir Herbert Samuel, British High Commissioner from July 1920, with the heads of the principal religious communities of the city.

Arab demonstrations in August 1928 against the measures of Hospitality accorded to Jews.

The Grand Mufti, leader of the Moslems.

1939: the thunderbolt of the White Paper causes a storm. 'We shall never agree! We demand immigration, unlimited immigration!'

The growth of the city was imperilled by the disturbances which broke out on several occasions: in 1920, 1928 and 1936–39. In 1920 the disturbances had as their foundation the crowning of the emir Feisal as King of Syria. Although Feisal had officially supported the Zionist point of view in a celebrated meeting with President Weizmann, the Arabs of Jaffa and Jerusalem started riots with cries of: 'Long live King Feisal', which produced casualties among both the Jews and the Arabs. The British forces directed all their efforts against the Jewish groups of self-defence, thus initiating a policy which was to cause greater and greater bitterness among the Jewish community. The first British High Commissioner, Sir Herbert Samuel, although himself a Jew, was surrounded by officials who were hostile to Zionism and the appointment to the position of Grand Mufti of Jerusalem of Hadj Amin el-Hussein, who was known for his intransigence, only increased the doubts of the Jewish authorities concerning the good intentions of the mandatory power.

In 1928 disturbances broke out over the rights of the Jews over their most sacred holy place: the Wailing Wall. This wall belonged to the Moslems but the Jews had always been allowed to come and pray unmolested. In 1928, however, the police removed a screen which, in accordance with tradition, was intended to separate the men from the women, on the pretext that the Jews were exceeding their rights. This incident roused the Jews even more profoundly in as much as it was followed by other acts of provocation and by an Arab campaign which inflamed religious hatreds. In August, stirred up by agitators, the Moslem crowd overran the new quarters of Jerusalem, looting and massacring without the police being able to take effective action. It was a week before the arrival of reinforcements from Egypt and a return to order.

In 1936 the policy of capitulation of the western powers in the face of Nazi provocations and successes put people into an acute state of alarm and gave the revolt a national character. Over the next three years disturbances broke out ceaselessly in Palestine, and at Jerusalem in particular. The British decided to send a commission headed by Lord Peel to study the situation there and take steps for the future.

The commission proposed the partition of Palestine: certain regions, including Bethlehem and Jerusalem, would remain under British control. The very people who were inclined to accept the scheme were compelled to refuse it when it was complemented by the White Paper of the Macdonald government, limiting Jewish immigration at the precise moment when, fleeing the rising tide of Nazism, the Jewish population of Europe was most desperately in need of refuge.

During World War II the Jews, preoccupied above all with the defeat of Hitler, relegated their bitterness against the British Government to second place, but not before stating, quite categorically, in the words of David Ben-Gurion: 'We shall fight against Germany as if there were no White Paper, and we shall fight against the White Paper as if there were no war against Germany.' In fact many Jewish volunteers enlisted in the ranks of the British Army. Despite the ill-will of the War Office, and thanks to a decision taken by Churchill himself, they formed a Jewish brigade, the Hayil, or Jewish Combat Force, which had as its flag the star of David and took part in the principal battles on the western front, in the African desert and in Italy. During this period the Grand Mufti of Jerusalem was recruiting Moslem volunteers to fight on the side of the Axis, and having himself photographed with the Führer at Berlin.

Jerusalem took on a more international character than ever with troops and officers of so many countries. Now an important administrative centre of the Middle East, the town developed rapidly. But the whole story of the British mandate was that of the confrontation of the conflicting interests of the English, Arabs and Jews. The disturbances continued to increase in violence, and the English troops were sometimes forced to supply certain beleaguered districts with food.

The relations between the Jewish community and the British authorities were becoming increasingly strained. In protest against British policy, the Zionist movement organised a meeting in New York, at the Biltmore Hotel, in the course of which it proclaimed the Zionist determination to obtain a sovereign and independent Jewish state.

A convoy of English supplies is distributed to the population of the Jewish zone during the disturbances.

On 22nd July 1946 a wing of the King David Hotel, the British headquarters, was blown up.

The British administration. In spite of a telephone call announcing the imminence of the explosion, the British authorities forbad the evacuation of the offices. The result was more than ninety casualties: Christian, Jewish and Moslem. The outrage was condemned by the Zionist authorities but the British general, Sir Evelyn Barker, commander of the forces of occupation, gave vent to his anti-Semetic feelings and proclaimed that the Jewish community in Palestine should be punished 'in the manner which it dreads the most: by attacking its purse'. This profession of faith shocked members of the Attlee Cabinet, and General Barker was transferred. Reprisals, counter-reprisals and outrages multiplied. The British were no longer able to maintain order. They shut themselves up behind barbed wire entanglements in the administrarive quarter of Jerusalem, which they fortified and the population called derisively Bevingrad.

Meanwhile the transports of 'illegal immigrants' continued. When they were intercepted by the British Navy these clandestine immigrants were sent to camps and then deported to Cyprus. The epic of the *Exodus* was to bring the attention of the whole world to this affair and its repression. Curfews, shootings and outrages increased. The situation in Palestine was becoming unbearable; the problem had become international. The United Nations was asked to intervene and a Commission U.N.S.C.O.P. (the United Nations Special Commission on Palestine), with representatives from eleven countries, was appointed to study the situation and find a remedy for it. It recommended to the United Nations the partition of Palestine into two states, a Jewish state and an Arab state, and a zone under international administration for Jerusalem and its environs. These proposals were adopted by the United Nations on 29th November 1947. Jerusalem was to be a *corpus separatum* placed under international trusteeship and its governor appointed by the United Nations. The Jews accepted the resolution concerning international administration and the plan of partition. The Arabs rejected them categorically, and announced their intention of opposing their application by force.

At Jerusalem the commercial quarter was attacked and set on fire six days after the United Nation's resolution.

The Biltmore programme was to form the basis of Zionist claims in the face of British hesitations and Arab policy. On the morrow of World War II the Jews realised that the British were not even going to allow the survivors of the concentration camps to enter Palestine, and the conflict broke out openly. The conduct of the mandatory government and the wave of hatred and pogroms in certain Arab countries (at Tripoli, in Libya and at Aleppo) drove certain groups, who had escaped the control of the Zionist authorities, into action. Denouncing the truce which had been established between the military organisation of the Jewish Agency, the Haganah, and the British army for the duration of the war, two groups, the Irgun Tzevai Leumi and the Fighters for the Freedom of Israel (the Stern group) proceeded to action.

The Anglo-American commission entrusted with seeking a solution acceptable to all ended by suggesting the granting of 10,000 immigration visas for the 'displaced persons' who were still in the European camps, and recommended that things should be so arranged that the Jews did not predominate over the Arabs and vice-versa. It was a question of maintaining British presence by ensuring that Palestine should be neither completely Jewish nor completely Arab. A plan of partition provided for the division of the country into four sectors. It was to remain a dead letter. In retaliation for a series of outrages, British forces entered the offices of the Jewish Agency at Jerusalem, proceeded to arrest the political leaders of the Jewish community and interned them in the camp of Latrun. Throughout the country the kibbutzim were searched, and the Jews saw the arms being confiscated which they relied on for protection against the attacks which the Arabs, emboldened by the British bias, made on their villages.

The Irgun decided to strike a major blow and, on 22nd July 1946, succeeded in blowing up a wing of the King David Hotel at Jerusalem which was the seat of

Jews who are in our native-land will fight. We shall not retreat.'

The debris of the King David Hotel.

Once more the Jews return, clandestinely, to Jerusalem: blockade runners from the *Intrepid*.

Sir Allan Cunningham, High Commissioner for Palestine, and the city's chief of police, inspect the commercial quarter set on fire on 5th December.

The United Nations adopts the resolution for the partition of Palestine: fierce and bloody fighting between Jews and Arabs . . .

During the six months of fighting which followed, up to the proclamation of the State of Israel, the situation deteriorated rapidly and escaped from British control. The Holy City was in fact isolated from the rest of the country. The supply lines were cut by the Arab troops and the 100,000 Jews of Jerusalem were encircled and besieged. The fifteen hundred inhabitants of the Jewish quarter of the old city held out for some time thanks to the fresh supplies of provisions and arms which the inhabitants of the new city managed to get through to them, though the situation in the new city was not much better. There was rationing of water, motor-fuel and food. Commanded by British officers, themselves under the

command of the celebrated Glubb Pasha, the Arab military harassed them continually. The convoys that attempted to reprovision the city were ambushed. The British troops were powerless; the Jews even thought that they were accessories to the outrages committed against the offices of the Jewish Agency, the premises in Ben Yehuda Street, and those of the *Jerusalem Post*. 'The explosion was caused by a military vehicle filled with dynamite which had been left in front of the building . . . The Arabs denied all responsibility for it. In spite of the absence of definite proofs, it was generally believed even in non-Jewish circles, that those responsible for this outrage were the British police.'

The United Nations, who had decided

on the partition of Palestine, did nothing to enforce it. The Jewish population of Jerusalem could only count on itself, while waiting for aid from the rest of the Jewish population of Palestine, and this did not fail, in spite of the inferiority of their armaments. In the course of the fighting that took place in the city and its environs, the front line was fixed on the demarcation lines between the various quarters. The old city remained in the hands of the Arabs, including the Jewish quarter, which had been practically destroyed, and whose population was evacuated, together with that of the northern districts. All the rest of the city was in the hands of the Jews. From then on the story of Jerusalem is the story of two cities.

Sir John Bagot, more famous under the name of Glubb Pasha, commander of the Arab Legion.

On 29th December a bomb exploded at the Damascus Gate

The offices of the Jewish Agency, the centre of the Zionist organisations, seriously damaged on 11the March 1948 by an explosion that killed twelve people.

killing fifteen people: twelve Arab civilians, two British and a terrorist. The taxi from which the missile was thrown was seized and burned.

The monument erected to the 'Davidka', the little David, the motor symbolising the courage of the Zionist forces during the War of Independence.

From 13th May to 15th May 1948: 'During the sixty hours from Friday morning to Sunday evening the city was a single battle front.'

The Jewish forces succeeded in seizing the heights of Castel, commanding the approach road to Jerusalem, and began, in the face of the enemy, to build a mountain road—since called the 'route of courage' or the 'Burma road'—so that fresh supplies could reach the city. Ramat Rachel, the kibbutz to the south of Jerusalem, resisted all attacks and thus saved the new city. The entire Jewish artillery, moreover, consisted of a single gun, a mortar mounted on wheels which was rapidly moved from one district to another in order to reassure the population and make it believe in the existence of a full complement of artillery.

On the proclamation of the independence of Israel, made at Tel Aviv on 15th May 1948, the British troops left Jerusalem. 'Tanks, light armoured-cars, truckloads of soldiers and staff-cars descended King George Avenue. The sidewalks and windows were black with people (sufficiently prudent to remain out of sight of the snipers hidden behind the walls of the old city) who stood in silence and watched the dramatic spectacle of the final departure of the English. Joy, irony, bitterness, animosity and incredulity could be seen upon the faces of the crowd . . .'

Although they were masters of Mount Zion, the Jewish forces were unable to relieve the Jews shut up in the old city who capitulated on 29th May. The historic synagogues went up in flames. The resistance of the kibbutz of Ramat Rachel prevented the liaison between the Egyptian forces and the troops of the Arab Legion, whose tanks were unable to enter the new city. After various truces the Jews remained in possession of Jerusalem, the provisioning of which was now assured, and which was no longer cut off from the rest of the territory controlled by the State of Israel. Everything had been tried to avert this war. Golda Meyerson (who later became Golda Meir and Israel's Minister of Foreign Affairs) was detailed to see King Abdullah in order to persuade him not to allow himself to be drawn into war. Disguised as an Arab woman, she managed to reach him, but King Abdullah—although he had no real wish to make war nor any interest in pursuing it—had to support the member countries of the Arab League. On 15th May 1948 itself, a meeting was arranged at the French consulate at Jerusalem. Only the Israeli delegate arrived and, for four hours, the Consular Truce Commission, presided over by the French Consul, M. Neuville, waited for the Arab delegates. The day after Independence Day, 16th May, the villages of the Etzion block, which had been completely surrounded and isolated, fell into the hands of the Arab Legion. A group of thirty-five young students, who attempted to reach them, were killed on the way.

The English burn their secret papers before leaving the city.

Colonel Tell, commander of the Arab Legion, on his way to discuss a truce.

The soldiers of the Haganah, a clandestine organisation, engaged in fierce fighting in the city in May 1948 and took Mount Zion by storm.

The 'Burma Road' built by the Jewish clandestine forces.

All round the old city, which was spared, the no man's land between Israel and Jordan,

What has become of the Jerusalem of Abraham? Israelis and Arabs engage in fierce fighting; the truce is only brief and precarious.

In the city itself the various quarters were the object of fierce fighting: The Haganah seized Mount Zion where tradition locates the tomb of King David. Mount Scopus, on which stood the university and the Hadassah hospital finally, after being bombarded by the Arab Legion, came under United Nations control. Police replaced the military. The zone remained an Israeli enclave in Jordanian territory and was policed by United Nations personnel.

The city was subjected to systematic artillery bombardment. The Arab Legion shelled the Notre Dame de France hospice and the Carmelite convent. On 11th June a truce was made and fighting ceased. Convoys with supplies reached Jerusalem . . . by the 'Burma road' whose existence was officially announced to the world.

But on 10th July, at the expiration of the truce (which the United Nations were unable to extend), fighting was resumed throughout the country and in the city. On 11th July Jerusalem had her first air-raid. The village of Ain Karim, birthplace of John the Baptist, was evacuated by the Iraqi forces on 17th July and the front was established in the region. An Israeli attempt to penetrate the old city failed as a result of a new cease fire which the troops decided to observe.

If at one time the government of Israel had considered accepting the project of internationalisation of the city, this no longer had any value, particularly in the face of the inability of the United Nations to do anything to save the Jewish inhabitants of the old city when appealed to. The State of Israel had it demonstrated to her that only the endurance of her armies and the courage of her people would ensure her survival, and that her future security could only be guaranteed in the same way.

Although the question of the status of Jerusalem has been the object of numerous debates in the United Nations, it nevertheless remains 'academic' in the face of the agreement, on this topic, of the Israeli and Jordanian points of view.

blind and mute, testifies to the violence of the bombardments and fighting which, for close on two years, opposed Jewish and Arab forces.

The Israeli-Jordanian armistice agreement which divides the city awaits the peace treaty of tomorrow. Tomorrow?

Count Bernadotte, the mediator of May 1948.

Count Bernadotte, the United Nations mediator, who suggested that the entire city of Jerusalem should be placed under Arab control, paid with his life for this proposal, and was shot by a group of dissident Jewish terrorists on 17th September in Jerusalem. This assassination shocked the whole world and the Israeli authorities used every possible means to break up the dissident groups and discover those responsible.

With the signing of the Israeli-Jordanian armistice agreement the demarcation line between the two cities acquired a more definite character. Israel was to retain all the Jewish part of the new city, while the Arabs were to keep the old town and the suburbs of Sheik Jerrah, with the exception of Mount Scopus. The armistice agreements pro-

vided for free access for the Israelis to Mount Scopus, while the Jordanians were allowed to use the road to Bethlehem which passed through Jerusalem. In the same way the Wailing Wall was to be accessible to the Israelis. But all these provisions of the armistice agreements have remained a dead letter because, if it is true that the first clause of the agreement states that it was being signed with a view to concluding a definitive peace, this peace has not yet been signed. The magnificent buildings of the university and the hospital (which were then almost new) were abandoned and the Israelis have built a new university and a new hospital. The new university is very modern and now includes the buildings of the National Museum and the administrative centre.

To replace the magnificent buildings erected on Mount Scopus, henceforth Jordanian territory, the Israelis have built a new University and a new National Museum.

The Jews do not have access to the Wailing Wall, but Arabs residing in Israel can cross over into the old city and go to Bethlehem at Christmas. The problems of the demarcation line have given rise to endless discussions. But misfortune has served some purpose here: in order to meet its vast programme of expansion, the young state has had to create trained personnel and technicians in every department. The new University of Jerusalem has faculties of law, medicine, philosophy, sociology, administration and economy.

Arab soldiers mounting guard in front of the Wailing Wall, now closed to the Jews.

The commanders of the Jewish and Arab forces discussing the demarcation line in July 1948.

279

Before the Parliament of Israel, the Knesset, assembled at Jerusalem on 14th February 1949, the first President, Chaim Weizmann, takes the oath. On the wall is a picture

'When the State of Israel is founded, everything will appear simple', said Herzl.

Slowly the city—or rather the two cities—returned to a normal way of life. Modern Jerusalem had been cut off from the rest of the country for months and the provisional government of Israel installed itself at Tel-Aviv. The officials of the former Jewish administration were transferred there in their hundreds to form the nucleus of the new administration. Their departure, together with that of a certain number of the inhabitants, the difficulties of the siege, privations and restrictions seriously affected the economic situation of Jerusalem. Buildings were demolished. The students, mobilised for the most part, were absent from the city. Jerusalem was going through a painful crisis when the state itself had many difficulties.

But the State of Israel could have no other capital but Jerusalem: great sacrifices were agreed to and it was proved that the statute proposed by the United

Nations had no grasp of reality. After the very survival of the state had been ensured and the initial difficulties overcome, the first parliament of Israel, the Knesset, met at Jerusalem on 14th February 1949. 'The State was a new link in the chain of history and we had been awaiting it for 1,835 years, that is to say since the defeat of Bar Kochba' (Ben Gurion). And it was at Jerusalem, before the Knesset, that the first President of the State of Israel, Chaim Weizmann, took the oath. In the course of 1949 the various ministries were transferred to Jerusalem. The Supreme Court installed itself there also, and the city became *de facto* not only the spiritual but also the political and administrative capital.

An administrative centre situated the ministries around the new Knesset building. Soon the broadcasting station will be built there also.

The government and the municipality

have done a great deal to develop the city. They have promoted the creation of industrial enterprises, while in the suburbs entire neighbourhoods—which are developing into small towns like the built-up areas on the outskirts of any Western capital—have been constructed in the immediate environs and on the hills. The water-supply, which had always been problematic, has now been definitively assured by the construction of pumping stations which bring water up from the plain and surrounding springs. Where once the Tenth Legion pitched camp—the same legion that destroyed the Temple—the 'palace of the nation', a congress and international conference centre, welcomes thousands of delegates each year from dozens of foreign countries for the most varied international conferences, from the Zionist Congress to that of the Administrators of National Lotteries. It also acts as the

of Theodor Herzl, originator of Zionism and the Jewish State.

The Palace of the nation dominating the city, an international theatre, music and cultural centre.

Adolf Eichmann in a glass dock hears the dismissal of his appeal against the death sentence.

A dream seeks fulfilment.

chief theatre and concert hall of Jerusalem pending the construction of the municipal theatre. Another theatre and assembly room has become very famous: the 'house of the people', a cultural centre which, before being put to its present use, and when scarcely completed, housed the tribunal charged with examining the case against Adolf Eichmann, who was being tried for having taken an active part in the slaughter of Jews during World War II.

Israel does not forget those who organised the most systematic and vile persecution in her history. Records from the various communities and Nazi and Neo-Nazi documents are gathered together in the administrative buildings of the memorial (see p. 283) which commands the valleys of Jerusalem where the great tree-planting schemes witness, in the most striking fashion, to the victory of life

The new synagogue of the university built after the loss of the superb buildings of Mount Scopus, part of Jordanian territory since the armistice.

On a hill behind Mount Herzl is the cemetery of the soldiers who fell during the War of Liberation, with the monuments to Jewish volunteers killed during world War II.

The flame of remembrance commemorates those who, by their blood and ashes, justified the creation of the young state.

New gardens, the Park of Independence, new buildings and hotels, the seat of the Chief Rabbinate and luxurious apartment blocks have transformed the face of the city. A campus site provides the 9,000 students of the Hebrew University with lodging facilities, and its synagogue with its daring architecture has fitted into the new city landscape.

The surrounding hills have been transformed. One of them bears from henceforth the name of Mount Herzl. On its summit, beneath a great stone of black basalt, lies the last of the prophets of Israel and the visionary of the return of the Jewish people to their land. All official ceremonies begin with a pilgrimage to the tomb of the man who wrote, fifty years before the proclamation of the state: 'If you wish it, it will not be a dream!'

On another hill-top behind it in the military cemetery are the graves of those killed during the War of Liberation and the monuments to the memory of the Jewish volunteers of World War II.

Finally, on the Mount of Remembrance, stands the Yad Vashem Memorial to the memory of the six million Jews killed by the Nazis. The crypt, in which a perpetual flame burns, contains the earth brought from the various concentration camps. A permanent exhibition reminds the visitor what the death agony of the Jewish communities in German-occupied Europe was like, together with the risings of the ghettoes and the resistance movements. Leading to the crypt, an avenue planted with carob-trees bears the name of the Avenue of the Just of the Nations. Each tree in this avenue has been planted in honour of those Gentiles who risked their lives for the persecuted Jews. The epic of courage and heroism is thus perpetuated and shows that Israel does not forget those who held out their hands to her.

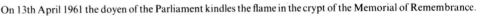
On 13th April 1961 the doyen of the Parliament kindles the flame in the crypt of the Memorial of Remembrance.

283

The *sabras*, prickly on the outside, so tender inside, always green beneath the sun, like the cactus which gave them its name.

The generation of girls and boys born in Israel smiles at the future with confidence.

The first act of the government of Israel, after the declaration of independence and the abrogation of the White Paper, opened up 'the State of Israel to the immigration of Jews from all the countries of their dispersion'. In addition, the new state guaranteed freedom of religion and conscience for all, and protection of the holy places of all faiths.

But the generation of *sabras*, who were born in Israel, is continually growing, and beside them the perpetual influx of immigrants sets a serious problem of integration. These new Israelis come from every part of the world, each being profoundly marked by his or her country or origin, and the frictions could be serious, particularly between Jews coming from the Mediterranean countries, who are sometimes of a less-advanced degree of civilisation, and the Jews of Europe. Temporary labour centres have been set up where immigrants are taught the country's activities.

All the Jews of the Diaspora support Israel in her endeavour, and it was one of the numerous international Zionist associations which made possible the building of Jerusalem's new synagogue, embellished by Marc Chagall.

A seventy-five-year-old pilgrim crosses the demarcation line.

The older immigrants still carry on their traditional handicrafts.

The Tribe of Judah, one of the stained glass windows in the synagogue of the Hadassah hospital designed by Chagall.

'Blessed be Thou, O my God, Thou who hast opened unto knowledge the heart of thy servant.' (The Manual of Discipline).

At Ain Karim—where John the Baptist was born—below the Medical Centre, is the synagogue designed by Neufeld, whose twelve stained-glass windows were designed by Chagall. Each of them is almost ten feet high and illustrates a tribe of Israel, in a different gamut of colours starting from red, green, yellow or blue. Since the Jewish religion still forbids the representation of the human form, the artist has transposed the texts from Genesis which inspired him into a saraband of donkeys, horses, birds, fish and flowers. 'Stained-glass', says Chagall, 'looks simple: matter and light. For a cathedral or a synagogue, it is the same phenomenon: something mystical which enters through the window. Nevertheless, I was very frightened . . .' In the centre of Israeli Jerusalem, forming part of the very modern complex of the National Museum, walls of black basalt and a dome in white porcelain stand in the midst of gardens: this is the Shrine of the Book. it is here that the oldest manuscripts of the Bible are preserved—the Dead Sea Scrolls—together with all the Biblical manuscripts and other historic parchment scrolls discovered by archaeologists. Taking his inspiration from one of the most precious manuscripts which describes The War of the Sons of Light against the Sons of Darkness, the architect of the shrine devised the contrast between the basalt wall and the porcelain dome which is directly inspired by the lid of the earthenware jar which contained the Essene treasure.

In contrast to this modern Jerusalem one finds at every turn signs of the Jewish religious tradition which permeates the new country. Close by the Israeli Parliament stands the wrought-iron seven-branched candlestick which has become the national symbol of the State of Israel. This relationship of the Israeli people to its God and its Torah is the very foundation of the state. Jerusalem the Holy must again become a capital of prayer. The religious message is taught there in dozens of schools (Yeshivot Rav Kook) in which the rabbis, religious magistrates and officials of the cult are schooled in the traditional discipline.

The seven-branched candlestick in wrought iron erected near the Parliament.

One of the numerous religious schools of the Old Quarter.

erior of the Shrine of the Book, part of the new National Museum.

Behind her walls, the old city of Jerusalem has not changed much. Historical sites and holy places, such as the Dome of the Rock and the church of the Holy Sepulchre, have been restored. Close by the Mount of Olives a large modern hotel offers pilgrims the marvellous landscape of the old and new cities while enabling them, on the other side, to admire the panorama of the Dead Sea. The two cities are completely separated from one another by the no man's land. A few frontier incidents break out now and then: mortar- or rifle-fire, or the throwing of stones. The former residence of the British High Commissioner is occupied by the United Nations observers. The meetings of the joint Israeli-Jordanian armistice commission are held at the Mandelbaum

Gate (which is called after a Jewish merchant who built a hotel there) or, according to its real name, the Gate of Simon the Just.

It is the only crossing point between Israel and Jordan, indeed the only crossing-point between Israel and the Arab world. The only people to pass through it are diplomats, United Nations observers, tourists and pilgrims. Tourists can enter or leave Jordan by the Mandelbaum Gate but on no account are they authorised to make a return journey. No Jewish Israeli has ever passed through this gate; only Christian Israelis have been authorised to do so on the occasion of religious pilgrimages. The Jews may not enter the old city, and no Jordanian has ever crossed over the border into Israel.

The cement fortifications are an unhappy witness to the split between the two cities.

The Mandelbaum Gate, the only crossing point between

rossing point, the Mandelbaum Gate, is silhouetted against a landscape of ruins and barbed-wire entanglements.

he old and new cities, flanked by blackened skeletons, relics of the war.

Jordanian soldiers on guard at the demarcation line.

Despite the ruins and the forbidden frontier, despite the tragic split between the two worlds, bright new spacious suburbs have been built, usually in the pink stone of the

The modern building of the Rav Kook Institute, a research centre specialising in the study of religious problems and the publishing of the sacred texts.

hills of Judah.

'Hearken Israel to the precepts of life, listen attentively in order to acquire knowledge.'

'Ten parts of beauty were allocated to the world by the Creator', say the rabbis, 'and Jerusalem received nine of them.' But 'ten parts of suffering were allocated to the world and Jerusalem received nine of them' and 'ten parts of knowledge were allocated to the world and Jerusalem received nine of them'. Divided by the folly of men, the city seems to be reliving its whole destiny anew and reincarnating its age-old tragedy. Side by side, two worlds are growing up which no longer communicate with one another. Barricades and barbed wire entanglements divide one of the most beautiful and uplifting landscapes in existence.

But the inhabitants of the city are conscious of the past of these places and of the historical importance they have for the world. Moreover, the Jerusalem of the past and the Jerusalem of the future mingle voices unceasingly. Dominating the Monastery and the Valley of the Cross, facing the Parliament, in the midst of gardens, the Israeli Architects Alfred Mansfeld and Dora Gad have designed the new National Museum. Opened in May 1965, this art centre not only integrates the Bezalel Museum, the Archaeological and Biblical Museum and the Shrine of the Book (*see* pp. 286–287), but also displays a very important collection of modern painting and one of the finest collections of synagogical objects of art and jewellery. The Rav Kook institute for researches into Jewish religious questions and publishing shows, in spite of the acuteness of the vital preoccupations of the country, the importance which the State of Israel attaches to cultural problems. But the sight of a parchment-tanner (*see below*) reminds us that here a book is certainly not a museum or library object.

This daily resurgence of the past, in the midst of a modern world, also appears in one of the most curious sights of the city. On the slopes of a hill which falls away towards a valley of pines, cypresses and eucalyptuses, a zoological garden exhibits the animals and plants mentioned in the Bible with, on each cage or in each corner of the garden, the verse in which they are mentioned.

Preparation of a parchment upon which religious texts will be written.

'Let a man meet a she-bear robbed of her cubs . . .' (Prov. XVII. 12.).

Under the eyes of the world an illustrious pilgrim carries away with him hopes of conciliation and peace.

The split between the two cities, between the two worlds, is total. Yet in recent times the situation was, for a time reversed, when Pope Paul VI visited the Holy Land and journalists and radio and television crews were exceptionally authorised by the Jordanians to enter Israel and leave it again.

Arriving at Amman on Saturday 4th January 1964, where he was welcomed by King Hussein, the Pope entered the city by the Damascus Gate. Everything was in perfect order for the reception of the sovereign pontiff. The soldiers of the Arab Legion in their red and white checked *keffiyehs* mounted guard, but the crowd was so enthusiastic that they rapidly became superfluous.

The Pope entered the Holy Sepulchre, went up to the chapel of Calvary and prostrated himself upon the slab of the Crucifixion. He then returned to the Tomb again and placed a gold olive branch there. From the basilica he made

his way to the Mount of Olives where, for the first time since the Council of Florence in the fifteenth century, a Pope met the Greek and Armenian Orthodox patriarchs.

The next day he crossed into Israel. He began his pilgrimage by visiting the holy places of Galilee, and at Megiddo, Zalman Shazar, the President of the State of Israel, welcomed him.

Beneath the blue and white flags bearing Solomon's seal and the yellow and white flags with the arms of the Holy See, the two worlds met. It ended with the words *shalom, shalom* (peace, peace) pronounced by Paul VI.

The Pope returned to Jerusalem via Nazareth, Lake Tiberias, Tabgha, Capernaum, the Mount of Beatitudes and Mount Tabor. He was received at the entrance to the city by the Mayor: Ish-Shalom (man of peace) who, surrounded by the leading figures of the city, offered him bread and salt as a

token of hospitality on the hill of Mount Zion, the symbol of the city and of Judaism, where the tomb of David is venerated. The Pope made his way to the Cenaculum, the site of the Last Supper, then to the church of the Dormition. Meanwhile Cardinal Tisserant, accompanied by the Israeli Minister of Religious Affairs, went to the crypt of the Martyrs where, on behalf of the Pope he lit six candles in remembrance of the six million victims of Nazism.

It was by the Mandelbaum Gate that the Pope left Israel to return to the old city, where he met the leader of the 'separated brethren', Patriarch Athenagoras I, primate of the Orthodox Church. The historic embrace between the two prelates took place at the Apostolic Legation. It marked the culminating point of the pilgrimage that took the Pope to Bethlehem before his return to Amman and Rome.

A group of students, carrying palms, enters Jerusalem by the Damascus Gate on Palm Sunday 1957.

On 5th January Pope Paul VI and the President of the State of Israel, Zabman Shazar, in friendly conversation.

The Pope and the Patriarch Athenagoras I.

On 6th January, before leaving the holy places, the Sovereign Pontiff visits the basilica of Bethlehem, which houses the grotto of the Nativity, as an ordinary pilgrim.

Hidden behind the trees on a spur of the Mount of Olives, the House of Abraham relief centre opens its doors to poor pilgrims.

At the request of Pope Paul VI a relief centre was built in the Holy City. On a spur of the Mount of Olives, in the midst of a huge park, a building in freestone displays as its arms three ears of corn and the motto 'shared bread'. This House of Abraham opened its doors to Christians of all rites on Christmas Eve 1964. By a singular coincidence the French School of Archaeology, with the British School of Archaeology, has brought to light, on the south of the city, the ruins of the Hostelry for Poor Pilgrims founded by Justinius.

Jerusalem rising anew from her heaps of stones and ruins after the outbreak of hostilities in 1967, may once again become *Yerushalayim*, the City of Peace. The tradition of welcome begun the day that Abraham met Melchizedek, may spring up again unchanged, despite the sounds of discord, for Jerusalem is the symbolic city *par excellence*, whose spiritual vocation has always exceeded her economic and political vocation. It was a book alone that gave her her unique place in the world and in which it is said:

'. . . . they shall beat their swords into ploughshares, and their spears into pruning hooks; nation shall not lift up sword against nation, neither shall they learn war any more; but they shall sit every man under his vine and under his fig tree, and none of them shall be afraid.'

The Pope celebrates mass at the Holy Sepulchre in the Latin chapel of Golgotha.

Following page: The restored dome over the bare rock around which the city originated and developed.

CIVITAS·IHERVSALEM